Children's Perspectives on Integrated Services

Interagency Working in Health and Social Care
Edited by Jon Glasby

Aimed at students and practitioners, this series provides an introduction to inter-agency working across the health and social care spectrum, bringing together an appreciation of the policy background with a focus on contemporary themes. The books span a wide range of health and social care services and the impact that these have on people's lives, as well as offering insightful accounts of the issues facing professionals in a fast-changing organizational landscape.

Exploring how services and sectors interact and could change further, and the evidence for 'what works', the series is designed to frame debate as well as promote positive ways of interdisciplinary working.

Published titles

Kellett: *Children's Perspectives on Integrated Services: Every Child Matters in Policy and Practice*

Forthcoming titles

French/Swain: *Working with Disabled People in Policy and Practice*
Williams/Johnson: *Learning Disability and Inclusion*
Baggott: *Public Health and Wellbeing*

Children's Perspectives on Integrated Services

Every Child Matters in Policy and Practice

Mary Kellett

palgrave
macmillan

First published 2011 by

PALGRAVE MACMILLAN

Palgrave Macmillan in the UK is an imprint of Macmillan Publishers Limited, registered in England, company number 785998, of Houndmills, Basingstoke, Hampshire RG21 6XS

Palgrave Macmillan in the US is a division of St Martin's Press LLC, 175 Fifth Avenue, New York, NY 10010.

Palgrave Macmillan is the global academic imprint of the above companies and has companies and representatives throughout the world.

Palgrave® and Macmillan® are registered trademarks in the United States, the United Kingdom, Europe and other countries.

ISBN: 978–0–230–23039–2

This book is printed on paper suitable for recycling and made from fully managed and sustained forest sources. Logging, pulping and manufacturing processes are expected to conform to the environmental regulations of the country of origin.

A catalogue record for this book is available from the British Library.

Library of Congress Cataloging-in-Publication Data
Kellett, Mary, 1955–
Children's perspectives on integrated services : every child matters in policy and practice / Mary Kellett.
p. cm. — (Interagency working in health and social care)
Summary: "Launching Palgrave's new Interagency Working in Health and Social Care series, this book provides one of the first reflective assessments of the Every Child Matters legacy of New Labour. Woven through with the voice of the child, it addresses the history, successes and limitations of the ECM agenda, in terms of both principle and practice"— Provided by publisher.
Includes bibliographical references and index.
ISBN-13: 978-0-230-23039-2 (pbk.)
ISBN-10: 0-230-23039-3 (pbk.)
1. Children—Government policy—Great Britain. 2. Children—Services for—Great Britain. I. Title.
HV751.A6K45 2011
362.7—dc23
2011024433

10 9 8 7 6 5 4 3 2 1
20 19 18 17 16 15 14 13 12 11

Printed and bound in Great Britain by
CPI Antony Rowe, Chippenham and Eastbourne

For my amazing daughters Elizabeth and Helen

I am very grateful to Jon Glasby for helpful feedback on draft chapters

Contents

List of Boxes, Figures and Tables

List of Abbreviations

ASB	antisocial behaviour
CAF	Common Assessment Framework
CAMHS	Children and Adolescent Mental Health Services
CCKS	Common Core of Knowledge and Skills
CfBT	Centre for British Teachers
CP	Children's Parliament
CRAE	Children's Rights Alliance England
CRC	Children's Research Centre at the Open University
CWDC	Children's Workforce Development Council
DCATCH	Disabled Children's Access to Childcare Programme
DCMS	Department for Culture, Media and Sport
DCS	director of children's services
DCSF	Department for Children, Schools and Families
DfES	Department for Education and Skills
DFP	Dundee Family Project
DH	Department of Health
DWP	Department for Work and Pensions
ECM	Every Child Matters
EDCM	Every Disabled Child Matters
EEC	Early Excellence Centre
EYFS	Early Years Foundation Stage
FCE	First Children's Embassy
FIP	Family Intervention Project
GSCC	General Social Care Council
ICS	Integrated Children's System
IQF	Integrated Qualification Framework
IRO	independent reviewing officer
ISA	Independent Safeguarding Authority
LACS	Looked After Care System
LCSB	local children's safeguarding board
NCH	National Children's Homes
NHS	National Health Service
NVQ	National Vocational Qualification

PCT	primary care trust
SATs	standard attainment tests
SCAA	School Curriculum Assessment Authority
SWPs	Social Work Practices
UNCRC	United Nations Convention on the Rights of the Child

1 Introduction

In this chapter we discuss:

- A brief introductory rationale
- The parameters of the book
- How the book is structured

Introductory rationale

There have been many books written on and about Every Child Matters (ECM) on a number of themes – political foci, critical practice, effective communication, early years' perspectives – and a number of texts exploring aspects of multi-agency working. To the best of my knowledge, none have explored integrated children's services specifically through the lens of the child. A principal aim in writing this text is to value and give voice to the perspectives of children and to illustrate the impact that ECM is having on their daily lives. This cannot be done in isolation, there has to be a framework in which to situate the lived experiences of children. Hence this volume necessarily depicts historical, theoretical and practice-based background canvases on which children have painted their own stories in a co-constructed platform of communication. Some children's voices are direct and first voice, others are accessed through advocates or child-focused research.

The axis of this book is a measured review of children's services and I do not shy away from praising or critiquing ECM in accordance with the experiences of diverse groups of children. History will be the ultimate judge of the value and durability of ECM, but if we wait for history to pronounce its verdict we will lose an opportunity to inform policy and practice in the here and now. Given the change of government, this is a fitting time to take stock of where we are with children's integrated services and to ensure that the views of children play a part in shaping future directions.

The parameters of the book

It is increasingly common to differentiate between 'children' and 'young people' because of the vast difference in their experiences. Generally this is divided along the lines of primary and secondary school age groups or across the 'teens' and the 'pre-teen' years. Sometimes this is further divided by separating off the early years. This volume relates to children aged 3–12. It would be too large a work to incorporate the whole 0–18 age range in any meaningful way. I have chosen the younger age group because they have a more marginalized voice and there is greater scepticism about involving them in the business of decision-making in matters affecting their lives.

The second parameter to flag is that ECM primarily relates to England although there are similar initiatives running in the other nation states. Therefore the content of the book is centred on English policy and practice, although some case studies are drawn from the nation states and references are made to relevant sources and suggested further reading where appropriate. Occasional illustrative material from around the world is also cited to further contextualize the central tenets under review.

A final limiting factor is the timescale in which this has been written. The coalition government of the Conservatives and Liberal Democrats came to power in May 2010, so this review only goes as far as the end of the regnum of New Labour. There is limited comment on early initiatives of the coalition government and these are framed speculatively.

How the book is structured

The book is organized into three parts. Part I depicts the ECM journey. Chapter 2 charts the main historical events that have led to ECM, beginning with the first known welfare, in the form of the Poor Laws, up to legislation that finally embedded ECM into the English constitution. By contrast, Chapter 3 examines the main theoretical and conceptual frameworks that underpin ECM. Key to this is a range of discourses on childhood and the exposition of political activity especially around the application of neoliberal thinking.

Part II moves to contemporary practice and to a real-world evaluation of how ECM is working as an interagency initiative. Different fields of children's services – social care (Chapter 4), education (Chapter 5) and health (Chapter 6), once separate departments – are explored in the light of their amalgamation into a single Department for Children, Schools and Families. Tensions arising in multidisciplinary approaches, concerns about the dilution of specialist professional expertise, and the outcomes of various practice models are reviewed from different professional perspectives and, crucially, from children's perspectives. Chapter 7 addresses broader issues of disadvantage, diversity and marginalization and how these translate into children's services at grass-roots level, dominated by the overarching theme of child poverty. Chapter 8 focuses on children in the domestic arena of the family unit, on how this landscape is changing, and the importance of children's services reflecting the needs of whole family units. Chapter 9 looks at ECM and the third sector and the nuances that a value-based sector brings to children's services. Chapter 10 is concerned with safeguarding children. The change of nomenclature from child protection to safeguarding children is indicative of the broadening of the area to include impairment of development and optimization of life chances. The impact on the specialist expertise of child protection is discussed at some length.

Part III considers ECM in the light of critical issues which are gaining momentum on the global stage. Chapter 11 probes the hot topic of children's rights and explores where the ECM agenda sits on the global spectrum as ensconced in UNCRC. It looks at agency and how this can translate into children's citizenship. Chapter 12 addresses participation and voice, deconstructing the rhetoric and reality in different models, and underlines one of the central tenets of the book – the imperative of listening to children. This leads naturally into Chapter 13, which considers the role of children as researchers in their own right. It sets out a rationale for empowering children as researchers, the value we can place on their research contributions and the potential to influence policy and practice. The final brief chapter draws together the main threads of the book and looks beyond ECM to future directions.

A characteristic feature of the book is the illustrations of children's experiences and perspectives which provide a running commentary on the efficacy of ECM. These are boxed to distinguish them and to afford them value. Reflection exercises at the end of each chapter encourage you to reflect on what you have read and apply it to your own circumstances and/or your own practice. Each chapter also has suggested further reading.

You will gain most from this book if you read it chronologically and in its entirety. However, the parts of the book have distinctly different purposes and the chapters within them are self-contained and constructed so that they can be read in isolation. There is clear interchapter signposting to show you where you can follow up an area of interest in its primary chapter.

Part I

The Every Child Matters Journey

2 The Historical Context

In this chapter we discuss:

- The United Nations Convention on the Rights of the Child (1989) and its impact on children's services
- The historical context of children's services
- How ECM is changing the children's services landscape
- New roles and organizations to embed integrated children's services
- Criticisms of ECM

The first decade of the twenty-first century has seen extraordinary changes in policy and practice relating to children's services, encapsulated in the Every Child Matters (ECM) agenda. In order to be able to evaluate how integrated children's services are functioning and evolving, it is important to have an understanding of the historical context that has brought this about. There have been two main drivers which brought us to ECM and to the current reforms we are witnessing in children's services. The first is the United Nations Convention on the Rights of the Child (1989) and the seismic shift in perspectives on children's status in society that it brought about. The second is a number of high-profile child deaths, notably Maria Colwell in 1973, Jasmine Beckford in 1984 and Victoria Climbié in 2000, which shook the nation and exposed catastrophic failings in the way children's services were operating. Similarly, high-profile homicides by individuals with mental health conditions drew attention to the need to review mental health policy (see Appleby et al., 2001). The government was galvanized to instigate sweeping reforms that collectively formed *Every Child Matters: Change for Children* (DfES, 2004). ECM is an ambitious agenda which seeks to ensure that every child, irrespective of background or circumstances, is enabled and supported to live a happy and fulfilled childhood, personified in the five intended outcomes: be healthy; stay safe; enjoy and achieve through learning; make a positive contribution to society; and achieve economic wellbeing. This chapter charts the historical and legislative processes en route to ECM and the major events that have influenced contemporary thinking on integrated children's services.

The impact of the United Nations Convention on the Rights of the Child (1989)

The 1989 United Nations Convention on the Rights of the Child (UNCRC) was ten years in the making. Representatives from all religions, cultures, organizations and societies were consulted and it went through numerous iterations before being finally adopted into international law in 1989. It was the first legally binding document to accrue human rights directly to children. In 1959, the United Nations General Assembly produced a Declaration of the Rights of the Child, but this was only an advisory document setting out ten principles for working in the best interests of children. Prior to UNCRC (1989), children's rights had been incorporated into general rights edicts, for example the Universal Declaration of Human Rights (UN, 1948). All countries in the world except the USA and Somalia ratified the UNCRC and in doing so agreed to implement its articles. It was a landmark proclamation which covered all aspects of human rights – social, cultural, civil and economic – and was the first proclamation to specify what children were entitled to expect in a quality childhood:

> The Convention is a comprehensive instrument which sets out rights
> that define universal principles and norms for the status of children.
> It not only sets out these fundamental rights and freedoms, but also
> takes into account the need for children to have special assistance and
> protection due to their vulnerability. It is the most complete statement
> of children's rights ever produced. It is also the first legal instrument to
> focus solely on the child, regardless of where the child was born and
> to whom, and regardless of sex, religion and social origin. (Human
> Rights Nexus, n.d.)

The content of the UNCRC reflected a shift in the status of children, an acceptance that they are children in the here and now, not adults in waiting, and an acknowledgment that they have agency in relation to their rights. Table 2.1 summarizes most of the articles of the UNCRC in simple language and shows how they are linked to the five intended outcomes of ECM.

The UNCRC was enforceable in international law. States which signed up to the Convention (the UK ratified the treaty in 1991) were required to furnish regular reports to the Committee on the Rights of the Child, which had been set up to monitor how states were implementing the Convention. This committee is made up of 18 independent children's rights experts who are elected to four-year terms. It meets three times a year in Geneva, Switzerland. The committee is responsible for examining the progress made by state parties in fulfilling their obligations under the Convention. However, it does not have the jurisdiction to examine issues relating to individual children. The UK government did not construct any new legislation to embed the 41 substantive articles, claiming that the requirements of the UNCRC

Table 2.1	How ECM is linked to UNCRC articles

Summary of UNCRC article	ECM link
3 Organizations concerned with children should work towards what is best for each child	a, b, c, e
4 Governments should make UNCRC rights available to children	a, b, c, d, e
5 Governments should respect the rights and responsibilities of families to direct and guide their children so that, as they grow, they learn to use their rights properly	b, c
6 Governments should ensure that all children survive and develop healthily	a, b, c, d, e
9 Children should not be separated from parents unless it is for their own good. Where parents have separated, children have the right to stay in contact with both, unless this might hurt them	b
10 Families who live in different countries should be allowed to move between those countries so that they can stay in contact, or get back together as a family	b, d, e
11 Governments should protect children from being taken out of their country illegally	b
12 Children have the right to have their opinions taken into account and to say what they think should happen when adults are making decisions that affect them	a, b, c, d, e
13 Children have the right to information as long as it is not damaging to them or to others	b, c, d
14 Children have the right to freedom of thought and to practise their religion as long as they are not stopping other people from enjoying their rights	c, d
15 Children have the right to meet together and to join groups and organizations, as long as this does not stop other people from enjoying their rights	c, d
17 Children have the right to reliable information from the media that they can understand	c
18 Where there are two parents, both share responsibility for child-rearing and should always consider what is best for each child. Governments should provide services to support them	b, e
19 Governments should ensure that children are properly cared for, and protect them from violence, abuse and neglect by their parents, or anyone else who looks after them	a, b, c e
20 Children who cannot be looked after by their own family must be looked after properly, by people who respect their religion, culture and language	b
21 Children's welfare is the first concern in adoptions. The same rules should apply whether children are adopted in the country where they were born or taken to live in another country	b

22 Refugee children should have the same rights as children born in that country	a, b, c, d, e
23 Children who have any kind of disability should have special care and support so that they can lead full and independent lives	a, c, d
24 To stay healthy, children have the right to quality healthcare, nutritious food, and a clean environment. Rich countries should help poorer countries achieve this	a, e
25 Children looked after by a local authority should have their situation reviewed regularly	a, b, c, d
26 Governments should provide extra money for the children of families in need	e
27 Children have a right to a standard of living good enough to meet their physical and mental needs. The government should help families who cannot afford to provide this	a, e
28 All children and young people have a right to a free primary education and to reach the highest level of education they are capable of. Wealthy countries should help poorer countries achieve this. Discipline in schools should respect children's human dignity	c, e
29 Education should develop each child's personality and talents to the full. It should encourage children to respect their parents and their own and other cultures	c, e
30 Children have a right to learn and use the language and customs of their families, whether these are shared by the majority of people in the country or not	c, d
31 All children have a right to relax and play, and to join in a wide range of activities	a, c, d
32 Children must be protected from work that is dangerous or harmful to health or education	b
33 Governments should protect children from dangerous drugs	b
34 Governments should protect children from sexual abuse	b
35 Governments should make sure that children are not abducted or sold	b
36 Children should be protected from any activities that could harm their development	a, b
37 Children who break the law should not be treated cruelly. They should not be put in prison with adults and should be able to keep in contact with their families	b
38 Governments should not allow children under 16 to join the armed forces	b
39 Children who have been neglected or abused should get special help to restore self-respect	a, b
40 Children who are accused of breaking the law should receive legal help. Prison sentences for children should only be used for the most serious offences	b

Key: a = be healthy, b = stay safe, c = enjoy and achieve, d = make a positive contribution, e = achieve economic wellbeing were already covered in the Children Act 1989. However, at the United Nations Special Summit on Children's Rights in 2002, the UK government was criticized for not doing enough to enact articles relating to children's participation and not stating explicitly how this was being achieved. In response to this criticism and in tandem with the fallout from the death of Victoria Climbié in 2000, the *Every Child Matters* Green Paper (DfES, 2003) was fashioned and ultimately adopted into English legislation in the Children Act 2004. In the nation states, similar legislation was adopted: in Wales, *Children and Young People: Rights to Action* (Welsh Assembly Government, 2004); in Scotland, *Getting It Right for Every Child: Proposals for Action* (Scottish Executive, 2005); and in Northern Ireland, *Our Children and Young People – Our Pledge* (Office of the First Minister and Deputy First Minister, 2006).

Historical context of children's services

Poor Laws and the welfare state

Children's services evolved out of a deficit model epitomized by the Poor Laws, the first being traced back to 1388 in England and Wales in response to the widespread poverty caused by the Black Death. The turn of the seventeenth century saw the introduction of almshouses to support those unable to work or support themselves. These were paid for by contributions – known as alms – collected in each local parish. In 1832, a Royal Commission undertook a review of the whole poor relief system, resulting in an amendment to the legislation in what became known as the New Poor Law of 1834. This brought into being the workhouse arrangements of the nineteenth century, where parishes were required to make available an establishment to provide basic shelter, food and clothing for the destitute in return for their labour. If a man had to enter the workhouse, his whole family had to accompany him. It was a harsh regime where men, women and children were separated and housed in different parts of the institution. Only children under the age of seven were allowed to stay with their mothers. They were at the mercy of those who ran the workhouses and many children suffered cruelty and malnutrition.

> " **Children's Experiences**
>
> 'One day I saw a little girl with red eyes at our school (for they had no school-mistress at the workhouse) whose heart seemed bursting, and on enquiring the cause, she said, "Missus has roped me." Her back and arms were red and covered with great weals and marks of rope. The child told me that it was done for the merest trifle, and that all the union children told how it was the "missus's" constant habit to beat them with a thick hair rope, made on purpose. It had two knots at the end and a loop for the hand.'

By 1839, almost half the workhouse population – 42,767 out of 97,510 – were children (www.workhouses.org.uk). The institutions were not abolished until 1930. The welfare state came into being in the early 1940s with a duty of care for vulnerable children and those living in poverty. However, it took the death in 1945 of Dennis O'Neill, a 12-year-old child, from the abuse and neglect of his foster carers to spark real institutional change (Home Office, 1945). It led to the Children Act 1948 and the setting up of the first local authority children's departments with their own children's committees and children's officers.

Maria Colwell

Through the 1950s and 60s, children's services continued to be organized via local authorities, the needs of children being addressed by separate social service and education departments. Another high-profile child death, Maria Colwell in 1973, initiated a major inquiry which drew attention to serious institutional failures. Maria was known to social services and frequent concerns had been raised by neighbours. In the months leading up to her death, there were 50 official visits to her home – from the NSPCC, the police, school welfare officers, housing officials, social workers and health visitors. Information was not being shared between them and Maria's injuries were not picked up by medical practitioners. Poor communication between professionals, compounded by medical misdiagnoses, had tragic consequences. Maria met an agonizing death at the hands of her parents. Among these many mistakes made by professionals was a failure to seek information from Maria herself, despite the fact that she was almost eight years old. Parton (2004: 82) refers to a 'considerable failure to engage and communicate directly with the children themselves about their feelings and circumstances' as a significant failure of the professionals involved in several child abuse deaths, despite legislation in the Children Act 1989 which made listening to children a legal requirement.

However, the Maria Colwell inquiry (Secretary of State for Social Services, 1974) did usher in some significant reforms and effectively introduced the modern child protection system in the UK. The inquiry accepted that individual errors were an inevitable part of human activity but stated that failsafe systems should have been in place to prevent individual errors leading to such devastating consequences. The inquiry report focused on poor training, particularly the absence of critical, sceptical analysis on behalf of the professionals as to what information was being presented to them by Maria's parents, chaotic administrative systems (even basic record keeping relating to visits and phone calls were not logged), and ineffectual supervision as major failings. But the primary criticism was reserved for the ineffective communication and liaison between agencies which led to Maria slipping though an extensive and sophisticated social care net. The fallout from the Maria Colwell case resulted in the establishment of child protection registers and a multi-agency case conferencing system:

> It is not enough for the state as representing society to assume responsibility for those such as Maria. It must also provide the means to do so, both financially and by ensuring that the system works as efficiently as possible at every level so that individual mistakes, which must be accepted as inevitable, do not result in disaster. (Secretary of State for Social Services, 1974: para. 242)

Jasmine Beckford

A decade later similar system failures were to lead to the death of four-year-old Jasmine Beckford. At least 66 carers were involved with the welfare of the Beckford family, including nine nurses, nine doctors, seven preschool educationalists and seven social workers, but once again the different professionals were not sharing information (Oliver, 1988). Jasmine's parents had themselves been victims of abuse as children and had both attended a special school. One of the criticisms raised in the inquiry was that too much attention was diverted away from Jasmine, as the vulnerable child in need, by a preoccupation with the needs of the parents:

> In its conclusion the report accuses Jasmine's social worker of 'focusing her gaze on Beverley Lorrington and Morris Beckford; she averted her eyes to the children to be aware of them only as and when they were with their parents, hardly ever to observe their development, and never to communicate with Jasmine on her own. The two children [Jasmine had a younger half-sister, Louise] were treated as mere appendages to their parents who were treated as the clients.' (Dale, 1986: 175)

There were 78 visits to the family in ten months from the social worker but in all those visits Jasmine was seen only once, and that was in the presence of her parents. The telltale signs were there – inadequate parenting, spasmodic attendance at nursery, Jasmine's invisibility to visitors, and a known history of violent behaviour in the stepfather – but were not being picked up or communicated between professionals. A few months before her death, Jasmine was taken into foster care under a care order but the procedures were bungled. When the parents requested her return, this was granted despite the stepfather's recent conviction for assault against Jasmine's younger half-sister. The inquiry later castigated social workers for their lack of understanding of care order procedures and their relative ignorance of child abuse. Tragically, Jasmine was returned home to spend the last few months of her life in near starvation and horrifying abuse. She died aged four and a half weighing only 23lbs.

A number of recommendations were implemented from the Beckford inquiry (Blom-Cooper, 1985):

- Abused children under five who are returned to abusive parents must be brought to a local child clinic at least monthly.
- Schools had to designate a member of staff as liaison officer with the local social services department for every child in care.
- Place of safety orders became emergency protection orders, which were limited to a maximum of 8 days and open to challenge after 72 hours (compared with the original 28-day place of safety order).
- Magistrates in juvenile courts became legally bound to provide reasons for their decisions in care proceedings.
- A specialist paediatrician must be consulted whenever serious non-accidental injuries occur.
- A tightening of the criteria for solicitors working on childcare cases.

The Children Act 1989

Getting the balance right between professional negligence and excessive interference did not prove easy. The public outcry from high-profile child abuse deaths led to a marked increase in the number of children taken into care, particularly through the use of place of safety orders. At times there was too much zealotry from some professionals. This was the case in 1987 with the Cleveland sexual abuse scandal, where 121 children were taken into care on the recommendation of two paediatricians, Marietta Higgs and Geoffrey Wyatt, using the now discredited anal reflex and dilation method to detect sexual abuse. Of the 121 cases, 96 were subsequently dismissed but not before untold emotional damage had been wreaked on the unfortunate families. A loss of confidence in child protection services followed, which was partly restored by the introduction of the Children Act 1989 (see Box 2.1).

Box 2.1	Greater protection afforded by the Children Act 1989

Main principles included:

- making children's welfare a priority
- protecting the rights of children
- establishing that professionals have a duty to listen to children
- promoting partnership between children, parents and local authorities

- improving the way courts deal with children and families, with the right of appeal against court decisions
- providing services for children and families in need
- recognizing that children are best brought up within their families wherever possible
- ensuring that a child cannot be removed from their family without the parents' consent unless the child is at risk of harm
- establishing that children in local authority care and their parents have rights, including the right of appeal
- providing support for vulnerable children and those with a disability.

New rights afforded to children:

- having their voices heard, and, if appropriate, to have a voice in some court cases
- being allocated their own solicitor who was to act on their behalf and to whom they could impart their own wishes about what they want to happen.

Additional rights for some children, according to their age and competency:

- right of appeal against a court decision
- right to refuse to be assessed or medically examined
- right to be kept informed about decisions that are taken about them while they are in care.

A number of reforms were instigated following recommendations from the Beckford inquiry. Prominent among these were tighter regulations permitting children in care to go home on a trial basis and additional training for magistrates involved in making these decisions. An urgent review of the assessment and supervision of social workers handling child abuse cases was called for. Henceforth, senior staff, in consultation with other agencies concerned, would be involved in any decisions to return a child home on a trial basis. Procedures were also tightened for child abuse training and supervision of nursing and health professionals (Blom-Cooper, 1985).

Victoria Climbié

The public outcry that had engulfed earlier child abuse deaths was further intensified when details of the torture and murder of eight-year-old Victoria Climbié were released in 2000, not least because earlier lessons appeared not to have been learned. Similar weaknesses in policy and practice led to similar mistakes and similarly missed opportunities to save a child. Fierce criticism was levelled at the absence of interagency communication. There were cultural complexities in Victoria's case, who was born in West Africa but sent to live with her aunt in London. Such informal adoptions are not uncommon in African and African-Caribbean cultures but their children's opaque routes into the UK make it easier for them to fall through the safety net of routine childcare checks. Even when Victoria did become known to social services, cultural issues continued to throw up a smokescreen. Victoria's timidity was interpreted as the natural reserve and respect for elder relatives common in West African communities. When abuse was suspected, there was a reluctance to act in case this was interpreted as racial harassment. Religion also played a part. Victoria was taken to a pastor of the Universal Church of the Kingdom of God to be exorcized. He readily believed the aunt's contention that Victoria was possessed by devils and that demons preyed upon her to harm herself.

Victoria was admitted to hospital with serious injuries, twice, and on both occasions non-accidental injury was suspected. On the first occasion, staff had misgivings about Victoria's injuries but the attending paediatrician accepted the aunt's explanation that Victoria had scabies and that the injuries were self-inflicted scratches. The paediatrician passed her for discharge, noting that there were no child abuse issues, without even speaking to Victoria on her own. As a consequence of the paediatric report, the social services downgraded Victoria's case. On a second hospital admission, a paediatrician did suspect that Victoria was being abused but wrote 'able to be discharged' on the case notes. She later said that she did not mean that Victoria should necessarily be discharged back into the care of her guardians, simply that she could be discharged from hospital, and had fully expected social services to follow up the case. Equally, when social services saw the discharge notes, they interpreted this as no further action being required and expected that if there had been cause for concern, the hospital would have involved the police. Each was expecting the other to take responsibility, with the result that neither did. In Lord Laming's words (2003), this was 'inexcusable', especially when the Children Act 1989 had specifically put in place policies and practices to ensure that children's agencies work together and share information. The inquiry concluded that there were at least 12 opportunities for the agencies involved to have saved Victoria.

The institutional failings were further compounded by systems failings. At that time, the children's department was running two record-keeping systems, a manual system and a completely separate, client-based computer system. Somehow, Victoria acquired five different identifying numbers, creating abundant opportunity for the mismanagement of information. There were also failings of individual professionals. Incompetence included not keeping records, making visits to the home without seeing Victoria and, on the rare occasions professionals did see her, not conversing with her directly and making some very bad judgement calls (Carvel, 2001). Between December 1999 and January 2000, a social worker made three visits to Victoria's home, but failed to get a response. She speculated that the family must have returned to France and conveyed this to her supervisor. Despite having no evidence, the supervisor wrote on Victoria's file that they had left the area. On 18 February 2000, a letter was sent to the aunt saying that if social services did not receive any contact from her, they would close the case. A week later they closed the case – on the same day that Victoria died.

Lord Laming led the public inquiry and he concluded that:

the suffering and death of Victoria Climbié was a gross failure of the system and was inexcusable. It is clear to me that the agencies with responsibility for Victoria gave a low priority to the task of protecting children. (Laming, 2003: para. 1.18)

He identified weak accountability, poor communication and absence of integration as the critical factors to be addressed. He made 108 recommendations for sweeping changes to be made to children's services. It was clear that earlier reforms recommended and implemented via the Children Act 1989 were not being effective. Lessons simply had not been learned and a sea change in practice accountability was needed:

The single most important change in the future must be the drawing of a clear line of accountability from the top to the bottom without doubt or ambiguity about who is responsible at every level for the wellbeing of vulnerable children. (Laming, 2003: para. 1.2)

New multi-agency ways of working needed to be organized *around the child*. It was Laming's 108 recommendations from the Victoria Climbié inquiry that finally galvanized action towards the *Every Child Matters* Green Paper (DfES, 2003) and heralded the naissance of integrated children's services as we know them today. Table 2.2 provides a summary of the main legislation that brought us to this point.

Table 2.2	Summary of main legislation that led to ECM	

Legislation/ report	Main elements
1388 First Poor Law	First known state support for those unable to work due to age or infirmity
1601 Old Poor Law	Formalized funding of support for the poor by the levying of a local tax – known as alms – collected in parishes
1834 New Poor Law	Parishes required to provide a workhouse available to furnish basics of shelter, food and clothing for the destitute in return for work
1872 Infant Life Protection Act	First regulation of infant minding, known as 'baby farming', of working mothers
1889 Prevention of Cruelty to Children Act	Gave the state the right to intervene in families if they were being abused. Previously children were regarded as the 'property' of their parents. The Act made cruelty to children illegal for the first time

1894 Prevention of Cruelty to Children (Amendment) Act	Allowed children to give evidence in court. Mental cruelty was recognized for the first time. It became an offence to deny medical aid to a sick child
1908 Children Act	Establishment of juvenile courts. Registration of foster parents
1908 Punishment of Incest Act	Incest made illegal for the first time – it had previously been left to the Church to regulate
1932 Children and Young Persons Act	Greater powers to juvenile courts, introduced supervision orders for children at risk. Amalgamated existing child protection law into a single piece of legislation
1948 Children Act	Children's committee and children's officer established in local authorities
1970 Local Authority Social Services Act	Amalgamation of social work services and social care provision into social services departments
1989 Children Act	Gave every child the right to protection from abuse and exploitation and the right to inquiries to safeguard their welfare
1999 Protection of Children Act	Required childcare organizations to inform the Department of Health about anyone known to them suspected of harming children or putting them at risk
2002 *Safeguarding Children*	A report of the joint chief inspectors on local arrangements to safeguard children throughout England
2003 *Victoria Climbié Inquiry*	Chaired by Lord Laming, it made 108 recommendations
2003 *Keeping Children Safe*	A response by government to the *Victoria Climbié Inquiry* and the joint chief inspectors' report *Safeguarding Children*
2003 *Every Child Matters* Green Paper	Proposal of child electronic tracking system in England. Children's trusts (150) to be set up to amalgamate education, health and social services, each headed by a children's director. Creation of a children's commissioner for England
2003 *ECM: What Do You Think?*	A version of the Green Paper for children and young people
2004 Children Act	Sets the ECM Green Paper proposals into law. Several papers produced to show how ECM would be implemented across different sectors:
	ECM: Change for Children (2004)
	ECM: Change for Children in Health Services (2004)
	ECM: Change for Children in Social Care (2004)
	ECM: Change for Children in the Criminal Justice System (2004)
	National Service Framework for Children, Young People and Maternity Services (2004)
	Working with Voluntary and Community Organisations to Deliver Change for Children and Young People (2004)
	ECM: Change for Children in Schools (2005)
	ECM: Change for Children – Young People and Drugs (2005)

How ECM is changing the children's services landscape

Changes to training and professional development

With the introduction of ECM, national training organizations were replaced by five Sector Skills Councils to address welfare services in the UK. One of these, the Children's Workforce Development Council (CWDC), was created especially to address integrated children's services. A primary goal was to improve the training and qualifications of professionals working in children's services, emphasizing a joined-up approach across the children's workforce, and improving the support and advice provided for children and their families.

One of the first initiatives of the CWDC was to introduce a framework to embed the Common Core of Skills and Knowledge (CCSK; see Box 2.2) into the training of all professionals in the children's workforce. CCSK was set out in the CWDC Common Core prospectus (DfES, 2005), which aimed to:

- support the development of more effective and integrated services
- introduce a common language among professionals and support staff
- begin to break down some of the cultural and practice barriers within the children's workforce
- promote more flexible development and career progression, allied to a single, national framework of qualifications.

Box 2.2	Common Core of Skills and Knowledge

1. *Effective communication and engagement with children, young people and families:* including working with parents, carers and families; listening and involving children and young people; communicating with children and young people in ways that are appropriate to their age; understanding cultural and diversity preferences; learning how to explain options and decisions to parents, carers and families in different circumstances; learning how to involve children, parents, carers and families in the creation of provision to meet their needs; understanding best practice in communication with people with disabilities.
2. *Child and young person development:* the ability to understand the full range of child development (physical, emotional and mental); understand different approaches for those with physical or mental health difficulties; recognize and understand a wide range of different behaviours; know when and how to ask for assistance.
3. *Safeguarding children and promoting the welfare of children:* understanding protocols for promoting and safeguarding the welfare of children and young people; knowing who to contact to express concerns; understanding protection factors; and understanding how children and young people manage risk themselves.
4. *Supporting transitions:* including children and young people's rights and responsibilities, maximizing their achievements and opportunities; understanding the effects of change in children and young people as they grow older, face new experiences

and challenges, move between different settings, rural areas, foster and other homes, and school stages.

5. *Multi-agency working:* working across professional boundaries and understanding the values of other professions; the vital importance of people working collaboratively to safeguard and support children and young people.

6. *Sharing information:* ensuring that individuals understand assessment frameworks; and develop awareness of the law, code of conduct and other guidance applicable to information sharing.

Source: Adapted from DfES, 2005

All vocational training within children's services was subsequently built around CCSK. Professional training was to be standardized via an Integrated Qualification Framework, a set of approved qualifications that would allow progression, continuing professional development and mobility across the children and young people's workforce. It would constitute a comprehensive set of qualifications agreed as appropriate for all people who work with children and young people, integrating shared values and learning approaches across the different sector bodies and occupational groups.

Improving the efficacy of multi-agency working

Key to ECM was effective multi-agency working and legislation which could embed this at local and national levels. Previously, responsibility for children had been shared across a number of departments: Department for Education and Skills (DfES); Department of Health (DH); Home Office, Department for Culture, Media and Sport (DCMS); and the Office of the Deputy Prime Minister (Barker, 2009). The creation of the Department for Children, Schools and Families (DCSF) in 2007 was intended to bring this within the remit of a single government department. Other initiatives were introduced with the goal of securing information in one central place, easily accessible and shared by appropriate practitioners. The Common Assessment Framework (CAF) was one such instrument.

The CAF is a standardized tool used in England to conduct an assessment of a child or young person's additional needs if it is thought that they are not able to meet the five intended outcomes of ECM without supplementary support. It provides a common assessment across services, thus reducing the number of different assessments – and different terminologies – used by various children's services. It is a voluntary process and can only be conducted with the consent of the children and parents concerned. The CAF is not used in high-risk situations or where abuse might be suspected – it is important to make the distinction here between children 'in need' and children who have 'additional needs' – and the CAF merely provides a generic base of fast, accurate information that can facilitate early intervention if it is needed. The target is for a CAF assessment to be completed within ten days of referral. Information is gathered on a standard form collated by a key worker based on discussions with the child and family.

Information is recorded on a single form, stored electronically and shared with other practitioners, where appropriate.

The CAF was piloted in 12 local authorities and an evaluation commissioned by the Department for Education and Skills (Brandon et al., 2006), with mixed outcomes. Some of the enthusiasm for a single generic assessment was offset by unease about how the concept of a holistic assessment was being interpreted and how the process was being completed in partnership with families. More deep-rooted concerns were expressed about additional workload, lack of professional support during the completion of the assessment, and an inability to secure any additional services requested. In some cases, the CAF was being used as a referral system rather than an assessment.

❝❝   Children's Perspectives

Despite the hype, rhetoric and clear guidance that CAF assessments were voluntary and to be completed in partnership with children and families, children were not included in the evaluation study of the pilot, not even by the proxy of their parents, since the remit of the DfES pilot evaluation excluded any consultation with families (Walker, 2008: 61):

> The research brief from the Department for Education and Skills did not include eliciting the views of children and families as to the benefits of the process. The authors of the report refer to this as a 'major omission' and it seems especially so in light of the apparent focus the government has placed on listening to children and families. One can draw several conclusions from this, including that the Department for Education and Skills wanted a quick and limited evaluation with which to support the rhetoric of the CAF; another conclusion could be that they were somewhat apprehensive of what children and families might say about the process.

Legislation to embed ECM

The *Every Child Matters* Green Paper appeared in 2003 and was followed by legislation to embed its principles into law and into practice, principally the Children Act 2004 and later the 2007 Children's Plan.

The Children Act 2004 was the legal enactment of the reforms proposed in the ECM Green Paper. The first part of the Act relates to the establishment of a children's commissioner for England, who would work closely with the children's commissioners already established in the other nation states, to advocate on behalf of children and young people. The children's commissioner was required to report annually to Parliament. Fundamental to the role was fostering a listening culture and examining how public and private sector bodies went about listening to children. The second part of the Act concerns the promotion of integrated working across children's services and the placing of responsibility for this on local authorities. For the first time it would be possible to pool resources across previously segregated services such as health and education. A third section of the Act addressed communication and information sharing and legislated for the setting up of a national database to contain basic information about 11 million children under the age of 18, which could be shared between professionals, facilitate early intervention, and prevent the kind of communication failings that led to the death of Victoria Climbié. This database, known as ContactPoint, finally went live in 2009 after a series of delays and was made available to 150 local authorities in England and around a third of a million practitioners across children's services.

There were mixed reactions to the introduction of ContactPoint. Ever controversial, it was one of the first initiatives to be scrapped by the coalition government that came to power in May 2010. Nevertheless, in the historical context of ECM, it is important to review this policy as it epitomizes many of the tensions and complexities that abound in the integration of children's services, not least the inadequate representation of children's perspectives.

Some saw ContactPoint as an inevitable necessity if further tragedies such as the death of Victoria Climbié were to be prevented. Indeed, the death of Baby Peter in 2007, which was a similar tale of bungled multiple agency communication and a failure to implement recommendations from Laming's 2003 inquiry, added fuel to this argument. However, others were concerned about the infringement of privacy and civil liberties and that the storing of basic data would be the thin end of a wedge which would lead to ever more sensitive information being made available to large numbers of people (Batty, 2003; Ward, 2004). There were further concerns about the high cost of collating and maintaining a national database of children and many argued that this high cost could be better spent on targeted support (for example Searing, 2007). ContactPoint cost £224 million to set up and £41 million per year to operate (www.silicon.com). A national database brings no guarantees of increased child protection, since it is not information itself that will save children but how the information is used, specifically how it is understood and interpreted. Anger was also expressed by some parents who claimed that their rights as parents were being infringed. Perhaps the greater concern is the minimal consultation with children themselves, given that this was putatively an initiative to embed ECM; clearly, every child did not matter sufficiently to be consulted about how their personal details are stored and who has access to them.

❝❝   Children's Perspectives

Children's views about ContactPoint were confined to one small consultation project (Morgan, 2007). It was commissioned by the government and undertaken by the Children's Rights Director for England Roger Morgan. Of 11 million children affected by the introduction of ContactPoint, only one small web survey (n = 47) and one focus group (n = 15) were carried out to elicit children's opinions. All 62 children consulted were in the care system. While this is an important and vulnerable group to survey because their details are likely to be accessed more frequently than most children, it was a token gesture that excluded whole swathes of children from having a say about ContactPoint. Moreover, the remit of the project did not allow for the eliciting of children's views about whether ContactPoint was a good idea or not.

Morgan's (2007) consultation exercise was confined to the administrative aspects of the database, how it would work and what children perceived to be good and bad points about it. A range of views was captured through the web survey and the focus group. Many concerns were raised by the participating children but the overriding anxiety was around the security of the database and measures to ensure that their details were safe and could not be accessed inappropriately. Some genuine fear was expressed, for example one child commented: 'I will be scared my dad could find me' (p. 11). Children appeared to have little faith that the security of the database would not be breached or that adults would not divulge information to others who did not have legitimate access to ContactPoint.

There were misgivings about promises being broken and adults not following rules:

> 'How many times has the government promised things, put it on paper but do not follow them – do you know that there are young people who do not get visited by their social workers, yet it is written on paper. Make sure that this happens for real, please' (p. 11).

Others were frightened by the prospect of paedophiles getting hold of information about them:

> They thought that paedophiles would spend a lot of time and effort trying to break into ContactPoint. They thought that one day, eventually, the system would either break down, or its security would be breached (p. 10).

Children wanted strong security measures put in place and thought that electronic tags and passwords would not be enough because adults would give others their passwords. Children were unhappy that people they did not know would be able to look up information about them and wanted adults to seek their permission before this could happen. They were anxious that people could find out where they lived and stressed the importance of safety: 'my safety should come first'; 'because I want to be kept safe at all times' (p. 11). Data from the focus group revealed similar concerns:

> all children who could understand should have the choice of having their details kept more safely so that people could not look them up easily on ContactPoint. They too thought that people being able to look up any child's address put children generally in danger (p. 10).

Other issues raised by the consultation included:

- letting children know what information is going to be held on them before it's up and running
- making sure all staff are fully trained before putting ContactPoint into force
- making sure there are no errors
- the computer might break down and lose information on young people – 'u can't put too much trust in a machine'
- wrong information might be circulated
- children should be informed of who is using ContactPoint.

One would like to think that the coalition government's decision to terminate ContactPoint was informed by children's concerns about their privacy but my own opinion is that this decision was more likely to have been driven by budgetary constraints.

Leadership and management

One of the recommendations of the Laming Report (2003) was to remove ambivalence and improve accountability in the leadership and management of children's services, particularly where this relates to child protection. The more senior the role, the more the focus appears to lean towards strategy and budgets and less about accountability for individual cases. The Laming Report also indicated that senior managers can lose sight of their primary goal, that is, providing quality services for children, in the rush to meet organizational and procedural targets. Laming was quite clear that senior managers did have responsibility for what happened at the grass roots of their departments and therefore shared some of the responsibility when things went wrong in individual cases:

> The Enquiry saw too many examples of those in senior positions attempting to justify their work in terms of bureaucratic activity, rather than in outcomes for people. (Laming, 2003: 6)

The Children Act 2004 set up statutory local safeguarding children boards (more on this in Chapter 10), made up of key child practitioners plus lay members to oversee child protection issues in local regions. Tighter regulations were introduced for the inspection of children's services, which henceforth were to be carried out through an integrated inspection framework rather than separate inspection bodies. Each local authority was required to set up joint area reviews to evaluate how effectively integrated children's services were functioning. The Act also strengthened provision for looked-after children, particularly in relation to their educational achievements and that this should be an important factor in placement decisions. It brought into being a statutory notification scheme for private fostering arrangements – a direct response to the private fostering issues that had been a factor in the Victoria Climbié case.

Annual children and young people's plans

The Children Act 2004 put in place a requirement that every local authority produce a single children and young people's plan, which was to replace the separate plans (some statutory and some non-statutory) from different children's agencies. This was a clear steer towards integration of children's services not just at delivery but at the earliest planning stages too. It was replicated at national level with the launch in December 2007 of *The Children's Plan* (DCSF, 2007), which set out the government's ten-year plan to deliver high-quality integrated children's services. Interestingly, this followed the publication of the 2007 UNICEF report on children's wellbeing, which placed British children bottom of the 'happiness' rankings. The stinging impact of the UNICEF research is evident from the very first sentence of the secretary of state's Forward: 'Our aim is to make this the *best place in the world* for our children and young people to grow up' (DCSF, 2007: 3, emphasis added).

The Children's Plan is based on five underlying principles:

1. government does not bring up children – parents do – so government needs to do more to back parents and families
2. all children have the potential to succeed and should go as far as their talents can take them
3. children and young people need to enjoy their childhood as well as grow up prepared for adult life
4. services need to be shaped by and responsive to children, young people and families, not designed around professional boundaries
5. it is always better to prevent failure than tackle a crisis later (DCSF, 2007: 5–6).

The Children's Plan was organized into seven chapters around these principles:

1. Happy and healthy
2. Safe and sound
3. Excellence and equity
4. Leadership and collaboration
5. Staying on
6. On the right track
7. Making it happen.

Each chapter set out goals for children's wellbeing, how these would be achieved and what resources would be provided.

The role of parents was elevated in a number of ways, including the appointment of two expert parenting advisers in every local authority. Training was identified as pivotal and the upskilling of the children's workforce declared a priority. Children's happiness and wellbeing were ensconced in commitments to eradicate child poverty by 2020, prioritize children's needs in housing decisions, and regenerate 3,500 playgrounds. Research was commissioned into how to keep children safe on the internet and protected from toxic commercialism. More support was highlighted for disabled children and additional funds made available for them to have respite breaks. Better education was targeted through more support in the early years, more involvement of parents, focused one-to-one support for literacy where needed, and more investment in technology. To achieve these goals, the government stated that it would:

- expect every school to be uncompromising in its ambitions for achievement, sitting at the heart of the community it serves
- set high expectations for Children's Trusts to:
  - deliver measurable improvements for all children and young people
  - have in place by 2010 consistent, high quality arrangements to provide identification and early intervention for all children and young people who need additional help
- monitor the difference Children's Trusts are making and examine whether Children's Trust arrangements need to be strengthened to improve outcomes, including by further legislation
- publish a Children's Workforce Action Plan in early 2008, covering everyone who works with children and young people, which will strengthen integrated working across all services (DCSF, 2007: 14).

The Children's Plan is an initiative that attempts to tailor integrated services to meet the needs of children and families, with an emphasis on early intervention and prevention. But what do children think about it?

> **❝ Children's Experiences**
>
> A few months before the Children's Plan was launched in December 2007, the government undertook a consultation exercise in four locations in England. Approximately 100 people took part in each location: 40 children's professionals, 30 parents and 30 young people aged 16–19. *No one* under the age of 16 had the opportunity to express a view about the proposed Children's Plan other than through a parent. Once again the absence of child voice and agency in processes operating under the mantle of ECM is shown to be at best ironical and at worst cynical. The listening culture so widely touted as essential to a better understanding of children's worlds and children's needs appears to have completely bypassed a ten-year plan to deliver them a brighter future.

New roles and organizations to embed integrated children's services

Children's trusts

Children's trusts are a primary vehicle of ECM and the embodiment of integrated working. They bring together all local services for children into one area, typically at a children's centre or an extended school. The ministerial guidance on setting up children's trusts clearly puts the child at the centre of the governance structures, with four rings of integrated service activity emanating out from this, beginning with delivery of integrated frontline services (see Figure 2.1).

| Figure 2.1 | Putting the child at the heart of governance structures |

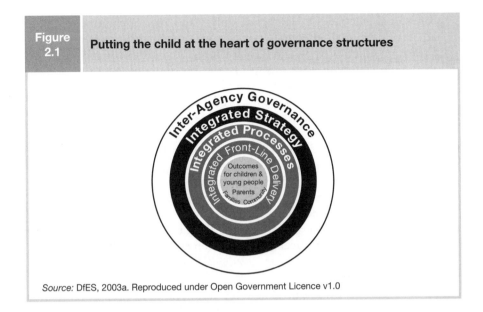

Source: DfES, 2003a. Reproduced under Open Government Licence v1.0

Purposely configured multidisciplinary teams replace individual professionals operating from multiple agencies. Previously, education, health and social services, the 'giants' of children's services, were run as separate organizations with their own autonomy and their own funding. Combining three such large bodies into children's trusts, pooling resources and sharing funding has proved challenging. Professional identities and boundaries became blurred as specialists worked alongside generalists in multidisciplinary teams. This new-look children's services needed strong leadership and management to hold the glue in place. A director of children's services (DCS) role was created to replace the previous two roles of director of education and director of social services. The DCS would now be responsible for delivering integrated children's services in a designated local area. These included education, social services and any children's health services delegated to the local authority by the NHS. The demands of the role and the accountability across such a wide breadth of services have not made them easy appointments to fill. Moreover, a noted tendency to appoint former directors of education into the roles has created some unease and resentment. Consternation expressed about the dominance of education personnel in DCS roles may yet result in a loss of senior managerial experience in child protection. This has added fuel to some existing dissatisfaction, particularly in the health domain, about the locus of children's services being positioned in the education arena. Other problems were highlighted in data collected for the National Evaluation of Children's Trusts in 2004, as detailed in O'Brien et al.'s research on the early pathfinder trusts (2006: 385):

arrangements for co-operation on governance and strategic
developments were more advanced than for procedural or frontline

professional practice. On aggregate, only 6 and 14% of pathfinders had 'developmental' integrated governance or strategic arrangements in place, in contrast to 34 and 23% for integrated processes and integrated delivery indicators respectively. For instance, all 35 pathfinders had a children's trust board or equivalent structure, whereas only 15 had a protocol for professional groups to share pupil, client, or patient level data.

O'Brien et al.'s research discusses mixed responses to shared budgets. These worked well for some aspects, such as pooling budgets to set up single safe-guarding units, but not for others, with major conflicts ensuing over how different professionals regarded needs as deriving from social care or health: 'Negotiations could become intensely strained when scarce resources combined with expensive interventions, for example the need for "out of area" child fostering or other specialist placements' (O'Brien et al., 2006: 388).

Children's centres

Children's centres evolved out of national early years and child development initiatives. The first of these were the Early Excellence Centres (EECs), which appeared in 1997. EECs were intended to provide a one-stop provision for young children and were early models of integrated services. They provided child daycare, early years education and adult learning. The concept of EECs was built on to provide targeted support into the most deprived areas, the new establishments being launched as Sure Start centres from 1999. Service provision was extended to include support for minority ethnic families, language and literacy projects, parenting advice, health clinics, drop-in centres and support for children with special needs. The Sure Start initiative was broadened out from areas of deprivation into universal children's centres. By 2010, the government aimed to have a children's centre operating in every local community. Integrated services on offer include integrated early education and childcare, parenting advice, childcare options, child health services, parents into work support with links to training programmes and job centres. An Ofsted (2009: 6) evaluation of 20 Sure Start children's centres found that:

- In 11 of the 20 centres visited, the impact of the integration of services on improving outcomes for children, parents and families was good or outstanding. In only one centre was the impact inadequate. Nearly all the centres had established an effective balance between providing integrated services that are open to everyone and those that are targeted towards potentially vulnerable families.
- Parents strongly preferred a single site, one-stop shop model for children's centres. This is impractical in rural areas, where families, especially disadvantaged families, may not be able to afford to travel to a centre remote from their homes.

- In the centres visited, children with early learning difficulties and/or disabilities were well provided for, with good early interventions and prompt referrals.
- The centres were successful in involving many aspiring and motivated parents from minority ethnic groups, including Eastern European families. They were sometimes less successful in gaining the confidence of white British families in disadvantaged communities.
- The key work of the centres in reaching the most potentially vulnerable children and families was developing well. However, early successes in integrated working with the most vulnerable families were revealing the scale of some of the problems, particularly of domestic violence.
- Children's centre teachers, speech and language therapists and daycare staff were successfully improving the quality of daycare provision in the centres visited. However, onward links with far too many primary schools remained weak. With notable exceptions, the survey found that primary schools did not yet engage fully with children's centres.
- A weaker feature of all centres visited was their link with Jobcentre Plus.
- Despite the growing use of the Sure Start self-evaluation form, centres often lacked the data about outcomes to evaluate rigorously their present and longer term impact on children and families. Data at national, local authority, locality and school levels were inadequate to support the centres in effective self-evaluation.

Issues relating to extended schools are covered in some depth in Chapter 4 and are mentioned here simply in relation to the historical chronology in the evolution of integrated children's services. Their purpose is similar to that of children's centres in providing a one-stop shop for wraparound services.

New roles

The emphasis on integrated working was also facilitated by the creation of new professional roles. One of these, the children's commissioner, was alluded to earlier in relation to the Children Act 2004 where the English role was announced. Significantly, children's commissioner roles were already in place in the other nation states where they had all been given a clear remit linked to children's rights. This, however, was not to be the case for the children's commissioner in England. This role was defined as promoting the needs and views of children. So, not only was England the last nation in the UK to have a children's commissioner, it also endowed its commissioner with the least power. However, one positive was that children were directly involved in the process of appointing the first English commissioner in 2004, Sir Al Aynsley-Green. He created 11 Million (depicting the 11 million children in England) as the organizational arm of his office.

Another important role fashioned to embed ECM is the lead professional. This role is intended to be a single point of contact for children and their families to help them cope with the multiple agencies they might engage with – a child with complex needs might be seen by as many as 20 or more different organizations – to improve communication and reduce overlap. A lead professional is identified and agreed from among the group of practitioners working with the child. It is generally someone from an agency that has the main responsibility for supporting the child's needs and is likely to be a professional who has an advocacy role or has already built up a rapport with the family. There are still some tensions in this role and some of these will be debated when the role is discussed in more detail in Chapter 5.

The integration of children's services into one large department required changes to be made to inspection services which had previously been spread across several agencies in three former departments. The Children Act 2004 made provision for inspection to be collated into one service. This organization was named as Ofsted, the agency that had formerly inspected schools. The new inspection regime was tasked with examining how integration was working, how multidisciplinary teams were performing, how effective the protection of vulnerable children was, how well service providers can identify their strengths and weaknesses, and the level to which children and parents' views are considered. Success indicators were based on the degree to which the five ECM outcomes were being achieved. There was widespread criticism of the impossible scale of this charge (Anning et al., 2006) and the inappropriate measures being employed (Fitzgerald and Kay, 2009), especially as the five ECM outcomes are not easily defined for evaluative purposes since they are framed in aspirational terms. The educational legacy of Ofsted also influenced the interpretation of the outcomes, sometimes in very narrow ways, such as 'enjoying and achieving' being measured in terms of school attendance and 'making a positive contribution' measured as an absence of antisocial behaviour (Hudson, 2005). The other major area of tension is that education has retained a significant level of autonomy despite the collation of children's services. Ofsted might not be best placed to identify poor interagency working in schools despite the inspectorate's supposedly multidisciplinary teams – review teams are made up of representatives from Ofsted, the former inspectorate commissions for social care and healthcare (CSCI and HCC) and adult learning (ALI). Equally, questions have been raised about the ability of Ofsted to inspect the complexities of social service departments, not least when the tragedy of Baby Peter revealed there had been a recent Ofsted inspection of Haringey council that reported 'good' levels of child protection. Christine Gilbert, head of Ofsted, admitted inadequacies in the system, as reported by Polly Curtis, editor of *Education Guardian* (Curtis, 2008: 1):

In her first major interview since the verdict on Baby P's death was returned, Christine Gilbert admitted to failings in Ofsted's oversight of Haringey council, acknowledging that officials in the local authority where Baby P died were able to 'hide behind' false data last year to earn themselves a good rating from inspectors just weeks after his death.

It would appear there is a long way to go before integrated children's services are either working optimally or being evaluated effectively.

Criticisms of ECM

It is important not to assume that ECM was a golden solution. There are many critics who consider the tight structural approach to be too rigid, especially in relation to assessment processes such as CAF (for example White et al., 2009). Others are wary that the impetus is emerging out of safeguarding children at the expense of preventive practice, with resultant tensions that ensue between professionals: 'Balancing keeping children safe within such a universal approach is structurally complex, and at a delivery level, often emotionally difficult for professionals' (O'Brien et al., 2006: 393). Hoyle (2008) is concerned that the shift in accountability to local authorities and children's trusts enables government to take all the credit for the oratory and vision, while diverting blame for any failures onto local councils and providers. From children's perspectives, and supported by researchers such as Hilton and Mills (2006), is the unease that the reporting and assessment processes of ECM threaten the privacy rights of children and young people. They fear that sensitive information will find its way inappropriately onto databases and be vulnerable to misuse. Perhaps the deepest criticism is the oversimplicity and universal acceptance of ECM that fails to acknowledge it as a social construction, what Thorpe (1994) refers to as 'situated moral reasoning'. In other words, theoretically, the moral imperative of ECM is not contestable but the reality is that ECM has been socially constructed on unconscious social and moral beliefs which reflect white, heterosexual, Christian ideals. Despite all the rhetoric and the clearly well-meaning intentions, critics would maintain that ECM may actually exclude some of the very groups it aspires to provide for.

Conclusion

There is a long historical trail leading up to ECM. This chapter has summarized the main chronological events that have contributed to the shaping of its agenda. The rights-based perspective encapsulated in the UNCRC and high-profile child death cases were the main drivers of ECM reform. Interagency working, joined-up thinking and pooled resources became cornerstones of an agenda that sought to shift children's services from autonomous silos to collaborative provision 'around the child'. The central premise was that integrated services should start from the needs of children, not the structures of organizations, departments and teams which provide them. ECM required significant changes to systems and processes, including the compiling of controversial electronic child databases with shared access for professionals and ambitious training programmes for upskilling the children's workforce. It was essential that every member of the children's workforce had a common core of knowledge about children's development and needs, which gave rise to CCKS. Children's trusts became organizational hives with Sure Start children's centres – 3,500 by 2010 – providing the 'worker bees' to get children off to a flying start in pursuit of the five ECM outcomes. ECM is not without its critics and some of the main debates were briefly outlined. As this book unfolds, these debates will be expanded on the service issues raised here and examined in greater detail in themed chapters. Before that, Chapter 3 provides some theoretical background to complement this historical overview.

Reflection exercises

1. For all readers

Jot down what you think the main pros and cons of ECM are. What are the main benefits and drawbacks? Do you think the criticisms outlined are well founded? Are there other issues that you consider to be pertinent which have not been explored?

2. For staff working with children and young people in multidisciplinary teams

Look again at Figure 2.1, the diagram of concentric circles with outcomes for children and their families at the heart. Where is your own practice located? Are you in the first circle of frontline services or one of the outer organizational circles? On a large piece of paper, draw the five circles leaving plenty of space to write in each one. Put yourself and your team on the diagram and then add in all the agencies, organizations and departments you work closely with into the circle you think is most appropriate. Once you have done this, look at where you have put them and reflect on the liaison required. How many overlaps are there? Is there any duplication? Are there ways in which it could be improved?

3. Children's perspectives

Take some time to reflect on the accounts of the deaths of Maria, Jasmine and Victoria. Compare and contrast their experiences. Were there any common themes? What were the main lessons? Why do you think we failed to learn from them?

Suggested further reading

1. Frost, N. and Parton, N. (2009) *Understanding Children's Social Care: Politics, Policy and Practice*, London: Sage

   Chapter 2 has a good depiction of children's services in the postwar period, which I can only refer to briefly in this chapter because of limited space. Provides useful supplementary material.

2. Laming, H. (2003) *The Victoria Climbié Inquiry*, London: TSO (also available as a free download at http://www.londonscb.gov.uk/files/library/climbie_inquiry.pdf)

   So fundamental to the evolution of ECM that it is worth dipping into the original inquiry report. Section 3 is entitled 'Victoria's story' and provides the facts of the case as seen from her perspective.

3. Hoyle, D. (2008) *Problematizing Every Child Matters*, www.infed.org/socialwork/every_child_matters_a_critique.htm.

   Articulates the main debates generally cited in critiques of Every Child Matters. It is quite philosophical in style but makes some weighty and eloquent arguments that are thought provoking.

4. Chand, A. (2008) 'Every child matters? A critical review of child welfare reforms in the context of minority ethnic children and families', *Child Abuse Review,* 17(1), 6–22

   Focuses particularly on the evolution of ECM in respect of minority ethnic children. Draws on research studies that have considered the experiences of different minority ethnic groups from the point of referrals through to long-term services, including those children who have been looked after in local authority care and those families that have been subject to care proceedings.

3 The Theoretical Framework

In this chapter we discuss:

- What is childhood?
- A child's perspective of childhood
- Interdisciplinary approaches to childhood
- Discourses on childhood
- Theories of power and the effect on adult–child relations
- Classical liberalism, embedded liberalism and neoliberalism
- The Third Way and concepts of 'capital'

The intention of this chapter is not to provide a treatise on theories of childhood, there are many texts that do this much better (see Suggested further reading), but to summarize the main theories that have contributed to scholarship about children and childhood, so that the influences these have had on policy and practice can be mapped to the journey that has brought us to Every Child Matters (ECM). Policies are shaped by the dominant theories of an era. The integration of children's services can be better understood and contextualized if we have a grasp of the complexity and contradictions of the underpinning theoretical frameworks. ECM, in aiming for a holistic, equitable, joined-up approach to children's services, is tasked with making sense of, and harmonizing, the various contradictions that successive policies have spawned. This chapter explores the interweaving of those theories and policies and their influence on ECM. I begin by reflecting on the meaning of childhood and how theory has moulded the evolving status of children in society.

Box 3.1	What is childhood?

- Has the concept of childhood always existed?
- Is childhood a separate stage or part of a human continuum?
- Can children ever just 'be' or are they always in a state of 'becoming?
- Do children have an exclusive identity or is their identity subsumed within adult apprenticeship?

The questions in Box 3.1 are typical of those that have shaped perspectives on childhood over time, constructed from a variety of standpoints – philosophy, psychology, biology, sociology and anthropology (Kellett et al., 2004). There is a degree of oversimplification in separating out perspectives into opposing schools of thought. All of them at one and several times have influenced policy in relation to childhood.

The main arena for debate has been between psychological and sociological disciplines. The dominant theory in developmental psychology is that children move from child to adult status in defined stages in a model that is adult-centric and based on measurement against norms of competence (Woodhead and Faulkner, 2008). The dominant sociological theory assumes that children are socially competent and autonomous within their own cultural worlds, an assertion of the integrity of the child perspective. They are beings, not becomings. This model depicts childhood as a transient stage in life during which children engage in everyday activities as social actors in their own right. Children ultimately become adults, so childhood, while it has a separate and unique identity, is also dynamic and transient where children are agentic in ever-changing social and cultural contexts.

This paradigm became known as the 'new sociology of childhood' (James et al., 1998). It acknowledges that children have an active role to play in the determination of their own lives. It widens the scope of childhood to a societal level, puts a new emphasis on children's rights, participation and voice, and an increased focus on childhood as a social category and children as a distinct population group. The watershed of the United Nations Convention on the Rights of the Child (1989) signalled that a clear, discursive space had been delineated for children. They have an autonomy that exists outside family, school and institutions and a voice conditioned neither by competence nor chronological age.

The status of children in society is also closely bound up with a rights discourse, but one that is full of contradictions. Children have a right to education but no right to choose which school they might attend and must rely on parents to include them in any decision-making processes. Children have rights to welfare, and necessarily rely on adults to provide this. They also have rights to self-determination (Wyness et al., 2004) and are not only shaped by their social setting but also actively help to shape it (James and James, 2004). Prout (2001) suggests that children need to be viewed as occupying a position within a network of relationships rather than being seen at the bottom of a hierarchical model of networks.

A child's perspective of childhood

Children are key stakeholders and service users. This is not confined to specifically child-oriented provision such as schools and child health clinics. Children are part of families who access a much broader range of services. The efficacy of those services can have just as big an impact on the quality of childhood and one must not assume that children will view them in the same way as their parents. Manasa Patil is an able-bodied, 11-year-old girl whose father is a wheelchair user. She tells her own story about how this impacts on the quality of her childhood (Patil, 2006).

" Children's Perspectives

Getting around as the child of a wheelchair user: a small-scale research project – Manasa Patil, aged 11

Introduction

There is quite a lot of research about wheelchair users, young and old, but what is rarely researched is what it's like to be the child of a wheelchair user and the impact of this on childhood itself. Because my dad is disabled and relies on a wheelchair, I have an understanding of this. So I decided to investigate this in more depth and focus on transport issues.

Methodology

I used a combination of methods to investigate this,

- I did some close observations of three different types of journeys: bus, pedestrian and train.
- I kept a research diary.
- I put together a life narrative from my memories and experiences.

My findings

The findings of my research are in three parts, each one relating to one of the modes of transport.

1: Getting around by bus

On the bus journey I made some observations and recorded them onto a Dictaphone. This is a summary of what I found out along with my research diary data and my life narrative data:

We waited at the bus stop but my dad was not allowed onto the first bus. The bus driver slowed down at the stop but as soon as he saw my dad's wheelchair he started to pull away shouting that there was already a pushchair in the wheelchair space.

It was very cold and we had to wait another 15 minutes for a bus. This made us late. I felt really upset that the bus driver hadn't even stopped to explain properly why we couldn't get on the bus. From my memories I know that this happens quite a lot. Sometimes if it's raining and the bus driver doesn't want to have to get out and put up the ramp they just don't stop even though there is a space for the wheelchair on the bus. This affects what I can do as a child out with my dad. For example once I was really excited to be going to the cinema with my dad. Everyone in my class had already seen Harry Potter and I was dying to see it too but Dad is often unwell and we hadn't been able to get out. Anyway, once he was well enough he promised to take me and I was so excited to be going at last. We waited at the bus stop but we were refused entry onto the bus even though I could see there was a free wheelchair space. We weren't allowed on the next bus either and by the time we got to the cinema we had missed quite a bit of the film. This spoilt the whole occasion for me and I had been so looking forward to it.

There are some really helpful bus drivers but I wish it could be all of the time. For example once a bus driver didn't allow my dad on the bus because his wheelchair was battery-powered; however, my dad has always been travelling on buses with his battery-powered wheelchair and has not had a problem; therefore, I think that the bus drivers should be more well informed about these kinds of things.

There are some really nice bus drivers but sometimes some can be quite rude in the way they talk to us and I think this is because they don't actually want to have to get down to lower the ramp for the wheelchair.

Another big problem for my dad is that there are only two buses in our area that have a ramp and a wheelchair space which makes it even more likely that we will be unable to travel. I really love going out with my dad but I am constantly disappointed and this makes me feel sad and angry. Even though I am not disabled myself it feels like my childhood is disabled because I can't do normal things with my dad like other children can do.

All the buses that we have travelled on in the past (and now) have a really narrow wheelchair space, so my dad has difficulty positioning his wheelchair in it. Sometimes the bus drivers get impatient of waiting and drive off before he has properly adjusted the wheelchair.

Lastly, it is hard for my dad to put the bus tickets into the machine that checks them, because the machine is too high and my dad cannot reach it.

From this first part of my research study I would like to make some suggestions to the bus company that would help people like me and my dad.

- All buses (not just a few) should have wheelchair ramps
- All the ramps should be electronic so that bus drivers don't have to get out of the bus to put it in place
- There should be a space for a wheelchair AND a pushchair not one or the other because too often the wheelchair can't get on because of pushchairs.
- There should be more training for bus drivers about disabled people and wheelchair users so that they might be more understanding about our difficulties particularly about trying to manoeuvre the chair into a very narrow, awkward space.
- For the future design of buses, these problems should be taken into consideration and the necessary improvements should be made. This may result in better facilities on buses for other wheelchair users.

I hope these suggestions are not too much to ask for because they would make a really big difference to the quality of my childhood. I could do more things with my dad more easily and more often – just like other kids do!

2: Getting around on foot

It was easier getting around on foot than travelling on the bus although there were a few difficulties. The roads were bumpy and rocky in some places which meant that my dad's wheelchair got punctured and sometimes the pavement was too high for us to get the wheelchair up onto it. In some places, the pavement was too narrow and it was difficult for my dad to ride on it. These things mean that we had to find an alternative route and it made the journey a lot longer but otherwise getting around on foot as the child of a wheelchair user is not difficult.

3: Getting around by train

The train journey I collected data on was from Banbury to Oxford, which takes about 30 minutes each way and has three stops. I made some observations and recorded them onto a Dictaphone. This is a summary of what I found out along with my research diary data and my life narrative data.

My dad had to book 24 hours in advance for a place on the train. This is because the train staff need this time for safety reasons and seat availability in both departure and arrival trains. The train had four second class carriages but only one wheelchair space. If someone else had booked that space we would have been unable to travel. Having to always think ahead and always wondering if we will be able to get a space on a train makes some social outings very difficult and it is impossible to be spontaneous. Other children can be spontaneous with their family. If it is a nice sunny Saturday and they decide to have a day out on the train, they will generally be able to do this without any difficulty. For me as the child of a wheelchair user a fun day out on the train can never be a spontaneous event. This makes me feel sad especially as it is not me who is disabled but my dad but it still affects the quality of my childhood.

It was hard for my dad to position his wheelchair in the space provided because the space is very narrow. The passage leading to the wheelchair space is also narrow and very curvy, so it is hard for my dad to move around the train.

The staff were very kind and polite but they didn't seem to be very well informed about what it's like for wheelchair users and particularly what it's like for children of wheelchair users.

Another major problem was that when our train arrived back at the station, nobody came with a ramp to help my dad get down. Luckily someone helped us and my dad was able to get down. However, this has happened to me before, when I was travelling with just my dad: no one came to our stop to help my dad get down, even though we had informed the staff. As I was quite young, I couldn't really help my dad and so we ended up missing our stop. We got down at the next stop but then it was difficult to get a train back home. I felt anxious and scared and I started to cry. I hear my friends talk about the excitement of train journeys and feel a bit envious because so many of my memories are of being frightened and anxious. It's easy for other children. People forget how hard it is for children whose parent is a wheelchair-user.

On the occasion when I collected my data the train was not very busy so I was able to stay next to him. But on other journeys I have done with my Dad when the train is crowded it is difficult to sit close to him because the wheelchair has to go in a special place and only the wheelchair space itself is reserved not any seat nearby. For a child this can be quite upsetting. I felt nervous and scared sitting next to a stranger when my Dad wasn't close by.

I know there are not many problems with the train, but the existing problems are very serious and should be taken into consideration for the future.

- I think that there should be better communication between the train services;
- I think that ALL trains should have an electric ramp installed into them because this would make it a lot easier for wheelchair users, as the existing ramp can only be put down by a member of staff but sometimes they may not be informed and wheelchair users may miss their train/stop.
- Only some trains have a ramp facility so that limits the transportation for my dad and other wheelchair users.

The train is the hardest and riskiest way to get around because there is no guarantee you'll get a ticket when you want or need to travel especially if you want to do something spontaneous. You might miss your stop because of poor communication about needing a ramp and this is very frightening for a child. This has given me a bit of a phobia of travelling on a train even when I'm not with my dad.

Overall, the train journey was quite convenient, but it is also quite risky because of all the serious problems, nevertheless, the staff are very helpful and polite. This was only a short local journey and I feel daunted by the thought of a longer train journey as the problems could be even greater. This is a shame because I would like to be able to visit other places with my dad.

Conclusions

I felt it was important to explore how children like me get around with a parent who is a wheelchair user and the impact of this on childhood and how this will impact on my feelings about transport when I'm older. There are some things that are hard to forget and will stay with you a long time. The experience of being shouted at by bus drivers and felt to be a nuisance is upsetting and embarrassing and this will stay with me a long time even when I'm older and not travelling with my dad. The fear of missing my stop because no-one will get the ramp that will enable us to get off the train has given me a bit of a phobia about travelling on trains. Many of my childhood treats have been spoiled by transport difficulties but I hope that my research has raised awareness about some of these things from children's viewpoint. I hope that it might help other children like me might have happier experiences getting around in the future.

Source: Patil, 2006

Interdisciplinary approaches to childhood

The growth of childhood studies as an academic discipline has extended childhood research into other fields, notably cultural studies, anthropology, social policy, applied education, the law and economics (particularly child labour), with an increasingly global perspective. In accepting the notion of children as co-constructors of society, we are accepting that childhood is a permanent part of this social structure which invites empirical enquiry into how childhood relates to wider social forces (Christensen and Prout, 2005).

Difference emanates from discrete theoretical frameworks underlying the various disciplines. Research techniques emerge from theoretical positions which reflect researchers' beliefs, values and dispositions towards the social world (Gray and Denicolo, 1998). Where is the value base located for childhood research? What does it mean to be a child? Should we think in terms of childhood or childhoods? What are the cultural implications? When is a child a child? Childhood cannot be expressed in simple homogeneous terms. An interdisciplinary approach accentuates difference and perspective. A child has an identity as a child but may also have other multiple identities, for example as black, female and/or disabled.

Sociologists view child development as unpredictable rather than universally periodic and acknowledge that it is influenced by cultural goals

(Smith, 2002). Generational ordering provides a more systematic pattern of social relationships, acknowledges diversity and avoids disconnecting the study of childhood from general social theory (Prout, 2002; Mayall and Zeiher, 2003). This broader framework blurs the boundaries between childhood and adulthood:

> The range of possibilities and opportunities to move between identities seem to be fewer for adults, and in this sense social change mirrors physical change rather than being in opposition to it. As we age and grow there are more 'fixed points' and a greater degree of certainty, based on decreasing pace of change and increasing resources in terms of knowledge and physical capacity. (Smith, 2010: 81)

Discourses on childhood

Daniel and Ivatts (1998) assert that representations of children in society fall into one of three categories: victim, threat or investment. This classification underlines the complex nature of childhood discourses that have evolved over time.

Box 3.2	**Primary discourses on childhood**

A *needs* discourse that seeks to identify children's basic needs, and where action is directed to ensuring that those needs are met

A *rights* discourse that seeks to establish children's rights and entitlements, and where action is directed to promoting these rights

A *quality of life* discourse that seeks to determine what constitutes, for children, a 'good' quality of life, where action is directed to improving the quality of children's lives.

Source: Stainton-Rogers, 1994: 127

With such an internecine array of discourses, it is not surprising that child welfare policy is full of contradictions and tensions. Policy emanating from the needs discourse identifies the biological and psychological needs of infants and children. Here, the child is entirely passive and the state is paternalistic in its value-driven determination of those needs, seeking to provide solutions to the problems created by need. Play is a good example of the conceptual tussle here. A needs-based policy legislates on the basis of play being *good* for children, for example learning through play, whereas a rights-based policy is predicated on *entitlement*, for example enjoying play for its own sake.

" **Children's Perspectives**

Kapasi and Gleave (2009) carried out some research about play based on eight focus groups with children aged between 7 and 14 years old across England, Scotland, Wales and Northern Ireland.

Children from most of the groups stated that playtime was often taken away from them as a result of not completing a piece of homework. They were often made to finish any incomplete homework during school playtimes.

'If you don't do your homework you get less golden time [free time awarded to children for good behaviour] or you have to miss a playtime.'

This tendency to reduce playtime as a punishment could reinforce the idea that time for play is a reward rather than a right to which children are entitled.

The consequences of juggling competing demands on children's play opportunities is noted in one child's account, where she describes her emersion in her play and the difficulty of returning to this state of deeply involved play once it had been broken:

'I stop playing mostly ... because of homework. My parents say "stop doing that for now, do your homework and come back to it later" but I would forget what I was doing and where I was up to' (p. 8).

'I have swimming and dancing and I am starting jazz, now I only have Wednesdays and the weekends off.'

'I'm too busy, I have to practise music and it's too much.'

'First I go to my friend's house, then I have piano, then I have swimming, by the time I get back I'm really tired.'

For these children, extracurricular activities and clubs seemed to threaten their free time, which they would otherwise spend in less structured forms of play. The national opinion poll also reflected a significant proportion of children would rather play than spend time in extracurricular activities (p. 11).

Some children in the groups claimed that they would like more time to play at school, either longer break times or an extra break in the day. Children frequently spoke about lunchtimes being 'rushed' and there was usually not enough time to eat lunch and play outside. Children used strategies, such as eating their lunch quickly or throwing it away, in order to have a longer time to play:

'If you don't eat fast you miss your playtime.'

'I have a big lunch so I don't have enough time to play afterwards.'

'People will chuck their lunch away so they have they have more time to play and other people sneak out of the canteen' (p. 12).

Source: Kapasi and Gleave, 2009

Another layer of social policy seeks to promote *quality of childhood*, as arbitrarily defined by adults. This discourse acknowledges that children's happiness is dependent on more than having their developmental needs met and/or their rights exercised. It recognizes cultural contexts of families and communities that shape the lived experiences of children and contribute significantly to what translates into a quality childhood. Focusing on how to improve the quality of childhood directs policy-making to what services and provisions children need to achieve it. This is exactly what ECM aims to do – the 'every child' of its title signifying the importance of individual cultural contexts for different children. However, the convoluted discourse route that led to ECM presents some major implementation challenges. Few discourses entirely die out. They hang around, get reworked, reappear and ultimately cluster into factions. This faction clustering was evident in the three large departments of education, social services and health, where each department had closer allegiance to certain discourses linked to typologies of welfare whose underlying ideologies accorded with the disciplines of different professionals. The challenge, when fusing into one large department, was to iron out the discourse wrinkles and harmonize the policies so that all those involved in children's services were singing from the same hymn sheet. This needed to be done without losing individual professionals' specialist knowledge and expertise. Since discourse perspective is often integral to individual professions, the challenges of this are clearly evident. A way forward was to adopt quality of childhood as the dominant discourse into which all the professional welfare typologies could be subsumed.

Returning to Daniel and Ivatts' categories of child, we can see that all three feature in ECM:

> Subsumed under these aims [ECM] are notions of protecting children from harm ('victim' perspective) and ensuring that they behave responsibly ('threat'), and the mechanism for achieving this is to be a well-funded corporate and collaborative commitment from all those agencies with a responsibility for children's wellbeing ('investment'). In this sense, at least, there has been a discernible shift in emphasis towards the idea of a comprehensive approach to children in their role as the collective future of the nation. (Smith, 2010: 100)

Lansdown (2005) takes an even more individualistic approach with her concept of children's 'evolving capacities', whereby children's need for protection lessens as their agency and their social competency increases differentially.

Theories of power and the effect on adult–child relations

Giddens' (1995: 54) rendition of power is:

> the ability of individuals or groups to make their own concerns count, even when others resist. Power sometimes involves the direct use of

force, but is almost always accompanied by the development of ideas (ideologies) which justify the actions of the powerful.

Ideological justifications for adults maintaining power over children are readily found in their paternalistic assertions of acting in children's best interests, of protecting children and of their claim to superior knowledge. The term 'adocentrism' is sometimes attached to these ideological justifications, as described by Summit (1984: 179) in his reference to sexually abused children's struggle to be heard:

> The basic reason for disbelief is 'adocentrism', the unswerving and unquestioned allegiance to adult values. All adults, male and female, tend to align themselves in an impenetrable bastion against any threat that adult priorities and self-comfort must yield to the needs of children.

But this is only one dimension of power. According to Sullivan and King (1998), 'power-over' is a negative construction and the concept of power has two other, more positive orientations – 'power-to' and 'power-with'. Let's take a brief look at how these three representations play out in children's lived experiences. Issues that affect adult–child relations operate in three principal spheres: the regulation of childhood, generational ordering, and the confinement of children to private space with their consequent exclusion from public arenas. Traditionally, children have been confined to domains of home and school. They have limited power within the private area of family life and even less in the highly regulated space of school. Keeping children out of the public arena also limits any power they might develop in the political arena. ECM is changing this traditional landscape.

Box 3.3	**Generational power issues**

Adults have divided up the social order into two major groups – adults and children – with specific conditions surrounding the lives of each group; provision, constraints and requirements, laws, rights, responsibilities and privileges. Thus, just as the concept of gender has been key to understanding women's relationships to the social order, so the concept of generation is key to understanding childhood.

Source: Mayall, 2000: 120

Power is not all about authoritarian coercion. It is also about influence, especially power that influences the creation of knowledge (Hoyle, 2000). With their role as social actors becoming more widely accepted, the prospect of children creating influential knowledge and thus exercising power becomes more real. In theory, the more actively children share knowledge generation with adults, through increased participation and their own research, the more likely it is that the imbalance in power relations can be reduced. In reality, however, the situation can be quite different because of what Gallagher (2006) refers to as 'governmentality', the process by which governments use policy to control their citizens. This will become more apparent in the next section which looks at how these internecine discourses have been enacted in the political arena in the period since the Second World War.

Classical liberalism, embedded liberalism and neoliberalism

Classical liberalism originated from the late eighteenth century, a period of history commonly termed the Age of Enlightenment. The ideology grew out of dissatisfaction with authoritarian aristocratic rule and a desire for self-governance. Liberalism is characterized by self-determination, the right to free speech, free beliefs, free movement and free markets. Policy is based on the pre-eminence of the individual and the nation. Widespread hardship in the Great Depression (1930s) shook the foundations of liberalism. A new strategy was needed that could bring about economic growth while restoring full employment and social wellbeing. Political economists of the time were not convinced that liberalism, with its free markets and deregulation, could bring this about. The postwar government (1945 onwards) introduced a number of measures to achieve these aims, effectively using the power of the state to control market processes so that jobs and welfare were protected. This policy came to be known as 'embedded liberalism' (sometimes also known as social liberalism or modern liberalism). It led to economic prosperity in the 1950s and 60s until stagflation, a period of rising prices and unemployment where there is little growth in consumer demand, brought about its collapse in the 1970s.

Neoliberalism is the term given to the new approach which grew out of the collapse of embedded liberalism and is most closely associated with the Thatcher era (Margaret Thatcher, Conservative prime minister, 1979–90). It combined a deregulated economy and free-market enterprise with an ideology of individualism. It aimed to harness social wellbeing to the strength of an entrepreneurial economy by introducing competition into public service provision and shifting more welfare responsibility onto individuals and away from a government-supported dependency culture. Rhetoric was all about consumer power exercised through consumer choice but, in reality, consumerism came with an increasingly moral price tag and a more punitive attitude towards benefit.

Neoliberalism operated by applying pressure to the unemployed to bring about a change of culture from a welfare to a 'workfare' regime, where active measures had to be taken to get more job seekers into work. The application of free-market forces to activities that had previously been 'protected' in the embedded liberalism period resulted in what Garret (2009: 18) refers to as 'accumulation by dispossession'. In other words, public assets were targeted for commercialization in order to create new opportunities for capital growth out of hitherto 'protected' areas. This was a double-edged sword. On the one hand, the government sought to generate growth through creating jobs in social welfare domains but, on the other hand, created job insecurity in domains that had previously been protected from the uncertainties of a free market.

Another consequence was the tension it created in seeking to make value-based fields such as social care into sources of capital generation via the distribution of the work across free markets. A neoliberal approach takes little account of ethical considerations, targets the strongest areas of growth at the expense of the weakest and, concomitantly, increases poverty levels. Creating a competitive internal market within public services led to a focus on cost rather than quality of service. The demise of safe, permanent jobs and the increasing use of short-term contracts brought a level of hitherto unknown precariousness and also jeopardized the autonomy of professional service groups. This led to more fragmentation of services. The position worsened until 1997 when a change of government brought New Labour and the Third Way to the dispatch box.

The Third Way and concepts of 'capital'

The 'Third Way' is a term that has become attached to a centrist approach that tries to find the middle ground between free-market capitalism and democratic socialism. It adopts a position that the welfare state is best protected by economic integrity rather than economic idealism and that policies must reflect, and react to, contemporary growth opportunities. For example, in a high-tech world, investing in technological development and education has to be equally prioritized with the human capital investment in welfare services and both have to operate in a competitive market. Tony Blair (Labour prime minister, 1997–2007) saw modernization as a key driver in this and institutional frameworks were devised to create capital that reflected it. In the 1990s, this was achieved through interventions in the labour market to create jobs within a social economy of, for example, regeneration, inclusion, education, health and social care (Garrett, 2009), where much of the investment was focused on new technologies and new systems that would accelerate the modernization process. Flexibility of employment, provision of greater choice for users, and devolution of delivery to galvanize local innovation were central to the rollout of the policy (Whitfield, 2010). The Education, Health and Employment Action Zones, Excellence in Cities and New Deal for Communities were examples of programmes that were developed.

The Third Way did not reverse all the neoliberalist policies of the Thatcher era, but built on and adapted those that encapsulated the middle ground. New Labour continued with reforms that developed workfare rather than welfare dependency and adapted the individualism of neoliberalism to a culture that encouraged rights and responsibilities. Old Labour had been portrayed as a provider, whereas New Labour promoted itself as a regulator and enabler, thus shifting more responsibility onto families and communities than had been evident with Old Labour. However, a major departure from neoliberalism was New Labour's unwillingness to attribute accountability to the individual to the same degree, particularly in relation to disadvantage. In the Third Way, inequality and structural factors were accepted as part of the problem (Whitfield, 2010) and centralized systems, such as the Social Exclusion Unit, which was set up in 1997 and overseen by the Office of the Deputy Prime Minister, were set up as support agencies to work across departments and across regions.

New Labour did cling to some central neoliberal concepts that promoted internal markets, maintained competition and bestowed consumerist power. This can be seen in the way it persisted with policies of the Major era (John Major, Conservative prime minister, 1990–97), such as the back to basics campaign and national standard attainment tests (SATs) in education. New Labour's micromanagement of education services extended to the introduction of literacy and numeracy hours in primary schools and the launch of Key Stage 3 SATs for 14-year-olds. Education and training were key to the UK staying competitive in a global market, so investment in human capital at both ends of the spectrum – lifelong learning and early years – was bolted onto a new focus of proactive citizenship.

A central tenet underpinning childhood theory, particularly that relating to the family, is the conceptualization of 'capital', generally recognized as four types: economic, human, social and cultural. Economic capital refers to resources that can be used to leverage wellbeing such as using it to buy services, for example healthcare. Whether that purchase is enabled through a state tax system or by private means is dependent on the individual and unconstrained in a neoliberal approach:

> In a departure from previous welfare approaches, recent social policy has looked to support parents to generate economic capital for their children through work and saving rather than being provided directly with benefits. (Leverett, 2008: 58)

Human capital relates to the resources concentrated in human skills and knowledge. High levels of human capital equate with success in the labour market. Many parents want to share their human capital with their offspring to give them the best possible start, for example in using their knowledge and skills to help children with their learning. The more human capital children can acquire, the more likely they are to be successful. Social capital is much broader. It refers to the ability to get the most out of society through social contacts and networking. Who one knows and where one lives can be powerful influences. Bourdieu (1986) is renowned for his treatise on the unequal access to resources and power that come with capital, especially where one form of capital can access another, for example economic capital being used to purchase social capital. However, social capital is not all about wealth and privilege, family groups and neighbourhood groups are often rich in social capital because of the support networks they construct over time, for example setting up babysitting circles and shared school runs.

Before moving on, I wanted to consider briefly where children's services are heading beyond New Labour and tie this into the theoretical frameworks of ECM discussed in this chapter. Globalization and international market forces have usurped the traditional central role of the state. In 2011, swingeing cuts necessitated by the credit crisis that began in 2007 are having a major impact on public service provision, not least because of the volatility of global markets (Diamond and Liddle, 2009). New Labour concentrated on interventionist policies that supported the right conditions for economic growth such as technology, skills training and, where appropriate, competitive markets but this approach is no longer working. These strategies have failed to deliver education attainment goals, reach child poverty targets, improve employment prospects for the long-term workless, or enable a more equitable society. Service provision in the second decade of the twenty-first century is likely to be more affected by global issues than has been the case previously.

Conclusion

This chapter has explored the interweaving of the principal theories and concepts that have informed discourses on childhood. It began by examining the status of the child and how this led to discourses being constructed around needs, rights and quality of life. These theoretical frameworks were then linked to the political arena in postwar Britain, examining how theory translated into the reality of political governance and the impact this has had on welfare services and ultimately on ECM. The 1970s were predominantly protectionist, the 1980s shifted responsibility back onto families in a more 'laissez-faire' approach, the 1990s were more preoccupied with standards and achievements, and the 2000s became fixated on social control and the containment of the perceived threat posed by children. Inherent contradictions ultimately led to ambiguity, which translated into tensions around the ECM agenda:

> The labour government of the time which spanned the turn of the century is reported as being deliberately 'ambivalent', seeking to bring together a number of competing strands of belief and interest into some sort of alignment, but not into a state of perfect equilibrium or consensus. It might be said to have been trying to ride the post-modern tide rather than being submerged by it. As a result, polices for children can be expected to incorporate contradictions, perhaps even intentionally. (Smith, 2010: 89)

Theories of power and concepts of capital were shown to have contributed to the way in which services are provided and accessed. The principles, policies and theories set out in this chapter, along with the historical overview presented in Chapter 2, provide a framework into which we can now assemble individual elements of ECM. Part II is concerned with the delivery of ECM from children's perspectives with a focus on multi-agency working.

Reflection exercises

1. For all readers

Think of a child you know well – it may be your own child or a friend's – and map out a typical day for that child. Once you have done this, take each activity/action you listed for the day and reflect on how much of it is about the child in the here and now or the child as an adult in the making.

2. For staff working with children and young people in multidisciplinary teams

Take a little time to reflect on the three main discourses of childhood outlined in Box 3.2. Are you aware of any one of these discourses being more dominant than another in the way you interact with children in your own practice? If so, reflect on why this might be. Is it something that comes from within you and your values or from the perspective of the agency you operate in?

3. Children's perspectives

Reflect on Manasa's account of getting round as the child of a wheelchair user. In what ways was the quality of her childhood compromised by her family circumstances? Could her childhood have been improved if the services her father used as an adult had been conceived from a more holistic, whole family perspective? What changes would you make if you could influence policy?

Suggested further reading

1. Qvortrup, J., Corsaro, W.A. and Honig, M.S. (eds) (2009) *The Palgrave Handbook of Childhood Studies*, Basingstoke: Palgrave Macmillan

   Comprehensive volume that draws together a vast range of perspectives and disciplines within the field of childhood studies. It is divided into six sections: concepts, historical contexts, generational relations, children's everyday lives, practice issues, and children's rights. Chapters are written by different authors. A landmark publication that will review and extend your thinking.

2. James, A., Jenks, C. and Prout, A. (1998) *Theorizing Childhood*, Cambridge: Polity Press

   The seminal book that shifted theory on the status of the child and introduced what became known as the 'new sociology of childhood'. Features four typologies of the child and is an important text for anyone wanting to acquire a deeper understanding of the sociological frameworks and well worth a read.

3. Montgomery, H. (2009) *An Introduction to Childhood: Anthropological Perspectives on Children's Lives*, Oxford: Blackwell

   Takes a single discipline – anthropology – rather than the more common interdisciplinary approach in childhood studies texts. However, the richness of the different societies that are drawn on challenges you to reappraise your own approach to children and childhood. Provides a global and culturally diverse background to all the major issues that are addressed in this and other chapters that follow.

4. Alanen, L. and Mayall, B. (eds) (2001) *Conceptualizing Child-adult Relations*, London: RoutledgeFalmer

   Accessibly written book featuring a range of chapters by different authors who look at generational ordering issues and adult–child power relations. Addresses these in different childhood contexts and also explores where generational ordering results in adult versus child conflicts. A useful introductory text.

5. *Childhood: A Journal of Global Child Research*, http://chd.sagepub.com

   An excellent resource that brings a mix of cutting-edge research, challenging discourse and informative reviews. Anyone interested in children and childhood would find this journal absorbing. Available electronically in academic libraries.

Part II

Multi-agency Working in Children's Services

4 Social Care

In this chapter we discuss:

- Social care policy context
- Systems and service integration
- 'Social Work Practice' models
- Multi-agency working
- Looked-after children

Social care policy context

Social care inevitably overlaps with many other chapters in this book because its service provision is at the core of children's lives and there is no intention to duplicate or encroach into areas covered elsewhere. To this end, I address the policy context of social care, examine issues pertaining to systems and service integration, multi-agency working and the piloting of new 'Social Work Practice' models. Given the vast remit of social care, it is not possible to cover all children's lived experiences of Every Child Matters (ECM) in one chapter. I have chosen, therefore, to focus on one group of children – looked-after children – first, because they are at the intense end of the user spectrum and, second, because they are frequently marginalized in terms of voice. Readers are directed to sources where they can find additional material in the Suggested further reading at the end of the chapter.

Merging social services into the Department for Children, Schools and Families in 2007 was intended to enhance services for children by improving communication and multi-agency working around a framework that would deliver ECM for every child. As part of the restructuring, most of the work previously administered by social services was taken up by newly created children's trusts (see Chapter 2) in a child-centred approach, with frontline services organized around the child rather than around organizations or professionals. It required an integrated strategy with pooled budgets and joint commissioning and planning. To be effective, there had to be robust arrangements for interagency cooperation. So, while the legislative functions of former social services departments remained unchanged from the Children Act 1989, the Children Act 2004 altered the governance structures and built these around statutory directives, which placed a 'duty to cooperate' on all the agencies. This was articulated in a ten-point national framework (Box 4.1).

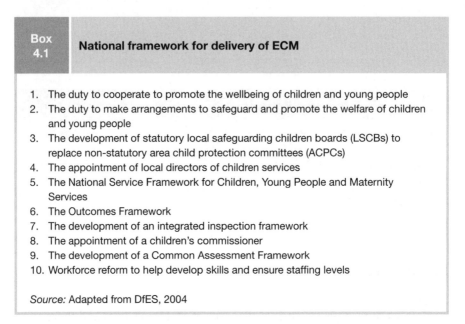

| Box 4.1 | National framework for delivery of ECM |

1. The duty to cooperate to promote the wellbeing of children and young people
2. The duty to make arrangements to safeguard and promote the welfare of children and young people
3. The development of statutory local safeguarding children boards (LSCBs) to replace non-statutory area child protection committees (ACPCs)
4. The appointment of local directors of children services
5. The National Service Framework for Children, Young People and Maternity Services
6. The Outcomes Framework
7. The development of an integrated inspection framework
8. The appointment of a children's commissioner
9. The development of a Common Assessment Framework
10. Workforce reform to help develop skills and ensure staffing levels

Source: Adapted from DfES, 2004

Children's Perspectives

To what extent was the rollout of the ECM agenda being informed by looked-after children's perspectives? Voice is a national advocacy charity for children and young people, supported by the National Children's Bureau. Not long after the 2003 Green Paper, it published *Start with the Child, Stay with the Child* (2004), a collection of looked-after children's views about their care, and these are some of the findings (p. 7):

> Young people said, a lot, that their friendships were not seen as being very important by professionals. They are!! Keeping friends is massively important and needs support (financial as well as time and space) from social services.

> Children and young people who are looked after need, at the very least, one constant relationship throughout their time in care.

> Managers must help workers to spend more time with children and young people, getting to know them, building relationships with them, planning for their future and supporting them here and now. To do this workers need to have less paperwork and more simple ways of doing things.

Government must help social services to spend more time 'doing' and less time 'talking about doing'. Children and young people should have one main worker who is supported in their work by a team. This team would all have different skills like education, health, and administration and more. All these workers should be easy to get hold of, open, honest and happy to explain their actions to children and young people.

Another Voice publication, *Try a Different Way* (2005), put together a set of reflection sheets, each based around a problem identified by looked-after children, in which they discussed problems and possible solutions from their perspectives. One such was an idea around child-led assessment.

Try A Different Way reflection sheets

What's the problem?

Children and young people say that social workers sometimes don't see what's important for them. They ask them questions which can feel too narrow, or leading in a certain direction. The areas they want to discuss may get missed. Plans are made which may not reflect the child's priorities, and therefore may not be followed. Professionals may not believe that children and young people have insight into their own situations. Children and young people have said they feel judged, and as if only the negative aspects of their lives are of interest. Forms with tick box answers can lead to a narrow definition of children's needs and their individuality can get overlooked.

What is it? Who is it for?

All children and young people can lead their assessments and define their own needs, to a greater or lesser extent. For younger children and those with communication needs, it may take more time, but it is still possible for a broader approach to needs assessment to be taken.

How will it work?

Child led assessments are based on more creative approaches to finding out a child's needs. Telling a story, drawing, starting with the child and asking open questions for example. It is based on allowing the child to lead the process by asking first what is important to them, going at their pace and gradually building a picture of their needs. In this way the child will determine the priorities, the order in which they come and their own needs. The information could still be transferred to categories, or dimensions back in the office.

What might stop it working?

There has been a huge investment in developing the assessment framework and associated materials. There may be a reluctance to use a different framework because of this investment. It will take longer to assess a child's needs this way. It could lead to inconsistent recording of a child's needs within care plans. The current assessment framework and looked-after children materials provide a comprehensive list of the areas of a child's life that need to be followed. It takes more skill to start from a child's perspective and build up a picture.

Source: Voice, 2005: 6

Systems and service integration

Children's trusts control all the core functions that had previously been handled by separate agencies, including education, looked-after children, child protection, youth work, adoption, care leavers and all aspects of children in need. Unsurprisingly, given the radical nature of the changes, there were teething problems. Revised guidance on the 'duty to cooperate' had to be issued in 2008 to emphasize the importance of agencies' duty to cooperate in early intervention work and in initiatives to narrow the gap for disadvantaged children. More resources were generated to assist with the implementation of ECM, primarily through *The Children's Plan: Building Brighter Futures* (DCSF, 2007). It set out a ten-year plan for children's integrated services including goals and priorities and attempted to provide cohesion and vision. Based on this model, children's trusts were charged with producing their own local children's plans followed by annual updates of progress against identified targets in each area of ECM. What were children's experiences of these? Tameside Children and Young People's Strategic Partnership (2007: 8) decided to produce its own version of the Children's Plan. Before doing this, it actively sought children's views.

❝ Children's Perspectives

ECM in Tameside: What children want

Being healthy

- The importance of a healthy diet and less junk food
- Better and more education on alcohol: drugs and smoking

Staying safe

- Reducing vandalism
- Stopping people being beaten up

Enjoying and achieving

- Feedback from children in Year 7 indicated that many of their fears about secondary school transition were rooted in myths spread by older siblings and friends. In response to this, children from vulnerable groups were identified from 4 primary schools and each visited 2 high schools in groups ... These children are reported to be more confident in school, and some are showing enhanced academic performance in Year 6.
- School attendance would be better if there were opportunities for good after school activities on site.

Making a positive contribution

- Young people want to play or just hang about safely, where they are not annoying anyone but say that there are less places to go because houses have been built or else there are 'no ball games' signs up.

- Young people want to tackle issues of bullying and racism.
- Young people would like better public transport so that they can take part in positive activities and not need parents or other adults to give them lifts.

Source: Tameside Children and Young People's Strategic Partnership, 2007: 8

Tameside incorporated these views into its version of the local Children's Plan, in which it set out nine commitments (promises) to Tameside children followed by six priorities (Box 4.2).

Box 4.2	Tameside's version of The Children's Plan

Tameside 9 Commitments (Promises)

1. Integrated Services:

If you are a child or young person all the different professionals and services involved in your life will be working together to meet your needs

2. Access to Services:

All the services involved in children and young people's lives will 'talk to each other' and be organised in a way that will make it easy for children, young people and their families to access these

3. Support and Information:

The information about children and young people is shared between services and recorded correctly and used when needed to provide suitable services.

4. Inclusion and Equality:

Tameside recognises that all children and young people are individuals and have different needs. Tameside is committed to tackle all forms of discrimination to ensure all Children and young people have equal opportunities in life.

5. Narrowing the Gap:

Tameside want to make sure that vulnerable and disadvantaged children and young people have better chances in life no matter where they live.

6. Early Intervention:

Tameside want to provide high quality children's Centres and extended school services. Through these services Tameside will be able to support children and young people at the earliest opportunity.

7. Local Provision:

Tameside is divided into 4 areas so that services can become locally based to suit the needs of the children and young people in that area.

8. High Achievement:

Tameside want to raise school standards so that children and young people are able to leave school having achieved the best of their abilities.

9. Involving Young People as positive members of the community:

Tameside are committed to involving children and young people in decisions that affect their lives. Tameside also want children and young people to be actively involved in their communities so that they can become valued members of their community.

Tameside's 6 Priorities

1. Promote healthy lifestyles with a focus on obesity and healthy gums and teeth.
2. Improve Emotional Health and Wellbeing for all young people.
3. Increase the amount of the young people moving into education, employment and training.
4. Continue to improve attainment at all levels of learning with focus on under-achieving groups and schools.
5. Reduce Teenage Pregnancy.
6. Continue to make Looked after children and other vulnerable groups have the same chances as other children.

Source: Tameside Children and Young People's Strategic Partnership, 2007: 6–7

Social Work Practice models

The Children and Young Person's Act 2008 further legislated on the delivery of social care services. One of the main concerns emerging from the Green Paper *Care Matters* (DfES, 2006) was the lack of consistency and continuity of care; some children reported that they had as many as 30 different social workers during their time in care. This reflected the low morale, dwindling recruitment and poor retention that had plunged social care into crisis. Working within education-dominated children's trusts led to social workers experiencing a loss of identity and erosion of core professional values as they found themselves caught between accountability to their employers and service users (Sayer, 2008). Concerns about the quality of initial training, recruitment and vacancy rates, and the status of the profession as a whole led the government to launch a Social Work Taskforce in 2008 to conduct a fundamental review of the profession.

In the same year, the 2008 Act introduced a new Social Work Practice model to be piloted from 2009. This remodelling of the way social work is delivered in local authorities is supported by the Children's Workforce Development Council (CWDC) and incorporates a new qualified social worker status. The Social Work Practices (SWPs) are intended to be groups of social workers working as independent organizations under contract to a local authority. One of the rationales behind the concept is a desire to improve retention – staff may be more likely to stay within an organization if they feel they have a stake in it. Widespread media coverage of a series of scandals, such as that surrounding the death of Baby Peter and the sacking of Haringey's director of children's services, has not only coloured public perception of social workers but has also exacerbated recruitment problems, with vacancy rates running at record levels. The smaller size of individual SWPs may encourage social workers to feel they have more control, more status in the community, and more personal involvement with children. In theory, SWPs could be run by professional partnerships of social workers, third sector or private organizations. Box 4.3 sets out what the proposed model entails.

Box 4.3	Social Work Practice (SWP) model

Undertaking social work functions for children/young people they support: This includes establishing and managing the relationship with the child, his/her birth family, foster carers and the foster carers' family (or residential social workers); developing and managing health and education plans; procuring specialised services for the child; organising holidays in conjunction with carers. The Social Work Practice would have all decision-making delegated to it in relation to children in care, except for major changes to a child's Care Plan which cannot be made outside of a LAC Review and with the agreement of the IRO.

Engaging with children/young people: This includes consulting children/young people and their parents/carers where appropriate; involving children/young people in decision-making and providing updates to them on decisions made; being attentive to their needs; and providing them with an element of choice in the decision-process involved in allocating a social worker and potentially involving them in the governance of the Social Work Practice.

Allocating a Lead Professional or a key worker for each child/young person: The Lead Professional will be selected from the Social Work Practice's partners or staff. The level of authority/power invested in the Lead Professional will be crucial to the role of Social Work Practices.

Implementing and reviewing a child/young person's Care Plan: This includes working with local services to ensure children's needs are met, maintaining compliance with Integrated Children's System (ICS) records and case files, preparation of information for reviews, liaising with the IRO with regards new Care Plans for all children/young people, ensuring the child is secure if he/she returns to their family as part of a revised Care Plan; and applies to all aspects of the Care Plan including the Pathway Plan, Health Plan, and Personal Education Plan where applicable. If any changes are to be made to the Care Plan and/or associated plans, the agreement of the IRO should be sought.

Placing children/young people: Choosing pre-approved foster carers or residential placements, or placing a child/young person with family or friends.

Notification of any safeguarding concerns to the local authority: Providing notification to the relevant local authority of any child protection concerns involving a child allocated to the Social Work Practice. The local authority must conduct the child protection enquiry and the Social Work Practice will be expected to co-operate fully.

Keeping case records in good order: including creating a database for inspection, research and development, and reporting on required performance indicators.

Source: DCSF, 2008: 16–17

> **66** **Children's Perspectives**
>
> Looked-after children's perspectives can make a valuable contribution to the piloting of SWPs. As part of the scoping work for modelling the SWPs, the DCSF (2008: 9–10) sought their views and a major concern they expressed was the absence of a social worker relationship:
>
> > 'The qualities my ideal social worker would have are: to be friendly and compassionate, to listen to what I want and what ways I can go around things to get it, to always be there for me, not to nag at me when I don't know what to do for my future.'
> >
> > 'I thought you were meant to get a working relationship with social workers, but it's like I don't even know her.'
> >
> > 'I have had around 30 social workers in 10 years.'
> >
> > 'You get to know one then they leave.'
> >
> > 'With children in care, they need to always know they have someone they can turn to and talk to. I never felt that. I ended up in and out of prison and felt like I had no support. The longest I had a social worker was 3 months, then from there I've had 14 different social workers. It's hard because you get to know and trust one and it leaves.'
>
> *Source:* DCSF, 2008: 9–10

The DCSF put together a prospectus for the piloting of SWPs and Table 4.1 summarizes the overarching outcomes and key goals expressed as an Outcomes Framework (DCSF, 2008: 15).

Table 4.1 **SWP Outcomes Framework**

Outcome	Key goal
Promote Stability and Continuity	Improved stability of placement Moves to permanence where in the child's best interests Increased stability of social worker or lead professional Reduced staff sickness and turnover
Be Healthy	Improved health care Reduced teenage pregnancy Better emotional and mental health

Stay Safe	Safe from bullying, discrimination or abuse Improved quality of relationships between child and foster carers Improved quality of relationships between child and birth family (where appropriate) Improved satisfaction by children's foster carers and birth family with services (where appropriate)
Enjoy and Achieve	Increased attendance of children in schools Improved educational attainment
Make a Positive Contribution	Increased participation Reduced crime
Achieve Economic Wellbeing	Increased chance of employment/career Avoid poverty

Source: DCSF, 2008: 15

In December 2009, the final report of the Social Work Task Force was published with a challenging set of recommendations for social work reform:

- a reformed system of initial training
- greater leadership and a strong national voice for the profession, led by a College of Social Work
- a single, nationally recognized career structure
- a system for forecasting levels of demand for social workers
- clear and binding standards for employers in how social work should be resourced, managed and supported
- a licence to practise system for social workers to acquire and maintain their professional status
- improved understanding among the general public, service users, other professionals and the media about the role and purpose of good social work and the contribution social workers can make to society (Social Work Task Force, 2009).

One of these recommendations – the creation of a College of Social Work – seeks to provide more leadership by, and for, the profession. This is envisaged as being similar to the Royal College of Nursing and the General Teaching Council. It will create a body that can lead the development of the profession and also represent it in discussions with organizations that regulate social work. A major consultation exercise began in May 2010 to develop a framework for this college.

Multi-agency working

ECM fundamentally changed the working practices of professionals employed within social services. Alongside new policies aimed to integrate children's services, consideration had to be given to harmonizing the various codes of practice, each with underlying values of the different professional bodies in their previous three big departments: the General Teaching Council (education), the Nursing and Midwifery Council (health) and the General Social Care Council (social services). These three bodies have adopted a common code of values to inform their practice. This integration has been further strengthened by adopting a common inspection framework and a single inspection body, Ofsted (for more on this see Chapter 5), although some would argue that this is now so big it is unworkable (Chandiramani, 2010).

Unlike previous practice, when social workers were based in teams in social service departments, they are now employed in a variety of settings and multidisciplinary teams, including the voluntary and private sectors. Some (for example Coughlan, 2007) are concerned about the dilution to the social work profession and specific expertise that might be lost because of this. Others, such as Sayer (2008: 30), wonder about lines of accountability:

> Despite the activities of the General Social Care Council (GSCC) which, through registration, the three-year degree and code of conduct, has sought to improve the status of social work as a profession the autonomy of social workers as professionals has diminished. There is an uneasy tension between the accountability a social worker feels to their employing agency, to their professional values and to their service users.

Fox Harding's (1997) seminal schema depicting four perspectives of working with children in social care services illustrates the potential for professional tensions as multi-agency working advances. Barker (2009) provides a helpful summary of these schema (see Box 4.4). While unified structures and systems can be readily erected, uniting value bases across different professions is not as easily achieved.

Box 4.4	Social care working perspectives

1. Laissez faire and patriarchy

This value position is characterised by a view that the role of state in child welfare should be a minimal one, and the privacy and sanctity of parent–child relationship should be respected. Underpinning this is a view that it is 'best' for society to have a 'slimline state' and 'best' for parents and children if the state 'leaves families alone' because 'parents know best' based on the special (biological) bond between parents and their children. In extreme cases, such as major child abuse, it is necessary that the state should intervene and (usually) find a permanent home for children. It should also be noted that a 'weak' state tends to align with, and reinforce, patriarchy in families.

2. State paternalism and child protection

In contrast to the laissez faire approach, proponents of the perspective favour more extensive state intervention, not least to protect children from poor parental care ... The child's needs are seen to be paramount; children are viewed as essentially vulnerable, with need for nurturing and care rather than self-determination. The importance of parental duties towards children is highlighted, rather than parental rights over children. The state and its representatives have the duty and the capacity to judge what is best for children and, where necessary, to provide it.

3. Modern defence of the birth family and parents' rights

This perspective is founded on the belief that birth/biological families are important for children and parents, and that psychological bonds should be maintained wherever possible. To facilitate this, however, the state should not have a minimalist role ... It is seen that class, poverty and deprivation have major impacts on parenting, so the state has a major role in providing support for families to counteract these. In the last resort, if children come into care, the state should focus on returning them if at all possible to their birth family and, in the interim support links and contact.

4. Children's rights and child liberation

This perspective emphasises the importance of the children's own viewpoints and wishes, and is more inclined to see the child as a separate entity with rights to autonomy and freedom, rather like adults. This stresses the importance of calling into question the control of children by state or by parents – the child is a subject, rather than an object, and there is an emphasis on their competence and strength.

Source: Barker, 2009: 187–8

The opening up of children's services to market forces through tendering and commissioning processes added another dimension to factor into overall efficacy and multi-agency working. Le Grand (2007) discusses choice and competition in public services. He concludes that it is the client (families) rather than the provider (local authorities/children's trusts) who prizes choice. Providers have to weigh up other considerations such as past performance of delivery and trusted relationships:

> Providers prefer alternative models of service delivery especially those that rely upon trust. Social democrats prefer voice and trust; conservatives want choice and competition to be exercised in the context of a full private market. Yet, so long as they are properly designed, policies aimed at promoting choice and competition can serve the interests of all these groups better than the alternatives.
> (Le Grand, 2007: 207)

Space does not permit a more detailed exposition of the motivations and situational factors surrounding the complex nature of competitive commissioning processes. Interested readers can explore this further in Le Grand's work and also that of Matosevic et al. (2007).

Looked-after children

If there is one group of children for whom the ideology and rhetoric surrounding ECM resonates it is surely looked-after children (sometimes referred to as 'children in care'). If *every* child really does matter and the policy is genuinely intended to narrow the gap between those who do and do not achieve the five intended ECM outcomes, then the experiences of looked-after children, as some of the most disadvantaged in our society, are an essential group to focus on. Services are planned and integrated through the Looked After Care System (LACS), which, since 2006, incorporates the Framework for the Assessment of Children in Need and is known as the Integrated Children's System (ICS). It provides a record of essential information for each looked-after child, a placement plan, a care plan and is supplemented by regular reviews plus 'assessment and action records', which measure progress against the care plan.

Two government policy documents, the Green Paper *Care Matters* (DCSF, 2006) and the subsequent White Paper response *Care Matters: Time for Change* (DCSF, 2007a), are central to the way services for looked-after children are evolving in the wake of ECM. In the 2007 White Paper (DCSF, 2007a), the government admitted that the gap between looked-after children and all other children was unacceptably wide, as shown in Box 4.5.

Box 4.5	**Mind the gap**

- Only 12% of children in care achieved 5 A*–C grades at GCSE (or equivalent) compared to 59% of all children
- Their health is poorer than that of other children
- 45% of children in care are assessed as having a mental health disorder compared with around 10% of the general population
- Over 50% of children in care responding to *Care Matters* said that they had difficulties accessing positive activities
- 9.6% of children in care aged 10 or over were cautioned or convicted for an offence during the year – almost three times the rate for all children of this age
- 30% of care leavers aged 19 were not in education, employment or training (NEET).

Source: Adapted from DCSF, 2007a: 6

Under LACS, one of the statutory duties of the field social worker is to organize contact with looked-after children's birth families. This can lead to some contentious situations and inconsistencies about the rights of children. Two contrasting case studies illustrate this point:

Two sisters aged 11 and 12 had been sexually abused by their father. On his release from prison he requested contact with his daughters.

The girls were adamant that they did not want any contact with him and the social worker felt that contact could be damaging, even dangerous. The social worker and the reviewing officer agreed that they were 'Gillick competent' and their views should be respected. The father made an application to the Family Court for a contact order, which was granted. The local authority appealed and the High Court overturned the ruling, accepting that the children's views, in the circumstances of the case, took precedence over the presumption of contact in the Children Act 1989. (Sayer, 2009: 115)

A father appealed against an order, made by a district judge, that there should be no contact between him and his son. This order was made on the basis of the son's view and an independent social worker's report, following a deterioration in the existing arrangements for the son to have staying contact with this father. On appeal, the most senior family court judge in England and Wales (Dame Elizabeth Butler-Sloss) overturned the order arguing that the child had a right to a relationship with his father, even if he did not want it, and his welfare demanded that efforts be expended to make contact possible. (James and James, 2004: 199)

In both cases, social workers supported the children's wishes for non-contact but this was only upheld by the judiciary in one of the cases.

Most looked-after children are accommodated in foster homes. After the scandals that engulfed the residential care sector in the 1990s, such as 'pindown' (Staffordshire County Council, 1991) and the 13-year period of abuse exposed in the Kirkwood Report (Kirkwood, 1993), policies have focused on providing children with a family placement wherever possible. However, foster care does not suit all children. It is imprudent to assume that it is always the first and best option, just as it is unwise to view residential care as a last resort. Placements need to be selections of choice, with children actively engaged in the decision-making processes. Foster care is cheaper than residential placements and we must be careful that consideration of children's wishes is not overridden by cost factors. If ECM is about building services around the child, then this should include meaningful attention to children's views about their care placements. An issue sometimes raised by children is the difficulty of managing conflict issues and divided loyalties between their birth and foster families, and in these circumstances children may feel that residential care would be a better option (Kahan, 1994).

Children resent the statutory medicals and adultist reviews (Morgan, 2005; Sayer, 2008) that frequently dominate their service provision and deny them any choice regarding their placement. A group of looked-after young people in North Tyneside carried out their own research about the care review system (Bradwell et al., 2009). They designed and distributed a questionnaire to all children and young people in care in North Tyneside and then collected evidence from 36 children and young people about their review meetings.

This was a substantial study, with fascinating insights into children and young people's perspectives. The young researchers adopted a balanced approach to their analysis, presenting both positive and negative findings and posited useful recommendations. Some extracts from their research are featured here.

> ## " Children's Perspectives
>
> Many are not asked about where and when they would like the [review] meeting to take place and one said
>
> > *'The social worker just decides'.*
>
> Most know that they should go to the meetings ... but often do not have the best experience:
>
> > *'I didn't want myself to be there to be honest. I don't like going to them but I can't not go to them because otherwise you don't get told what is happening.'*
>
> > *'I don't want to hear any thing bad I just get embarrassed'*
>
> Young people felt that in general they are listened to when they attend their meetings and that any views they have will be passed on.
>
> > *'I put my views across and they would listen'*
>
> although one person said that in meetings, the adults *'seem to talk amongst themselves'.*
>
> ### Recommendations
>
> - A checklist should be devised which social workers go through with a young person before the review meeting, to discuss and agree details. This would make sure that young people are asked for their views on the time and place of the meeting, who should be there and whether they would like to meet with their IRO. This could also cover whether certain adults should only attend relevant parts of the meeting, such as teachers.
> - Looked after children and young people should be given clear information about the roles and responsibilities of those involved in the review process. While most had a good idea about what the review meeting is for, many were not clear about the role of the Independent Reviewing Officer. They also need to be clear about their own rights and responsibilities.
> - There should be an ongoing opportunity for young people to evaluate their review meetings immediately afterwards. This could be done using a short questionnaire, similar to the one used in our research. If the Independent Reviewing Officer knew that a young person was not happy with the meeting, they could make sure it was better for them the next time.
> - Looked after children and young people should be given opportunities to be involved in the process at different levels if they choose to. Young people who are confident are more likely to get involved – we should find ways for those who are not very confident to be involved as well if they want to.
>
> *Source:* Bradwell et al., 2009: 10–12

Clearly evident from Bradwell et al.'s research is the honesty and balance demonstrated in the young people's research, in which they do not cherry-pick a catalogue of negative comments about the looked-after review system, for example it is clearly stated that 'Young people felt that in general they are listened to when they attend their meetings and that any views they have will be passed on', which makes their recommendations all the more powerful and deserving of attention.

Conclusion

Social care aspects of ECM are too broad and all-encompassing to cover comprehensively in a single chapter. The focus here has been on policy context, new systems and a practice spotlight on looked-after children as a group of service users significantly affected by ECM. The importance of interagency working was highlighted, along with descriptions of initiatives to improve the way children's social care services are provided such as the proposed Social Work Practice models. In privileging the perspectives of children, it was evident that they want to be more involved in their service care plans and consider their own expertise derived from their experiences to be underused and undervalued. Readers are encouraged to read other chapters in Part II, as they all incorporate social care elements not covered here.

Reflection exercises

1. For all readers
The Children's Workforce Development Council (CWDC, 2007) identified the following roles in social work with children: enabler, protector, assessor, networker, advocate, manager, commissioner, coordinator/broker, specialist, expert independent resource and practice assessor. Reflect on how many of these roles you can recognize in the cases and scenarios explored in this chapter. Are there any others you would want to include?

2. For staff working with children and young people in multidisciplinary teams
Revisit Barker's (2009) descriptors of Fox-Harding's (1997) four-part schema in Box 4.4 and reflect on whether any resonate with your own perspective and how your own value base influences your thinking and practice.

3. Children's perspectives
Reflect on the suggestions for child-led assessment made in *Try a Different Way* (Voice, 2005). Can you think of anything else that might get in the way beyond what the children have listed? How might this suggestion by children be received in a practice setting?

Suggested further reading

1. Howe, D. (2009) *A Brief Introduction to Social Work Theory*, Basingstoke: Palgrave Macmillan

   Ideal introductory text for those new to social work theory. Covers all the main theories that have influenced social work over time from psycho-analytic and attachment theories to anti-oppressive practices and feminist social work in a particularly accessible way.

2. www.voiceyp.org

   The website of Voice, a children and young people's advocacy charity supported by the National Children's Bureau. Produces a range of publications for adults and children, such as the two featured in this chapter. Worth surfing the website as it is a rich resource of children and young people's perspectives, including their comments on contemporary policy.

3. Smith, M. (2009) *Rethinking Residential Child Care: Positive Perspectives*, Bristol: Policy Press

   For anyone with an interest in residential care. Charts its renaissance in the wake of the scandals of the late twentieth century. Smith challenges the concept of residential care as dominated by discourses of protection, choosing to focus on the positives of children developing personal relationships. Comprehensive section on the historical context of policy and practice.

4. *The British Journal of Social Work*

   Leading journal for those interested in keeping up to date with new horizons of social work. Has a diverse readership, including academics, practitioners and students. Available as an e-journal in academic libraries and features a good mix of papers that reflect, challenge and extend thinking on all aspects of social work. Always worth browsing the contents page of each new issue.

5. Wright, P., Turner, C., Clay, D. and Mills, H. (2006) *The Participation of Children and Young People in Developing Social Care*, Social Care Institute for Excellence (available as a free download at www.scie.org.uk/publications/guides/guide20/references/asp)

   Compiled for SCIE by a team from Barnardo's Policy and Research Unit. Provides guidance to social care organizations in the form of a framework that aims to systematically develop effective and meaningful participation of children and young people in the design, delivery and review of their services.

5 Education

Education and the ECM context

Education was one of three giant providers of children's services (the other two being health and social services), each having considerable autonomy and their own funding. This all changed with ECM and the statutory commitment to integrated children's services. In this chapter I explore what changes integrated approaches have made to education and the impact these have had on children's school experiences. Is ECM assisting every child? What are the benefits and the shortcomings? Are any groups of children still falling through the net? Children's perspectives are crucial to such an exploration and feature throughout the chapter.

A principal aim of ECM is to gather support *around* the child, so that the child becomes the centre of the provision. Schools are places where children spend significant amounts of their time – much more, for example, than in health centres or social service offices. It was a logical step, therefore, to assemble a raft of extended services in and around schools and children's centres, effectively positioning the school as a community epicentre for integrated children's services. Logical, that is, if the focus becomes the community hub and not the school per se. There is a danger that wraparound services become tinged with educational overtones, making it impossible for some children to escape either the classroom milieu or educational personnel between the hours of eight in the morning and six in the evening.

The government pledged that every child would have access to extended school services provided by various partnership agencies and the voluntary sector by 2010, including:

- breakfast and after-school clubs
- access to childcare from 8am until 6pm
- study support and homework clubs
- sport, music and after-school activity clubs
- adult education classes
- parenting support programmes
- community-based child healthcare
- specialist social care services.

Early years education

Provision for children in their early years is inextricably bound up with the labour market and women returning to work before their children reach statutory school age. An array of free kindergartens, state-supported nurseries and private care arrangements co-existed throughout the twentieth century, with as many as 35 categories of provider by the 1990s (Siraj-Blatchford et al., 2007). When New Labour came to power in 1997, one of its first initiatives was a major expansion of preschool provision amid an initiative to get mothers back to work. It was billed as the *National Childcare Strategy* (DfEE, 1998) and aimed to provide quality childcare to support working mothers.

There is a general consensus that preschool provision benefits children both socially and cognitively (Santer and Cookson, 2009) and recent studies show that young children attending settings where a proportion of staff are qualified teachers benefit even more (Sylva et al., 2004). It is not surprising therefore that access to a qualified teacher in every integrated early years setting became a primary government target. The impetus started with Early Excellence Centres in the late 1990s, which evolved into Sure Start centres and ultimately into children's centres. These combined centres drew together childcare, family support, maternity services, health and education into one integrated setting. Working from the premise that if society gets its provision for young children working effectively, it pays dividends in the later childhood years, early years care and education became a flagship for New Labour, underpinned by a plethora of legislation.

The microcosm that is early years provision affords a model of how integrated services can work for other age groups of children, although it is doubtful that the coalition government can replicate the level of funding that was injected into the early years under New Labour. The cost of having 3,000 plus children's centres with at least one qualified teacher up and running by 2010 was considerable. A £250 million transformation fund was made available in 2006 to upskill an early years workforce – many of whom had no formal qualifications – to a minimum Level 2 qualification. An extensive training programme of NVQs, foundation degrees, professional status certifications (EYPS) and postgraduate leadership courses (for example, the National Professional Qualification in Integrated Centre Leadership) was instigated, with a further £300 million being provided for a Graduate Leader Fund.

Alongside the resourcing of premises and staff, early childcare and education also underwent a radical reform of policy. It began with the publication of *Desirable Outcomes for Children's Learning on Entering Compulsory Education* (SCAA, 1996). This was the first time a standardized learning experience framework had been proposed for preschool provision (aged 3–5 years). In 2002, standardization was extended to the youngest age range in the *Birth to Three Matters* framework (DfES, 2002) and a year later to childminding in the *National Standards for Under 8s Daycare and Childminding* (DfES, 2003b). The three documents were drawn together and updated to become the Early Years Foundation Stage (EYFS) for children aged 0–5 (DfES, 2007). From 2008, all providers were required to register with Ofsted and be inspected against the EYFS standards, which grew out of Every Child Matters. Box 5.1 illustrates how Santer and Cookson (2009: 70) describe these.

Box 5.1	Four themes of the Early Years Foundation Stage

- *A unique child:* every child is a competent learner from birth who can be resilient, capable, confident and self-assured.
- *Positive relationships:* children learn to be strong and independent from a base of loving and secure relationships with parents and/or a key person.
- *Enabling environments:* the environment plays a key role in supporting and extending children's development and learning.
- *Learning and development:* children learn and develop in different ways and at different rates, and all areas of learning are equally important and interconnected.

Concerns were raised about the increasing focus on outcomes rather than process in EYFS. Outcomes need to be interpreted skilfully and holistically otherwise they can lead to narrow target-setting right from birth. There was also disquiet that EYFS practice guidance notes would be interpreted as fixed norms rather than guidance. This makes the fourth EYFS theme relating to children learning in different ways and at different rates particularly important in professional practice.

This policy shift towards integrating care and early education, two halves of early childhood which had been approached as separate entities (care having previously been in the domains of health and social services), brought with it many challenges of multi-agency working. It also exposed issues of inequity when the early care workforce and the early education workforce were brought together under the newly created Department of Children, Schools and Families (DCSF). It exposed tensions and mismatched priorities in so far as one former half – the social care system – focuses on widening diversity and the embracing of more disadvantaged groups through social inclusion, while the other half – the schools system – is constrained by being measured solely on educational attainment. One consequence of this has been the entrenching of inequities in the early childhood field.

Historically, the early childhood segment is one of the lowest paid and lowest qualified workforces in the public sector, dominated as it is by female part-time employees. Until the mid-1990s, when *Desirable Outcomes for Children's Learning on Entering Compulsory Education* (SCAA, 1996) was released, the vast majority of preschool provision was *care*-based in state nurseries, playgroups, or private childminding, as the nomenclature indicates, for example nursery *nurse*, child*minder*, *play*worker. The descriptor 'teacher' was reserved for the minority of private nursery 'schools', which set themselves up as educational preschool establishments where the owner/manager was likely to be a qualified teacher. Sometimes these nursery schools were directly linked to private fee-paying schools. Care workers and playgroup workers might have no qualifications or training and might be appointed simply because they demonstrated a liking for or ability to work with children. Nursery nurses did have to study for qualifications but this was a shorter training than teaching and had a lower entry bar. Playworkers, childminders and nursery assistants were likely to be part-time, minimum wage earners. Nursery nurses were paid a little better but there was still a wide gulf between their pay and that of qualified teachers. Some tentative steps have been taken to narrow the parity gap between early years workers and early years educators but efforts towards this are likely to be stalled by current suggestions that teaching should move to a Masters-led profession.

The government recognized that early childhood was a vitally important time in children's lives and a rapid stage of development. The rationale was that money spent on their health, wellbeing and cognitive growth to give them a flying start in the early years would reap a rich harvest in subsequent childhood years. Thus began the mammoth task of pulling together care and education within a new integrated workforce.

The ideological link between early years provision and getting women back to work is at its most strained during school holiday periods when parents have to rely on alternative care arrangements. Finding quality, affordable, holiday childcare can be a postcode lottery, with considerable variations in standards and cost of care and large differences across the four nation states. The Daycare Trust's *Childcare Costs Survey 2010* gives some indication of the realities of this:

- Average childcare costs for 25 hours per week are £88 in England, which is more than half gross average part-time earnings of £153 per week.

- Parents in London are facing the highest reported costs, paying up to £11,050 per year for 25 hours childcare per week, or £22,100 for 50 hours.
- Average yearly expenditure on childcare is £4,576 for English parents, £4,368 for Scottish parents and £4,056 for Welsh parents for 25 hours of nursery care per week, for a child under 2.
- There has been a rise in costs above the rate of inflation for all types of childcare, despite the UK being in recession. In England the cost of a nursery place for children aged 2 and over has risen by 5.1 per cent – almost double inflation.
- The typical cost of a place for a child in a local authority-run summer play scheme is £82.60 per week in England, £58.89 in Wales and £104.28 per week in Scotland. The typical cost for private, voluntary and independent-run provision is £104.55 per week in England, £101.60 in Wales and £96.47 in Scotland (Daycare Trust, 2010).

Multi-agency working

Removing the distinction between childcare and education was put in motion with the Childcare Bill 2005, which placed a duty on local authorities to provide childcare for working parents. The Childcare Act 2006 added a further link to the labour market in a requirement to set up partnerships with Jobcentre Plus and NHS child health services. These partnerships grew organically. For children in the primary years, this translated into a network of children's organizations and voluntary groups hubbed around the school. These included, among others, educational psychologists, nurses, police, counsellors, social workers, school attendance officers, playworkers and youth workers. As well as links outside the classroom, additional roles were created inside the classroom to support a greater emphasis on the holistic needs of the child. This resulted in a significant increase in the number of teaching assistants, learning mentors and peripatetic teachers, for example sports coaches, who come from non-teaching backgrounds and bring with them a broader understanding of children's lives beyond the classroom. The multiple roles build a team around the child better equipped to deliver services that address the five ECM outcomes. One of the advantages of multi-agency teams is that workers can attend joint training programmes, learn about each others' roles, and adopt a common approach to providing for children in childhood. Multiple and interagency working also brings with it certain challenges and I want to consider, briefly, the implications of coordination and leadership for children's education where multiple professions are involved.

ECM introduced a new role defined as the 'lead professional'. This role is intended to provide a single point of contact for children and their families to help them navigate the different professional roles and input. Most children in receipt of services will have been allocated a lead professional in early childhood but once they begin full-time schooling, this may no longer be the most appropriate person. It is important to appreciate the extensive roles that primary classroom teachers already fulfil: coordinating a team of assistants and volunteers, working with parents, collaborating with professionals, in addition to delivering full-time, face-to-face teaching. It would be an overload to add a lead professional responsibility without taking anything away and may erode goodwill towards integrated practice. This is primarily a funding and resource issue. If the government is committed to the ideology of ECM and its stated goal of better providing for children's needs, then ECM has to be resourced properly. Earlier in the chapter I alluded to the transformation funding made available for early years staff training. Similar funding needs to be allocated to the lead professional role, as it cannot be assumed that it will just be bolted on to a professional's workload.

Impact of ECM on the primary curriculum

Schools are expected to incorporate the five ECM outcomes into their teaching. ECM puts the child at the centre of provision and provides for children's needs from a holistic perspective that emphasizes wellbeing as a human right. However, school assessment processes have been working against this ideology for more than a decade. Standard attainment tests (SATs) in core subjects were introduced for 7-year-olds in 1991, 11-year-olds in 1995 and 14-year-olds in 1998. With all the other external exams – GCSEs, A and AS levels – a typical student leaving school aged 18 could have been subjected to over 80 national tests. In an attempt to raise standards, the government set targets of attainment pegged to age not development stage. This meant that children who did not achieve a certain level on national tests were labelled as failing. Furthermore, their schools were labelled as failing. There was no hiding place. Outcomes were published in national league tables and schools were pitted against each other in the competition for parental approval that could boost their school admissions. Since literacy and maths – and, intermittently, science – were the only subjects externally assessed and the results published nationally, schools focused their efforts on teaching these subjects to the exclusion of others. In many primary schools, sport, music, art and humanities were almost denuded from the timetable in order to make way for extended programmes of literacy, numeracy and science. I would suggest it is somewhat ironic that in the run-up to the 2012 Olympics, we are now bemoaning the lack of sporting prowess among the younger generation and the critical levels of child obesity.

Schools, concerned to maximize their performance in national tests and their standing in league tables, were lulled into a culture of teaching to the tests.

Borderline pupils were targeted for extra support and booster classes arranged to get them over the threshold. Some schools even ran revision classes during the Easter holidays (children sit SATs papers in May). The fifth special report of the Children, Schools and Families Committee (2008) raised concerns:

> The evidence we have received strongly favours the view that national tests do not serve all of the purposes for which they are, in fact, used. The fact that the results of these tests are used for so many purposes, with high-stakes attached to the outcomes, creates tensions in the system leading to undesirable consequences, including distortion of the education experience of many children. In addition, the data derived from the testing system do not necessarily provide an accurate or complete picture of the performance of schools and teachers, yet they are relied upon by the Government, the QCA and Ofsted to make important decisions affecting the education system in general and individual schools, teachers and pupils in particular. In short, we consider that the current national testing system is being applied to serve too many purposes. (para. 44)

> We consider that the over-emphasis on the importance of national tests, which address only a limited part of the National Curriculum and a limited range of children's skills and knowledge has resulted in teachers narrowing their focus. Teachers who feel compelled to focus on that part of the curriculum which is likely to be tested may feel less able to use the full range of their creative abilities in the classroom and find it more difficult to explore the curriculum in an interesting and motivational way. We are concerned that the professional abilities of teachers are, therefore, under-used and that some children may suffer as a result of a limited educational diet focussed on testing. We feel that teacher assessment should form a significant part of a national assessment regime. (para. 58)

" Children's Experiences

Boyuan Xiao, an 11-year-old boy, carried out some research about the views and emotions of his peers regarding the Key Stage 2 SATs (Xiao, 2006). He designed his own questionnaire which he distributed in two schools, one positioned near the top of the SATs league table and one lower down. His research highlighted the anxiety and stress being experienced by his peers leading up to the Key Stage 2 tests. Interestingly, his research also discovered that the children had sophisticated knowledge about the league tables and were well versed in the position of their own school, possibly through hearing their parents or teachers talking about it. The worse their school had performed on a particular SAT paper in the previous year, the less confident they felt about their own impending tests. Boyuan's research showed that the majority of the children who participated in his research had negative attitudes towards SATs, felt they caused stress and put them under increasing pressure.

The introduction of ECM has brought about a gradual erosion of the testing regime as the focus shifts to services *around* the child. Another significant impact of ECM on children's primary education is the influence it is having on personalized learning. Achieving the five ECM outcomes requires a much more child-centred approach to teaching and learning. Educational philosophy ebbs and flows, different ideologies surf vacillating waves of popularity at different times but there is a wry inevitability about its cyclical nature. Suffice it to say that personalized learning is nothing new. We know it by another name, 'child-centred learning', and it prevailed in the early 1980s. It was replaced by subject-driven and assessment-based curricula (ultimately the national curriculum). Child-centred learning is experiential, it is learning through doing, where process is more important than product. Teachers are facilitators of learning and skill development rather than vehicles of knowledge transfer.

The Children's Plan (DCSF, 2007: 10) announced a root and branch review of the primary curriculum, to be led by Sir Jim Rose, to ensure:

- more time for the basics so children achieve a good grounding in reading, writing and mathematics
- greater flexibility for other subjects
- time for primary school children to learn a modern foreign language
- a smoother transition from play-based learning in the early years into primary school, particularly to help summer-born children who can be at a disadvantage when they enter primary school.

Assessment was conspicuous by its absence. When the secretary of state commissioned the primary review, he told Sir Jim Rose: 'Your review is focused on the curriculum and is not considering changes to the current assessment and testing regime' (BBC News, 20 October 2008). Indeed, when the review was published in December 2008 (Rose, 2008), one of the main criticisms was that it failed to look at a number of critical factors that were affecting the quality of children's primary school experiences, notably testing and assessment:

> On the one hand, it recommends six themed 'areas of learning', which – and Jim Rose is keen to emphasis this – will still include all the traditional subject areas. At the same time, the review says there should be greater emphasis on literacy, numeracy and ICT (information and communication technology), space should be made for modern foreign languages and schools should find more time to teach about personal skills and sex and relationships education. This is not 'de-cluttering' the curriculum. They have simply moved everything around, renamed a few things, and thrown a few more things on top.

> The second problem with the review is that it fails to take the testing regime into account. The greatest block to primary schools – and their

capacity to develop – is not the curriculum but the way they are tested and held to account by Government. Key Stage tests have proven clumsy, narrow and of no significant purpose for the children themselves. Primary schools already have a tremendous capacity and appetite for curriculum development; it is the tests, not the content of the curriculum that is holding most back. (*The Telegraph*, 8 December 2008)

By contrast, the report *Children, Their World, Their Education* (known as the Alexander Report), which was undertaken by Cambridge University and funded by the Esmée Fairbairn Foundation, came to very different conclusions about the primary curriculum:

The most conspicuous casualties are the arts, the humanities and those kinds of learning in all subjects which require time for talking, problem-solving and the extended exploration of ideas; memorisation and recall have come to be valued over understanding and enquiry, and transmission of information over the pursuit of knowledge in its fuller sense ... A curriculum should reflect and enact educational aims and values, but during the past two decades national aims and curriculum have been separately determined, making the aims cosmetic and the true purposes of primary education opaque. In a complex and changing world there is an urgent need for proper debate about what primary education is for ... Micro-management by DCSF, the national agencies and national strategies is widely perceived to be excessive and to have contributed to some of the problems above. Curriculum debate, and thus curriculum practice, is weakened by a muddled and reductive discourse about subjects, knowledge and skills. Discussion of the place of subjects is needlessly polarised; knowledge is grossly parodied as grubbing for obsolete facts; and the undeniably important notion of skill is inflated to cover aspects of learning for which it is not appropriate. There is an urgent need for key curriculum terms to be clarified and for the level of curriculum discussion and conceptualisation to be raised. (Alexander, 2009: 1–2)

The Alexander Report makes uncomfortable reading and suggests that we have collectively failed a generation of primary school children. Returning our central focus to the child, building the five ECM outcomes around the child and broadening education into more holistic, integrated provision is heading in the right direction. However, there is still little evidence that we are involving children sufficiently in decisions about their education. I would argue that had the last generation of primary school children been more involved in decisions about their education, they would have been unlikely to sanction a denuding of art, sport, music and topic work in favour of intensive maths and literacy lessons and endless preparation for tests. Children also have much to say about the way in which they are taught, how they are grouped and how education budgets are spent.

> **‟** Children's Perspectives
>
> In 2005, Dominic Cole, a 12-year-old researcher, when presenting to a group of government officers at the Cabinet Office, urged them to trust children and share decision-making in schools and society with them. He wanted more say in school budgets, school furniture, materials for lessons, as well as consultation on the curriculum, which he described as 'endless revision' and 'tests, tests and more tests' (Cole, 2005: 4). He asserted children's rights to express their views on:
>
> - War
> - Politics
> - Design of children's places
> - Organisation of children's events
> - School politics
>   - the way we are taught
>   - children's councils (Cole, 2005: 5).

Pupil voice

The school environment is one of the most governed childhood arenas outside youth offending institutions and a location where children are least able to assert their human rights. Devine (2002) maintains that the rights discourse focuses primarily on a child's right to education rather than on a child's experiences within the system itself. For example, children do not have the right to be consulted in decisions made about which school they might attend or to participate in tribunals making decisions about possible exclusion. While children have rights to welfare, and necessarily rely on adults to provide this, they also have rights to self-determination (Wyness et al., 2004).

Despite the requirements of the Education Act 2002 that schools consult with their pupils, engaging children's voices in an active and meaningful way in schools remains a challenge (Leitch and Mitchell, 2007). Citing the requirements of Article 12 of the UNCRC, Leitch and Mitchell note that encouraging such shifts by law is one thing but changing the culture of schools is another. Pertinent here is the liberal interpretation of Article 12, where adults (in this case, teachers) decide if a child is capable of forming their own views and how much weight can be given to those views. All this results in a system of top-down control (Wyness, 2006) that perpetuates the traditional hierarchical power relationships between adults and children. The danger is that lip service is rendered to pupil voice for reasons of a school's accountability (Robinson and Taylor, 2007) rather than for reasons of a pupil's human rights. Smyth (2006) proposes a shift of emphasis in pedagogic and leadership approaches away from the focus on standards and accountability towards 'relational reforms' which address the emotional and personal needs of pupils, thus engendering confidence, trust and respect. It is here that the broadening out of education to provide a hub for integrated children's services should work in favour of pupil voice because it will bring more professionals into the educational arena operating from a rights-based agenda.

The growth of school councils and the establishment of School Councils UK as an empowering organization have done much to raise awareness about the potential for children to play a part in the leadership and management of schools. As yet, participation by pupils in the machinery of schools has clustered around relatively uncontroversial elements such as improving the school environment and less on issues of teaching and learning. Close inspection of *Working Together: Giving Children and Young People a Say* (DfES, 2004b) reveals that while teaching and learning were listed as possible areas of pupil consultation, the practice example provided in the guidelines was the rather more innocuous topic of school uniform. Other references to teaching and learning in the document only refer to children planning and evaluating their *own* learning. The rapidity with which initiatives are put into place is also a point of concern. This is underlined by Bragg's (2001) contention that when rapid results are needed (notably performance league tables), it is easier to listen to those voices which accord with the establishment position rather than those which challenge it.

Nonetheless, a head of steam is building around pupil voice, carried by advocacy organizations such as School Councils UK (www.schoolcouncils. org) and Involver (www.involver.org.uk). The latter was established to help children and young people learn about democracy by doing democracy actively in their schools. Involver works closely with Little Heath School, Reading, as described in Box 5.2.

Box 5.2	**Student voice in action: spotlight on Little Heath School**

The school has six student voice groups, each of which have a special job in the school. These are:

- The Building group (looking at school environment)
- What makes a good lesson group (teaching and learning)
- The Independent Learning group (trying to define independent learning)
- Safe to learn group (Anti-bullying)
- STARS project (students as researchers).

It's clear from the style of relationships that teachers genuinely want to hear what students think, will take it seriously, and want to set up ways to encourage this more formally. Staff are willing to run with their ideas, and recognise that good school democracy/citizenship is often a bit of a step into the unknown. They also understand that trusting young people is not losing power – it's helping everyone to work together in the same direction.

Source: Involver, 2010

> ## " Children's Experiences
>
> A DfES study jointly funded by the Centre for British Teachers (DfES, 2006a) explored personalized learning in eight schools and focused particularly on children's views. In one school, student engagement in Year 8 (aged 12–13) was problematic. The researchers invited a group of ten Year 8 students to keep logs for a two-week period about their learning experiences. Teachers allowed them five minutes at the end of each lesson to record their views. For ethical reasons, the students were asked to record only positive comments and to leave the log blank if there was nothing positive to report. Analysis of the logs (p. 22) revealed that:
>
> i.   relatively few examples of encouragement were recorded
> ii. although advice was offered on how to improve, the comments were almost exclusively of a generalised and largely moralising nature – for example 'work harder', concentrate more', 'sit in your seat and don't stand up', 'don't giggle', 'try not to call out', 'put more effort into your work', 'don't get sent out' and so on. Whilst these exhortations, if acted upon, might well have improved the quality of pupils' work, it was hard not to notice the frequency with which they were reiterated and to sense something of their general ineffectiveness
> iii. where specific advice was offered on how to improve work it came exclusively – and then rarely – from practical subjects (for example 'point your toes', 'wear goggles'). Teachers were made sharply aware through the logs of the sense of inadequacy that feedback can generate if not well managed. In particular, the generalised advice to try harder, make more effort, etc., may simply serve, when repeated frequently, to emphasise students' lack of progress. Such generalised (as opposed to personalised) pointers to progress seem to reflect a generalised rather than personalised recognition of a student's strengths and capabilities.
>
> Teachers were surprised at the maturity and scope of the student observations and it increased their willingness to involve students more in teaching and learning initiatives, as these teacher quotes from the report testify (p. 36):
>
> 'This initiative has created a seismic shift in attitude and culture and sharpened our awareness of what it's like from the student perspective.'
>
> 'Their comments have dramatically changed the way I work – I have a much clearer idea now of the strengths and weaknesses of all the pupils I teach.'
>
> 'The most powerful evidence about changing teaching and learning is coming from the students.'
>
> 'Pupil voices make us look at things we don't normally think about.'

There are important implications for policy and practice. It is evident from the report that pupil voice helps to build a sense of membership and recognition and changes teacher–pupil relationships. This readjustment of power differentials can lead to shared constructions for school improvement that incorporate students' experiences and concerns.

Extended schools

Extended schools, in tandem with children's centres discussed earlier, are a major delivery arm of children's integrated services. There are two particular issues of concern: first, a risk that extended services will be diluted and not delivered by appropriate professionals and, second, a risk of overgovernance for those children who spend from 8am till 6pm, five days a week there. Will this simply lengthen school hours and school curriculum – more of the same diet for children in power-laden settings with limited personal space and personal autonomy?

> What choices will children have about this? Will they want to remain at school (albeit perhaps within a separate building in the grounds) in their uniforms after completing a full day's work? What if a child is being bullied and the bully also attends the after school club? (Walker, 2008: 166)

Children are already growing up in a risk-averse society where parents are too afraid to let them play out in the streets or go to parks unaccompanied for fear of stranger danger (Gill, 2007). Imaginative play, creativity and children exploring their own worlds are being increasingly marginalized as children are bundled from one supervised location to another. Extended schools must be organized carefully so that they offer a range of opportunities to children including creative and exploratory activities. There are opportunities, too, for disadvantaged children to bridge some of the attainment gap through well-run homework clubs. These had been operating in some schools, before ECM, particularly in deprived areas. They were run by teachers as after-school clubs and typically operated until 4pm. Such homework clubs are now being rolled up into the larger wraparound services operating until 6pm. The longer hours increase the likelihood that these will be facilitated by non-teaching staff which reintroduces a note of caution. Undoubtedly, extended schools offer an opportunity to improve the educational chances for some children through skilfully supported homework classes. It would be a missed opportunity if they become little more than supervised childcare sessions.

Conclusion

Children spend a large proportion of their waking hours in school and the extended schools programme suggests that this is set to increase even more. It is critical, therefore, that education systems meaningfully reflect the ECM ethos of support *around* the child and that they can deliver the five ECM outcomes. In exploring school systems within an ECM context, this chapter has highlighted the challenges of amalgamating education into the DCSF. The benefits of ECM are most apparent in the early years, and the 'one-stop shops' of children's centres. However, tensions result in attempts to marry provision of social care, for example quality childcare, with mounting pressure to evaluate outcomes on educational attainment. This invites debate about the appropriateness of school systems and curricula and the impact ECM is having. Pupil voice was explored, as was the contested notion of child citizenship. While these have links to education, they are broader issues that lend themselves to a rights-based analysis and are addressed in more depth in Chapters 11 and 13. Issues relating to children in the care system and those who have disabilities (including learning difficulties) are explored in Chapters 6 and 7. Illustrations of children's perspectives would suggest that adult–child power relations in schools are out of step with other service areas, where progress towards consultation and involvement in decision-making is more advanced.

Reflection exercises

1. For all readers

Take some time to reflect on the main issues and debates discussed in this chapter and then draw up a list of what you consider to be the positives and negatives of contemporary education provision for children in their early and primary years in relation to ECM objectives.

2. For staff working with children and young people in multidisciplinary teams

The traditional notion of the lone primary teacher ensconced behind closed doors with 30 or so children is long since past. A number of adults from a range of professions now work inside classrooms and/or are closely linked to education service provision. The number and diversity of adults are increasing as the extended schools programme gathers pace. As this chapter has shown, multi-agency working is not as affective as it might be. Evaluate your own, or your team's, contact with educational settings. Identify, and reflect on, areas of strength and weakness.

3. Children's perspectives

School councils are now an integral part of educational agendas and an important vehicle for pupil voice. If you could set up a school council from scratch, what would your drivers be? What value base would you adopt? How would you go about constructing a framework? Using a mind map or similar, sketch out what your ideal primary school council might look like.

Suggested further reading

1. Matheson, D. (ed.) (2008) *An Introduction to the Study of Education* (3rd edn), London: David Fulton

   Covers a wide range of issues such as race, gender and additional needs in education, along with an exposition of pertinent ideology and psychology of education. Presented at an introductory and accessible level with some interesting comparative discussions.

2. Siraj-Blatchford, I. (2007) 'The case for integrating education with care in the early years', in I. Siraj-Blatchford, K. Clarke and M. Needham (eds) *The Team Around The Child: Multi-agency Working in the Early Years*, Stoke-on-Trent: Trentham Books

   If you have a special interest in the early years, this helpful chapter will be invaluable in setting out the main debates and discussions surrounding the integration of education with care. Other chapters in the book include multi-agency issues related to the early years sector.

3. Middlewood, D. and Parker, R. (2009) *Leading and Managing Extended Schools: Ensuring Every Child Matters*, London: Sage

   A publication in three parts, the first has an excellent overview of what extended schools are and why they are needed. Chapter 1 is particularly useful if you are looking for a good source that contextualizes the concept of extended schools. The second part looks more particularly at the personnel who work in these settings and the leadership and management issues that are involved.

4. Cheminais, R. (2010) *The Pocket Guide to Every Child Matters: An At-a-Glance Overview for the Busy Teacher*, Abingdon: Routledge

   Highly recommended for educational practitioners. Rita Cheminais has written several books on Every Child Matters, but this is a particularly useful (and short) book that gives an overview of what practitioners in school settings need to know in order to deliver ECM. Also useful for student teachers or anyone considering a career change into teaching.

6 Child Healthcare and Wellbeing

In this chapter we discuss:

- Child healthcare in the twenty-first century
- Children with disabilities
- Children with chronic health conditions
- Mental health and wellbeing issues for children
- Early intervention health initiatives and interagency working

Child healthcare in the twenty-first century

'Be healthy' is the first of the five Every Child Matters (ECM) intended outcomes. These two small words belie the size of the challenge. The provision of healthcare for children in contemporary society is a mixed tale of success and failure. In some areas of child health there has been laudable progress. Better awareness of dangers in the home and tighter vehicle safety laws have reduced the number of children being injured or dying from accidents in the home and on the roads. There have been dramatic improvements in the survival rates from childhood cancers and the infant mortality rate has dropped to its lowest ever, at 4.9 deaths in 1,000 (DH, 2008). At the same time, we are witnessing a rapid rise in childhood obesity and alcohol-related problems – 30% of 11-year-olds have been drunk at least twice (UNICEF, 2007) – and allergies are on the increase. Perhaps the gravest concern of all is the significant escalation of mental health problems (Layard and Dunn, 2009). The root cause of many of these health issues can be traced to poverty, disadvantage and inequality:

> Our poorest children are more likely to be born too early and too small, less likely to be breastfed or immunised, more likely to suffer accidents in the home and on the street, more likely to have asthma, to be overweight and to suffer from chronic illness – all of which puts them on a lifelong trajectory of compromised health and wellbeing, which will spill over across generations. (Pickett, 2009: 11)

The White Paper *Choosing Health* (DH, 2004) was the first health-related policy response to ECM and identified children's health as a priority. It set out a number of measures:

- more children's centres to enhance the health and wellbeing of children
- an increased number of extended schools, to help make the school a force for health in every community
- encouraging healthy eating and restricting the promotion and marketing of food high in fat, sugar and salt to children
- providing more opportunities for sport and physical activity
- new support and information to young people on sexual health
- preventing the sale of alcohol to children
- preventing the sale of cigarettes to children
- the development of personal health plans for all children.

In this chapter, I explore, from children's perspectives, the extent to which these aims are being realized. The limitations of space restrict this to examples in three areas: disability, mental health and early intervention initiatives. The Suggested further reading recommends resources on other child health topics that it is not possible to cover in this chapter.

Disability

Estimates suggest there are around 770,000 children who are disabled in the UK, 7% of all children, and that they are among the most disadvantaged (Sharma, 2007). Approximately 57% of them live in poverty compared to 37% of children without disabilities (Disability Alliance, 2009). Families with children who are disabled are 50% more likely to be in debt and 50% less likely to be able to afford holidays, new clothes, school outings or 'treats' for their children (Emerson and Hatton, 2005). It costs about three times more to bring up a child who has a disability but only 16% of mothers are in work, compared with 61% of mothers with non-disabled children (Langerman and Worral, 2005), another factor which may account for why so many are caught in the poverty trap.

Aiming High for Disabled Children (DCSF, 2007b) was a major review of services to families with disabled children. This policy document introduced the 'core offer', a set of five principles (information, assessment, transparency, participation and feedback) which were promised as core standards against which disabled children's service provision would be monitored on an annual basis. The purpose of the core offer is to improve access to services by ensuring that disabled children and their families:

- are aware of services available to them in their area
- understand how those services can be accessed

- undergo only the minimum possible assessment to qualify for services
- are actively involved in the planning and delivery of services in their local area
- are aware of ways in which they can give feedback on their experiences of services (DCSF, 2007b).

Table 6.1 shows the 2009 monitoring data for each of the five standards collated from a survey of parents' experiences. These are presented as national headline figures for England. Scores are rated on a scale of 1–100 based on a subset of 15 indicators. Below each score is a base figure which represents the number of parents who were surveyed.

Table 6.1	Parents' experiences of services provided to disabled children		
Core offer standards	Health scores (out of 100)	Education scores (out of 100)	Care and family support (out of 100)
Information	69	70	69
Base	29,340	28,526	29.503
Assessment	76	77	67
Base	13,238	13,135	3,700
Transparency	96	92	89
Base	13,720	13,424	3,809
Participation	61	48	53
Base	13,698	13,435	3,808
Feedback	12	20	12
Base	23,321	23,993	13,773

Source: DfE, 2009: 14. Reproduced under Open Government Licence v1.0

The consultation process leading up to *Aiming High for Disabled Children* revealed that the top two causes of anguish to parents of disabled children were not being able to take short breaks and the difficulty in accessing quality childcare. The government sought to address this by providing additional funding – £340 million for the period 2008 to 2011. This funding was allocated to four specific service areas: short breaks (given the lion's share), childcare, transition, and parent forums. In December 2007, the Children's Plan in England committed an additional £90 million capital funding for short break services from 2008 to 2011, bringing the total funding allocation to £430 million. Legislation to underpin this initiative came with the Children and Young Person's Act 2008, which introduced a *duty* on local authorities to provide short break services for parents. The benefits of short breaks for parents and disabled children are well documented (Eaton, 2008; Robertson et al., 2008) but despite all the good intentions, many families are still missing out because the government failed to ensure that short break funding was ring-fenced by PCTs and tied to this specific purpose. Instead it went into a generic pot and some was then used for other competing priorities.

Revenue has been increased in other areas of child health. Funding for children's palliative care services was boosted following the review *Better Care, Better Lives* (Craft and Killen, 2007). In 2010, a further £12.5 million of funding was made available as part of the Disabled Children's Access to Childcare Programme. At one level, increased funding demonstrates a willingness to address inadequacies in services provided for disabled children. Translating this into meaningful practice is quite another.

> ## " Children's Perspectives
>
> Every Disabled Child Matters (EDCM) is a consortium campaign run by four of the leading organizations working with disabled children and their families: Contact a Family, the Council for Disabled Children, Mencap and the Special Educational Consortium. It campaigns to get rights and justice for every disabled child. It is a valuable source of information and a strong vehicle for authentic voice of disabled children. One of its publications (in print and DVD format) is a collection of disabled children's views on the theme of 'If you were Prime Minister for the day, and could change one thing, what would be it be?' Here is what some of them said (EDCM, 2007):
>
> > 'I would like to have more support so that I can do social activities with other children of my own age and more activities available in my area.'
> >
> > 'Just because my mum has a car to help with my mobility don't assume that I want to go everywhere with her. I want to experience different modes of transport.
> >
> > 'More buses, more routes, more transport, help with independence.'
> >
> > 'More respect for disabled people.'
> >
> > 'Tell people not to discriminate us, we are no different from other people. Let us decide what we want.'
> >
> > '"Average" is all a disabled child is allowed to be. We should have the same rights as the other children in schools.'
> >
> > 'Find meaningful activities for us to do in Games and P.E. Not timing others or collecting balls up.'
> >
> > 'Please stop the war and please no bombs please no guns.'

Mobility is an important part of any childhood and particularly important for normal development activities and autonomy. For disabled children who cannot get around, a wheelchair is essential. Yet many children experience difficulties with wheelchair provision, especially in sourcing one which is appropriate to their needs. Sharma and Morrison (2006) conducted a survey of 340 families whose children were immobile: 54% responded that their local services could not provide the equipment they needed and 47% had been told that budget restrictions prevented their child's individual needs being met. Whizz–Kidz is a voluntary organization which supports disabled children to live as active and independent lives as possible and provides equipment to children who cannot get what they need from statutory provision.

> ## " Children's Perspectives
>
> The following is a quote from a nine-year-old child who has severe impairments and epilepsy, cited in Sharma and Morrison (2006: 13):
>
> > 'Why does it take so long when someone says it's a priority? Does it take nearly a year to get a chair? I had to be uncomfortable and sometimes housebound because it took so long to supply my chair, which is still not complete. Ideally I need an electric wheelchair as I am really heavy now for mum to push'
>
> ### Sam's story
>
> Sam is a four-year-old boy who has cerebral palsy, which for him means he is unable to walk and is dependent on a wheelchair or being carried to get around. Before contacting Whizz-Kidz, Sam had an NHS wheelchair that he could only use inside. It was very difficult for his family to take him out and enjoy family activities together. He had to be pushed everywhere in a buggy. The NHS was unable to fund a wheelchair that would give him the freedom to become more independent.
>
> A Whizz-Kidz therapist assessed Sam for a powered wheelchair that he could use anywhere – from small spaces in the house to outside in the park. His new wheelchair also has a riser to enable him to reach his easel to paint at school and be the same height as his friends. As soon as Sam received his new wheelchair, he showed how bright and inquisitive he is. One of the first things Sam did was to explore the kitchen for the first time. He was delighted when he discovered that he could reach his drink and fruit on his own.
>
> *Source:* Sharma and Morrison, 2006: 16

There is a lack of consistency in criteria governing the allocation of wheelchairs to children. Some local authorities will not provide a wheelchair until a disabled child reaches 30 months of age, on the basis that parents can use a commercial pushchair until at least that age. This denies such children an entitlement to engage in activities commensurate with their development needs, one of which is independent exploration. An able-bodied, 30-month-old child may use a pushchair occasionally but at other times will be getting around independently – exploring, discovering and learning. Disabled children should be able to have similar experiences to their able-bodied peers. This can be facilitated, for example, by an electric tricycle or adapted wheelchair.

" Children's Experiences

The following is a quote from a young person, aged 10, who has cerebral palsy, cited in Sharma and Morrison (2008: 23):

> 'My new powered wheelchair means that I can go in the playground and not get so tired – it is fantastic! I can go shopping without someone having to push me all the time and I can play basketball at my Saturday Club all by myself.'

Jacob's story

Six-year-old Jacob recently received a Terrier Trike from Whizz-Kidz. Jacob, who has developmental delay, usually moves by shuffling on his bottom, now he is able to go outside and play with his two sisters, Abigail and Hollie.

Jacob's mum Jackie described how emotional she felt as Jacob tested the trike for the first time: "we couldn't believe it when we were told Jacob could take the trike home that day and kept checking in the car's rear view mirror, expecting someone to tell us it was a mistake!"

The trike was a perfect fit for Jacob, who didn't want to get off and with the sunny weather it could not have come at a better time. The family plan to take the trike into the park and since they received it friends have been giving them tips on other fun days out in their area.

Jackie feels the trike will have an impact on the whole family, as it will allow Jacob to keep up with his sisters. Watching Jacob sitting upright on the trike Jackie said she felt she was witnessing a day which her and her husband 'felt would never come'.

As the trike has dual controls which can be managed from behind, there is no need to run along side the bike and as Jacob becomes more independent he will be able to take over.

Source: Whizz-Kidz, 2007

Peter's story

Peter is a lively 7-year-old boy who has cerebral palsy, which affects his ability to walk; he can only walk short distances with assistance and gets tired very quickly. Before contacting Whizz-Kidz, he had a manual wheelchair supplied by the NHS, which meant that whenever he wanted to go outside, he relied on other people to push him. He was unable to join his friends for sports or at playtime at his mainstream school. Peter also has a disabled twin brother, which made it very difficult for his mum to take both boys out together since she could not push two wheelchairs at once.

The NHS was unable to provide the powered wheelchair Peter needed, primarily due to financial constraints. The powered wheelchair provided by Whizz-Kidz is suitable for indoor and outdoor use. It has a joystick so Peter is able to drive it on his own and his mum has her own joystick so that she can provide extra support if needed. Now the family can enjoy trips out together. For Peter the difference is huge as he has much more independence and can join in and play with his friends. At school he can join in at playtime, take part in PE and do the everyday things, like hanging up his coat.

Source: Sharma and Morrison, 2008: 20

Children with chronic health conditions

An underlying theme throughout this book is the acceptance of children being agentic and acknowledged as experts in their own lives. This is no different for children who have chronic health conditions. An initiative that is gathering momentum in the Leeds and Bradford area is the Getting Sorted programme. This project designs, delivers and evaluates self-care workshops to empower children and young people with type one diabetes (Webster, 2007) and asthma (Webster and Newell, 2008) to manage their own conditions and attain more life independence. Children and young people are involved in all aspects of the project, including advisory, co-researcher and evaluator roles. Findings emerging from the project suggest that many of the children and young people involved have negative experiences of paediatric clinics such as those that children attend as part of their diabetic care plans. They feel disempowered by consultants who either do not listen to them or give them no opportunity to express a view. Critically, they feel that professionals do not understand what it is like trying to live as normal a childhood as possible and manage their conditions. Medical staff appear to be only interested in the clinical management of blood sugar levels and seem oblivious to the emotional impacts of the condition. Children feel nagged, judged and criticized, to a point where their self-esteem becomes crushed. Many also feel suffocated by parental restrictions on their activities.

> ### " Children's Perspectives
>
> 'Depends on my blood sugar levels whether I'm allowed to go out or not'.
>
> 'I am not trusted'.
>
> 'Telling you what to do all the time'.
>
> 'Checking up'.
>
> 'Over-protective'.
>
> 'Not listening'.
>
> 'Need people to understand what Diabetes is about and how it affects me. People make assumptions'.
>
> *Source:* Webster, 2007: 26–7

In helping to design the Getting Sorted workshops, children and young people advised on the venue, timing and content. As a result of this consultation, an inspired training programme of self-care workshops was co-constructed using approaches such as games, drama, art, role play and so on to connect with the different age groups (6–17 plus). Children and young people were involved in the evaluation.

> ❝ **Children's Perspectives**
>
> 'that acting drama group came in and that really helped … I had something to relate to'
>
> '[I] drew a picture of a person and put arrows at different parts of the body where diabetes effects them, bruising from injections and things like that'
>
> 'we were blindfolded and had to trust … that was good … – trust building'
>
> '[When] I had another appointment at the hospital I was much more confident at talking to the doctor'
>
> 'I went to a doctor's appointment and told them the truth for once'
>
> 'I'm able to talk to my parents you know like to back off'
>
> *Source:* Webster, 2007: 32–3

The Getting Sorted project is an example of how the perspectives and experiences of children and young people can be directly harnessed to design processes. Bringing them on board at the concept rather than end-user stage acknowledges the capacity of children and young people to directly influence policy and practice.

Children's mental health and wellbeing

Children's mental health and wellbeing is integral to all five ECM outcomes. Children and Adolescent Mental Health Services (CAMHS) is the main service provider. It has four tiers of working, shown in Box 6.1.

> **Box 6.1** **CAMHS working tiers**
>
> *Tier 1:* generic support provided by professionals whose main role and training is not in mental health, such as General Practitioners, health visitors, paediatricians, social workers, teachers, youth workers and juvenile justice workers.

Tier 2: provided by specialist trained mental health professionals, working primarily on their own, rather than in a team. They see young people with a variety of mental health problems that have not responded to Tier 1 interventions. They usually provide consultation and training to Tier 1 professionals. They may provide specialist mental health input to multi-agency teams, for example for children looked after by the local authority.

Tier 3: provided by a multi-disciplinary team who aim to see young people with more complex mental health problems than those seen at Tier 2. In many areas the movement of young people and families between Tier 2 and 3 is fluid and seamless, with the same professionals working at both tiers.

Tier 4: very specialised services in residential, day patient or outpatient settings for children and adolescents with severe and/or complex problems requiring a combination or intensity of interventions that cannot be provided by tier 3 CAMHS.

Tier 4 services are usually commissioned on a sub regional, regional or supra-regional basis. They also include day care and residential facilities provided by sectors other than the NHS such as residential schools, and very specialised residential social care settings including specialised therapeutic foster care.

Source: York and Lamb, 2005: 15–16

The number of children suffering with mental health issues has risen alarmingly in the past decade to one in ten children and young people aged 5–16 (CAMHS, 2008). Much has been written about the Innocenti Report (UNICEF, 2007), an international comparison of children's quality of life and wellbeing. Particularly relevant here is the sixth measurement, in relation to children's own subjective sense of wellbeing – the UK was ranked bottom. Five years earlier, in a statement to the Joint Committee on Human Rights, David Hall (2002: 160), then president of the Royal College of Paediatrics and Child Health, warned that:

> Child and adolescent mental health services in this country are a total disgrace. There are many places where the waiting list is 18 months or more. If that were an adult service there would be a public outcry but this is just accepted as being the situation.

Considerable progress has been made since then. The Mental Health Act Commission undertook a review in 2003 which resulted in the construction of a *National Service Framework for Children, Young People and Maternity Services* (DH, 2004) to improve standards. Standard 9 articulates a vision to improve the mental health of all children and young people which stresses the importance of partnership and multi-agency working. Early intervention, by staff who draw on an appropriate range of skills and competences, is central to effective support for children and young people with established or complex problems. Standard 9 seeks to address two major issues persistently raised by parents and professionals: the admission of child patients to adult psychiatric wards and long waiting lists for a child mental health referral.

Despite clear guidance in the *National Service Framework for Mental Health* (DH, 1999) that children should only be admitted to adult psychiatric wards in exceptional circumstances, and where this did happen measures must be taken to safeguard children's interests, pressure on beds in CAMHS units resulted in this becoming much more common than the exceptional practice ruling had intended.

" Children's Perspectives

Shaun said most of his time on the [adult] ward was spent in his room listening to music and staring at his wall, walking the corridors, eating, sleeping and drinking tea. He was not offered the opportunity to take part in any activities, even though there were many on offer for patients. It emerged that despite living only half an hour's drive away from the unit, Shaun did not come from the right area of the county to be able to access the unit's activities that involved trips away from the ward. Shaun believes that not having anything to do, and being denied the opportunity to take part in unit activities contributed massively to how low he felt while being a patient at the adult psychiatric unit (p. 57).

'I need treatment to get over my treatment' (Hattie, p. 75)

Source: 11 Million, 2007

Bowing to increased pressure, the government finally agreed in 2007 to phase out all admissions of children to adult psychiatric wards by 2010.

In 2006, a government review of the implementation of Standard 9 revealed that some children were still waiting six months to see a CAMHS professional and that the referral system was a postcode lottery. Anecdotal evidence cites that, in some areas, CAMHS are suffering as a result of the financial problems within the NHS: 'There is concern that the good work to date risks being undermined by under-investment and poor planning in some areas' (11 Million, 2008: 13). This view is supported by evidence in the CAMHS Review Interim Report (2008), which identified a slowdown in service development relative to previous years and a lack of national consistency, in that some areas were experiencing improvements in services and others reductions. Despite evidence that children with mental health problems benefit from early intervention (11 Million, 2008), support is only available in some areas of the country in crisis situations. Younger children are also less likely to be able to be accommodated in CAMHS facilities. A survey by the Royal Psychiatrists Research Unit (O'Herlihy et al., 2007) found a reduction in the number of CAMHS units that admit children under the age of 14.

As indicated earlier, children's mental health services are a mix of positives and negatives. A strong theme emerging from all the comments and reviews is a real need for consistency across PCTs and equal access for all children:

In recent years, much progress has been made in improving the psychological wellbeing of children and young people and in recognising that this is the responsibility of everyone who works with children. There has also been considerable investment in mental health services. This has led to a more strategic approach to the commissioning and delivery of mental health services for children and young people, informed by a comprehensive analysis of needs. However, there is still a need for more concerted action focusing on effective prevention strategies, as well as for earlier and more sustained interventions, and more comprehensive and equal access to high quality evidence-based treatment. To achieve this will require sustained investment across children's services, closer alignment with adult services and an even greater focus on commissioning services jointly within children's trust arrangements. (11 Million, 2008: 27)

❝ Children's Perspectives

YoungMinds' VIK (Very Important Kids) panel was set up in June 2007. VIK is a group of 15 children and young people aged between 5 and 25, from across England, who have had experience of emotional support across tiers 1-4 of CAMHS. YoungMinds also have a virtual panel called Healthy Heads (set up in June 2007), which VIK consults with before meeting, and feeds back to following each meeting. This enables a larger number of children and young people with various experiences of mental health services to feed into national agendas, without the need to travel. VIK meet regularly to help find solutions to current barriers that prevent children and young people from accessing support. They inform us of current issues which cause children and young people to develop mental health difficulties and they work with us to make decisions about how YoungMinds and other NGOs and children's services/organisations can help. All the children and young people who are on the panel or board are trained by YoungMinds to make sure they can make democratic decisions and feel in control of their involvement.

Source: 11 Million, 2008a: 10

Effective interagency working is critical because children's mental health and wellbeing pervade so many aspects of their lives and are central to all five ECM outcomes. Barnardo's response to the 2008 CAMHS consultation highlights areas where improvements are still needed. Four areas of concern were raised:

- Opaque commissioning processes and the difficulties that come with the separate commissioning budgets across integrated children's services;
- The dominance of the medical model in access, diagnosis and treatment;
- Overlooking the participation of children and young people in commissioning and developing services; and
- The continued stigma attached to mental health difficulties (Barnardo's, 2008: 4).

Also, four areas were identified where significant improvements are needed:

- Increased strategic and financial support for early intervention and preventative approaches;
- A shift in culture to embed collaborative working and knowledge sharing;
- Improved information and access to services for vulnerable groups; and
- Improved monitoring and dissemination of service outcomes (Barnardo's, 2008: 4).

" Children's Perspectives

Eilidh was only nine when her parents started on heroin. Their home was chaotic and Eilidh and her three brothers were left to fare for themselves. When people came to visit, it was usually to take drugs. Eilidh says that the visitors never troubled her, but her mother and step-father – the man she calls her father – were both in and out of jail for supplying drugs. At the age of 12, Eilidh started running away, sometimes twice a week, usually staying with friends until the police picked her up and returned her home. At the same time, Eilidh started taking drugs. She tried heroin, stealing it from her mother, but settled for Valium, which was easily available on the streets. She paid for the drugs with money she was given to buy clothes. It was only when her mother went to prison, and money stopped coming in, that Eilidh had to conquer her dependence. Eilidh started to cut herself. Social workers were assigned to the family but weren't able to help her. She says: 'Everything was building up. My mum and dad were heroin addicts, I just couldn't cope. I more or less wanted to end it all.' Aged 12, she tried to kill herself. Her second suicide attempt followed not long afterwards.

Source: Action for Children, 2010: 66

Set against measures to improve children's mental health services is a consideration of some of the social constructs that may be contributing to the rise in incidence. Sayer (2008: 188) lists some of the labels that are applied to children within the mental health spectrum (Box 6.2).

Box 6.2	Mental health spectrum disorders

Behavioural or conduct disorders:

- ADHD, hyperkinetic disorder
- Tourette's syndrome
- Inappropriate sexual behaviour

Attachment disorders:

- Attachment deficit disorder

Emotional disorders:

- Depression
- Self-harming
- Eating disorders (anorexia and bulimia nervosa; some obesity)
- Anxiety disorder

Psychosis:

- Schizophrenia

Psychopathy (sometimes concerns about 'dangerous' personality disorders)

Autism spectrum disorders:

- Asperger's syndrome

Some of these presenting 'mental disorders' are a consequence of modern-day living. More sedentary childhoods spent indoors on multimedia activities have reduced levels of physical exercise and increased the likelihood of obesity and depressive-related conditions. The cocktail of chemicals in food additives is also known to induce bizarre behaviours (Kelleher et al., 2000) and the rise in the prescription of mind-bending drugs for hyperactivity to children as young as five is nothing short of alarming (Zito et al., 2000). In my opinion, additional funding alone will not improve children's mental wellbeing. It has to be accompanied by a rethinking of modern lifestyles, a raft of preventive measures, comprehensive healthy living education, and an acceptance that absence of wellbeing is directly linked to poverty and disadvantage.

Early intervention health initiatives and interagency working

Many of the health conditions that children develop, including mental health problems, can be prevented or limited by early intervention and support. This is why the integration of services and effective multi-agency working is crucial in the early years from prenatal services onwards. An example of this in practice is a children's centre in Essex.

The Carousel Children's Centre in Braintree is situated in one of Essex's highest areas of deprivation and has been described as 'trailblazing' in the media (Williams, 2009):

> We've seen that the only way we're going to get early intervention with families and support them is through working with health. It's about picking things up much earlier. That starts with early contact through midwives and continues as the child grows. Once mums have been to the breastfeeding group, they're likely to start going to the 0–1 group. Their children's centre becomes a normal part of their life, something they do all the time. If they've got a problem, they come here. It destigmatises it. (Tracy Lindsell, head of children's services at 4Children, cited in Williams, 2009)

At Carousel, appointments are available every morning with a community paediatrician, who works with the centre's specialist nursery to help devise educational plans for children with delayed development. Twice a week, a health professional runs a drop-in service for parents who have concerns or questions about their children but who might not otherwise see their GP. A health visitor is also attached to the centre's nursery and can be called in by staff if parents raise concerns with them. Outreach workers from Carousel work alongside the PCT's health visiting team to identify families who could benefit from help. Healthy living teams go into the centre to give advice on nutrition and exercise, and occupational therapy is provided once a week for children and parents. Children can also get their vaccinations with a school nurse, in an environment that is more friendly and comforting than a GP surgery environment.

Another initiative at Carousel involves training mothers to lead breast-feeding support groups. This is being piloted following suggestions that women are less likely to give up if they are mentored by another parent, rather than by a health professional. There are plans to start a postnatal depression group.

The London borough of Newham is a good example of early intervention initiatives and effective interagency working on child health. It is one of the most deprived areas of England and has the highest proportion of children in its demographic profile (28% of the population is under 20 years of age) and there is a projected 3% increase in population. As of 2009, Newham has the highest birth rate in the country and the second highest rates of child obesity in the country and there are rising numbers of children with type 2 diabetes. Understandably, the health of children is a key priority. It is estimated that over 50% of children are living in poverty and 10% are living in intense poverty.

The PCT worked together with Newham council to create a Joint Strategic Needs Assessment for health and social care needs. It was revised and updated in 2009. An extract in Box 6.3 illustrates some of the complex issues they face and the imperative of effective multi-agency working.

Box 6.3	Extract from Joint Strategic Needs Assessment

Breast feeding is important in giving a good start to life. Newham has high rates of breast feeding initiation. An innovative buddying support programme aims to improve uptake and duration of breast feeding.

Childhood immunisation rates have substantially improved in the last year and are now almost 90%. Newham has experienced small outbreaks of infectious diseases, mumps and measles, but with less severity than neighbouring boroughs.

Education is important as a potential pathway to social mobility. Children start off at a disadvantage with only a third at a good level of development at Foundation stage. Areas of concern are the low levels of achievement by boys – 52% of girls achieve the required standard compared to 38% of boys.

Newham has the highest numbers of children in care and one of the highest proportions of children in care for long periods. Health outcomes for young people in care have improved greatly but educational attainment for this group is still below average.

It is estimated that there are around 4,000 disabled children under 19 years in Newham and 2,500 children with learning disabilities. The Child Development Centre deals with children with complex needs and demand for their services has increased twofold since 2005.

The Child and Adolescent Mental Health Service has seen an increase in referrals of children with mental health problems. Referrals were mainly in the 10–14 year age group and boys were twice as likely to be referred as girls with disproportionate numbers of white children. Nearly two fifths of referrals were for emotional or conduct disorders.

Source: London Borough of Newham, 2009: 11

The ethos of ECM that services 'follow' the child has resulted in many more health initiatives being based in the community and this has required increased numbers of specialist children's nurses and maternity practitioners and greater levels of investment. In the main, this system is working more effectively for children and one can only hope that levels of funding will be maintained. There will always be occasions when a child's health problem requires hospitalization. As adults in increasingly busy health environments, we easily forget just how scary this can be. Even when funding is low and specialist resources are scarce, there is one early intervention that will make a difference – *actively* listening to what children are trying to tell us.

> **❝❝ Children's Perspectives**
>
> 'I was worried ... In the olden days you went into hospital and you lost one of your fingers ... they would chop your finger ... they would chop your hand off, right, and bend it like that, they would put this black stuff on and it heats it up and it hurts ... We got told in a book ... by our school and I remember it' (boy aged 7, cited in Coyne, 2006: 330).

Conclusion

This chapter has highlighted children's lived experiences of health issues, particularly what daily life is like for those who have disabilities, chronic conditions and mental health problems. In reviewing the child health policies that have accompanied ECM, some changes are visible, such as increased funding and greater involvement of parents and children. Interagency working is becoming more mainstream, although there are still difficulties where professionals are at variance in their specialist perspectives. The ECM goal of support provision that 'follows' the child has been shown to be possible where services are hubbed around children's centres. However, children are still telling us that they are not listened to and kept in ignorance of their treatment plans. Active listening and respect for children's rights continue to be major challenges in the implementation of ECM outcomes for child health. Fundamental to everything explored in this chapter is an irrefutable link to disadvantage. The urgency of eradicating child poverty is self-evident if ECM is to have any real impact on children's wellbeing.

Reflection exercises

1. For all readers
Why do you think it is so difficult for parents of disabled children to access quality childcare? What are the critical issues? What are the additional responsibilities and risks? Make a list of factors that might influence a prospective childminder's decision to accept a disabled child. Reflect on what can be done to help disabled families caught in this situation.

2. For staff working with children and young people in multidisciplinary teams
Bullying is a major problem for children who have disabilities. Imagine you have to lead a professional development workshop on this topic. How would you prepare for it?

3. Children's perspectives

'Just because my mum has a car to help with my mobility don't assume that I want to go everywhere with her. I want to experience different modes of transport.' What is this child trying to tell us? Reflect on the human right to be a child first and foremost, irrespective of any disability. Think through some of the barriers that prevent a child with a disability enjoying a quality childhood. What can you do to make a difference?

Suggested further reading

1. Cambell, S. and Hunter, J. (2009) 'Nursing and Every Child Matters', in R. Barker (ed.) *Making Sense of Every Child Matters: Multi Professional Practice Guidance*, Bristol: Policy Press

   An excellent chapter that addresses children's health and wellbeing from the perspective of nursing practitioners. Gives a brief overview of policy drivers and a good exposition of new roles within the nursing profession that directly address ECM. Straightforward and comprehensive.

2. Children with Disabilities Strategic Alliance (2009) *Manifesto*, http://www.cafamily.org.uk/pdfs/CAFNI.pdf

   Based in Northern Ireland, this is an alliance of 46 organizations across a range of sectors. Its manifesto takes an in-depth look at all the critical issues related to children's disability and sets each of these within a children's rights context and cites the articles from the UNCRC that directly underpin them.

3. NSPCC/ChildLine (2007) *ChildLine Casenotes: Calls to ChildLine about Depression and Mental Health*, London: NSPCC/ChildLine

   Anonymous compilations of calls made to ChildLine in the previous year and themed according to different childhood issues. A total of 14,463 children and young people spoke to ChildLine about mental health issues in 2005/06, and this gives a summary of children's lived experiences and useful tables of the distribution of different mental health concerns by age and gender.

4. *Happy + Healthy: Summary of Children and Young People's Views on What Makes Them Happy and Healthy* (2008), London: Office of the Children's Commissioner

   A short, readable document that expresses children's views about what makes them happy and healthy. Produced in a child-friendly format with colourful illustrations and a blend of information text and children's quotes.

7 Disadvantage, Diversity and Marginalization

ECM at the margins

A particular challenge for Every Child Matters (ECM) is reaching those children at the margins of society and affording them the same opportunities to achieve the five intended outcomes as all other children. Such children are doubly disadvantaged, first, because their minority status renders them less visible so they are more likely to fall through the social care net and, second, because their needs are more specialized, rendering resources scarcer and more expensive. The specialist expertise required in supporting, for example, refugee/asylum-seeking children makes multi-agency working more challenging because professionals operate on the fringe of mainstream multidisciplinary teams. Marginalized groups of children often have complex needs, which, in pre-ECM times, required multiple referrals to numerous service departments. If provision is to be genuinely socially inclusive, this suggests a *greater* imperative to engage with multi-agency working in the post-ECM era, whatever the challenges. In order to address both breadth and depth, I have chosen to present a broad view of disadvantage via the overarching theme of child poverty and then focus on diversity by spotlighting two specific examples of marginalized groups, refugee and asylum-seeking children and children with learning disabilities. Readers can find recommended sources for other groups of marginalized children in the Suggested further reading.

Child poverty

Whatever the circumstances of a child's marginalization, there is a common link which is typically (although not invariably) present – poverty. Time and again research has shown that where a child is prey to disadvantage or marginalization, poverty is one of the associated factors (Hirsch, 2007). Poverty is not an easy concept to define because of different cultural contexts and different ways in which measures and indicators are used. Townsend's definition (1979: 31) is a helpful one for our purposes:

> Individuals, families and groups in the population can be said to
> be in poverty when they lack the resources to obtain the types of
> diet, participate in the activities, and have the living conditions and
> amenities which are customary, or are at least widely encouraged and
> approved, in the societies in which they belong.

A common poverty indicator used in the UK is where a household has less than 60% of median income and is categorized as 'income poor'. This is rather a crude measure and not as flexible as Townsend's but at least it gives a base point for comparisons. Each year the government conducts an annual survey of households' below-average income. The latest available of these showed that 13.5 million people in the UK are in the category of 'income poor' (DWP, 2009). Of those 13.5 million, 53% are in households with children. Figures cited by BBC News (26 August 2009) show that the number of children in workless households had risen to 1.9 million by June 2009. This equates to one in six children living in homes where there is no adult in employment. In addition, the number of children in homes with a combination of working and workless adults over 16 has risen to 3.6 million (Allen, 2009). Box 7.1 shows the percentage chance of different categories of children living below the 60% median income poverty indicator.

Box 7.1	Percentage chance of different categories of children living below the 60% median income poverty indicator

- Nobody working in household – 77%
- Pakistani/Bangladeshi – 67%
- Inner London – 52%
- Black or black British – 51%
- Lone parent – 50%
- 4 plus children in family – 47%
- Disabled adult – 42%
- London (not inner London) – 41%
- Northeast England – 32%
- UK average – 30%

Source: Data derived from Sharma, 2007

As can be seen from Box 7.1, black and minority ethnic groups are at greater risk of poverty. Some of this is linked to employment: 72% of white women are in work compared to 27% of Bangladeshi and 30% of Pakistani women (EOC, 2006).

" Children's Perspectives

Minority ethnic case study

Anna is from mainland China and has two small daughters aged 5 and 9. The family received tax credits as her husband worked part time. When Anna and her husband separated, there was a mix-up on her income support and tax credits and she is paying back £2,000 from her weekly benefit of £180.75, which includes disability living allowance. Anna has limited English and really struggles with the letters regarding her benefits. She spends £60 a week on food and has very little left over for any extras. She is unable to take her children to any activities or on outings. The family is isolated from family and friends. Anna used to work in a Chinese takeaway but has not worked since her first child was born, as she has no childcare. As her children are now at school, she would like to work in the mornings but the barriers to this are her poor health and limited English.

Source: Sharma, 2007: 17

I would suggest that children living in poverty are the least likely to achieve the five ECM outcomes. The impact of poverty on children is far more extensive than the term 'income poor' suggests. Children living below the poverty line experience a poorer education, resulting in the achievement of less qualifications and inferior life chances (Hirsch, 2007). They live in substandard housing and enjoy less good health. Crucially, poverty prevents them participating in social childhood activities. In a study, 16% of the poorest fifth families in England could not afford to allow their child to have a friend for tea once a fortnight and 10% could not afford to send their child on a school trip once a term (Tomlinson and Walker, 2009).

New Labour indicated a willingness to tackle child poverty, with its bold pledge to eradicate child poverty in the UK by 2020 and halve it by 2010. It failed to meet the first of these targets and 2010 arrived without the trumpeted new dawn. Further measures were set out in the Child Poverty Bill 2009 to try and regain ground lost on the 2020 goal. These are mainly focused on getting more money into low-income families through increases in child tax credit and child benefit. Other measures have been aimed at narrowing the attainment gap by early intervention initiatives delivered through children's centres.

Children's centres

Children's centres are a central plank in the campaign to eradicate child poverty and narrow the attainment gap for the disadvantaged. The original Sure Start programme, which began in 1999, was formulated precisely to address the needs of families with young children living in disadvantaged areas to break the vicious circle of social disadvantage at birth, translating into educational disadvantage upon starting school and increasing margins thereafter. The inability to catch up on lost ground consigns children to an ever-widening attainment gap as they progress through their school years. By the age of three, children living in poverty are, typically, a whole year behind peers from wealthier backgrounds in terms of their readiness for learning. This gap increases to two years by the time they leave primary school (Marchant and Hall, 2003). Using free school meals as an index measure, figures from the DCSF (2008a) show that Foundation Stage children (age 3 and 4) are two and a half times less likely to reach their standard attainment targets. By Key Stage 1 (age 5–7) this has increased to three times less likely and by secondary school age, it has increased further to 3.5 times. Equally concerning is that primary aged children receiving free meals are seven times more likely to be excluded from school.

Some progress is being made towards narrowing the attainment gap but it is slow and in small measure. Statistics for 11-year-old children on free school meals achieving the Key Stage 2 national target (level 4) for mathematics show an increase from 54% to 60%. While the government would like to claim this as a 6% increase, attainment for children not receiving school meals also increased (from 77% to 80%), so the actual gap has only narrowed by 3%, a much more modest achievement.

Low family income is a major factor in child poverty. Parental earning capacity can be hampered by lack of access to childcare facilities. This is why quality childcare coupled with early learning was made the bedrock of children's centres. Children's centres were to be rolled out in four staged phases. The first two phases have focused on identifying areas of greatest need and providing target numbers of childcare places within tight guidelines. Requirements for achieving Sure Start recognized status in phases 1 and 2 (areas of high disadvantage) are set out in Box 7.2 (DfES, 2006b).

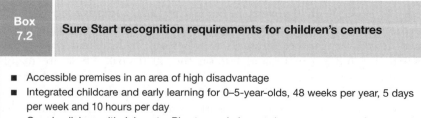

Box 7.2	Sure Start recognition requirements for children's centres

- Accessible premises in an area of high disadvantage
- Integrated childcare and early learning for 0–5-year-olds, 48 weeks per year, 5 days per week and 10 hours per day
- Ongoing liaison with Jobcentre Plus to maximize employment prospects for parents
- Ongoing liaison with local school(s)

- Suitably qualified centre manager – managers are now being encouraged to study for the postgraduate National Professional Qualification in Integrated Centre Leadership
- A minimum of 0.5 qualified teachers to lead the integrated learning element (Ofsted inspected)
- Community health facilities, for example midwifery, child healthcare, nutrition advice
- A range of drop-in services, for example childminder support club, parenting advice, counselling, playgroup, adult education classes, financial advice
- Special needs and disabilities early identification and support service
- Family outreach services, for example visits to all families within two months of a new birth and a comprehensive system of home visits for targeted support that includes a key worker and referral system to other services according to family needs
- An advisory board
- Evaluation system allowing parents and other service users to give feedback on the centre and be consulted about new initiatives.

Let us consider how this translates into real improvements for disadvantaged children.

" Children's Perspectives

Baby Olivia

Nineteen-year-old Leanne first found out about Sure Start West Riverside from her Health Visitor when her daughter Olivia was born. At first, Leanne was reluctant to join in the groups but finally decided to try out Fun, Play and Learn at Bridgewater when Olivia was nine months old. "I wanted Olivia to mix with other children, and thought that the groups would do me good as well, in terms of meeting new people. The Fun, Play and Learn group was really good and the staff were really nice and welcoming," said Leanne. Following her involvement with the group at Bridgewater, Leanne came into the Sure Start Information Point one day to find out what else she and Olivia could get involved in. Soon after, Leanne and Olivia were attending the Toy Library and Messy Tots sessions on a weekly basis, as well as popping into the Information Point regularly. "I started to meet new people and make new friends and Olivia's personality and development started to progress, which I believe is down to the fact that the Sure Start staff talked directly to Olivia and she began picking up words from them and other children," said Leanne. Shortly after Olivia's first birthday, Leanne decided she wanted to go back to learning and study a NVQ in Childcare at Newcastle College. "The first place I turned to for help with childcare was Sure Start. I spoke to the Childcare Access Worker, who found out about childcare options and gave me information about funding for young mothers returning to learning." Leanne is now well into her course and is really enjoying it. She is relieved to have found excellent childcare for 19-month-old Olivia at Bridgewater and Leanne believes her daughter is now 'thriving'. "Sure Start West Riverside Children's Centres are excellent because they offer everything from advice and support to places where Olivia and I can go to play and enjoy time together," said Leanne.

Source: Shout Out for Sure Start, 2010

Box 7.3 shows how one particular local authority, Northumberland, monitors ECM progress in its children's centres.

Box 7.3	Ways in which children's centres help disadvantaged children achieve the five ECM outcomes

- *Be healthy:* providing healthcare and wellbeing promotional advice such as nutrition guidance, anti-obesity and physical activity programmes, antenatal and post-natal services.
- *Stay safe:* tight regulation of childcare provision ensures high-quality service and minimizes risk to children's safety during the time they are cared for. Frequent contact with children from a young age increases the chance of early detection of any potential harm, neglect or abuse and early intervention.
- *Enjoy and achieve:* providing quality play experiences including toy libraries, playgroups, outdoor play facilities, learning through play activities and English language classes.
- *Make a positive contribution:* Childcare provision coupled with close ties to Jobcentre Plus optimizes opportunities for parents to find and retain employment, helping to raise them out of poverty and enabling them to make a contribution to society.
- *Achieve economic wellbeing:* The head start that children gain at the centres ensures they can make the most of learning opportunities once they start school and thus achieve more. Rather than starting from behind and never catching up, disadvantaged children have a chance of educational attainment that can lead to good employment prospects and economic wellbeing.

The government achieved its target of opening 3,500 children's centres by 2010 but there are fears that the current economic downturn and public service cuts will curtail the implementation of stages 3 and 4:

> Sure Start Children's Centres are one of the greatest achievements of modern Government. The Centres have helped thousands of families to become stronger and better able to cope with tough times. The concern now is that there may be pressure for Centres to become a service only for families in crisis as local budgets are reduced.
> (Longfield, cited in Cook, 2010)

Some confidence was restored when a parliamentary cross-party investigation recommended the continuation of the Sure Start programme, protection from any impending budget cuts and the launch of an All-Party Group to support this in March, 2010. However, the coalition government has signalled that the children's centre programme will be targeted at those children who are most disadvantaged, reversing any hope of more universal expansion.

Early intervention remains a key strategy in the campaign to eradicate poverty and reduce disadvantage. As can be seen in this and other chapters, children's centres are an important early intervention hub. There are many examples of initiatives which build on this as children move into their school years. A few examples are set out in Box 7.4.

- Springfields School (Wiltshire) is a behavioural, emotional and social difficulty (BESD) special school centre of excellence. It has reduced both fixed and permanent exclusions sharply by developing innovative outreach and in-reach packages. It is a completely non-excluding school that ensures real continuity of provision for its pupils – their aspirations and best interests come first in all decisions. Early identification of needs and swift referral is the key to preventing further disaffection.
- Blue Gate Fields Infant School (Stepney, Tower Hamlets) has run a range of initiatives designed to encourage parents to support their children's early years' development. Nearly all pupils have English as an additional language. Activities on offer are based on developing parenting skills and experiences in order to help develop children's learning. In addition, all parents are encouraged to become volunteers during the school day through a six-week parent volunteer programme. A toy library for parents with pre-nursery children develops parents' playing skills with their children. An oracy group encourages families to play games together and practise speaking English in a safe environment. Parents, pupils and school staff believe the work has had a positive impact.
- Lister Community School (Newham) set up parent support groups for Somali and Bengali parents to help involve them in the wider school community. The groups help the school share information on policies, curriculum issues and adult learning, as well as offering support and advice about services and entitlements. The success of the groups and contributions from parents have resulted in new initiatives – such as special family learning sessions for Bengali-speaking parents and children, joint social events and learning opportunities. The school is seeing regular attendance from parents who had previously been hard to reach. The school is extending this approach within the local school cluster.
- Handale Primary (Redcar and Cleveland) is already using the extended services disadvantage subsidy to fund activities for free school meals pupils. With the LA's support, the school carried out a consultation to identify new activities that would appeal to disadvantaged pupils, including an ICT animation activity, which the school now offers to pupils on-site using an external provider. Progression mentors work in schools with high socioeconomic deprivation within the borough of Redcar and Cleveland. The mentors encourage the identified target group of young people to participate in activities which will meet individual learner needs to raise their aspirations and awareness of higher education and progression routes.

Source: Adapted from www.teachers.tv

Children with learning difficulties

Historically, children with learning difficulties have been passed from pillar to post between the three former departments of education, social services and child health, each arguing over whether the child's need was educational, social care or health related and who should resource the need. This is a recipe for children to fall through the social care net or flounder endlessly in service limbo. An integrated approach to children's services should therefore be of particular benefit to this group of children, especially young children, whose learning difficulties might not otherwise have been addressed until compulsory schooling age. Despite all these measures and the ECM rhetoric, slow progress has been made to fully include children with learning disabilities in society. While we have seen considerable diversity in positions of influence in the past few decades, for example we have had a female prime minister, a visually impaired home secretary, minority ethnic MPs, gay and lesbian MPs, there is little prospect of an MP with learning difficulties. It is unlikely this will ever happen unless learning difficulties are better understood and some of the taboos that surround them are confronted. A good start would be ensuring that all children with learning difficulties get equal opportunities to achieve the five ECM outcomes.

> ## ❝ Children's Perspectives
>
> Achieving ECM outcomes is more challenging for children with learning difficulties, not least because they have to cope with a high incidence of bullying. Mencap's Don't stick it, stop it! research (2007: 2) revealed that *most* children with learning difficulties in Northern Ireland, England and Wales are bullied. This has a significant impact on the quality of their childhood:
>
> - Eight out of ten children with a learning difficulty are bullied
> - Eight out of ten children with a learning difficulty are scared to go out because they
> - are frightened they might be bullied
> - Six out of ten children with a learning difficulty have been physically hurt by bullies
> - Five out of ten children who had experienced bullying said that they stayed away from the places where they have been bullied in the past
> - Nearly four out of ten (36%) children surveyed said that the bullying didn't stop when they told someone
> - Nearly three out of ten (27%) children surveyed were bullied for three years or more.

How are integrated services and ECM working for children with learning difficulties? Since the Special Education Needs and Disability Act (SENDA) passed into legislation in 2001, schools can only refuse entry to a child if that admission would harm the education of other pupils in the school. SENDA places education within the remit of the Disability Discrimination Act and therefore it is now illegal to discriminate against a learner on the grounds of their disability. It puts the onus on the school to adapt its provision. This is the bedrock of the inclusion policy, which adopts the perspective that it is society that is disabling rather than a child's particular condition. Thus, mainstream schools are tasked with adapting their physical environment, teaching styles and curricular provision to meet the diverse needs of all pupils. However, the inclusion of children with learning difficulties in mainstream schools has been fraught with tension, especially in situations where the learning difficulties are severe and complex. In theory, it should be possible to include all children whatever their difficulties, but in practice, the absence of the resources needed renders this goal either unachievable or poorly supported. Attaining the five ECM outcomes for children with learning difficulties is patchy and subject to the resourcing priorities of different children's trusts and individual schools.

The context for inclusion is situated within a human rights' discourse (UNESCO, 1994), in which segregation of children from their peers is seen as a denial of human rights. The concept of inclusion extends beyond special educational needs and disabilities to the wider embracement of human diversity – gender, ethnicity, sexuality, cultural heritage and religion. Increasingly, 'equality and diversity' are replacing 'inclusion' as the preferred terminology. The emphasis on 'diversity' steers thinking towards the total learning environment rather than individual 'need' or 'difficulty'.

While there have been few ideological objections to inclusion, there have been many concerns raised about its feasibility in practical terms and resistance from some teachers who worry that they do not have the skills to teach at this level. However, this book is concerned with how integrated services are impacting on the ECM experiences of children, so it is not the place for an in-depth ideological discussion on inclusion. Interested readers can explore this in the Suggested further reading.

A strong message of ECM is the importance of early intervention and support. This was the thrust of the measures outlined in *Removing Barriers to Achievement* (DfES, 2004c), the government's strategy for special educational needs. This policy developed out of the *Every Child Matters* Green Paper (2003) and proposed the development of personalized learning for all pupils, along with improved teachers' skills to meet diverse educational needs so that more children can be taught in mainstream schools. The corollary was that many special schools were closed down, with only a small number being retained for children with the most complex needs and as centres of excellence to share their expertise with mainstream schools. Further support was provided in the Disability Discrimination Act 2006, which placed a duty on all schools and early years providers to take a more proactive approach to promoting disability equality and eliminating discrimination, recognizing the importance of parents being able to access quality childcare and stressing the imperative of interagency working.

Making ECM a reality for children with learning difficulties, particularly those with severe and complex needs, hinges around improving their ability to communicate and participate. In an inclusive setting, children with communication impairments benefit greatly from all the children around them having a basic knowledge of 'low-tech' ways of communicating such as the use of symbols and signing. There is some ground-breaking research currently being developed to facilitate this (see www.rixcentre.org).

> **Children's Perspectives**

'We are used to people saying we cannot communicate, but of course, they are wrong. In fact we have powerful and effective ways of communicating and we usually have many ways to let you know what it is we have in mind. Yes we have communication difficulties, and some of those are linked with impairments. But by far the greater part of our difficulty is caused by 'speaking people' not having the experience, time or commitment to try to understand us or include us in everyday life.' (disabled child, cited in Rabiee et al., 2005: 2)

Newham Schools Inclusion Project

The London borough of Newham and the North London Special Educational Needs Regional Hub are working with the Rix Centre (www.rixcentre.org) to carry out a research project in six primary schools called 'What constitutes good progress for children with special educational needs?' The project uses multimedia advocacy technology to enable children to be more involved in their own learning and have more voice.

We have been using talking mats*, disposable cameras, computers, microphones and photo stories. The children enjoyed the use of cameras and this definitely helped with their engagement. We found we were able to engage the attention of most children for much longer than with their usual activities, often for up to an hour and with minimal support (Gosia Kwiatkowska, www.rixcentre.org).

* Talking mats (www.talkingmats.com) were developed at the Augmentative and Alternative Communication Research Unit at Stirling University to enable individuals with cerebral palsy and communication difficulties to express their views and choices. Children position graphic symbols around a 'mat' or board and can use their own photographs to facilitate 'conversation'.

Making a Difference

The three-year research study *Making a Difference* was carried out by a team of researchers from the Norah Fry Research Centre, University of Bristol and the Family Fund (Townsley et al., 2004). The study investigated the impact of multi-agency working on disabled children with complex healthcare needs from the perspectives of the professionals involved, the families and the children and young people. Eighteen children from two to fifteen years old were visited, each with complex healthcare needs including communication impairments. Ten of the children and young people had no verbal communication, some of whom used signs, three had limited verbal communication supported by signs and five used limited verbal communication. All the children were dependent on medical technology, including seventeen who were tube-fed.

Methods

The study used a mixed methods approach tailored to the communication strengths of the individual child. A detailed picture was assembled of the children involved, including their views and experiences of having many different professionals involved in their lives. Visits took place in the children's homes and lasted about an hour. The visits were informal. Researchers used a topic guide as a basis for the conversations.

The guide covered: things I like, things I don't like; who lives at home with me; school; friends; adults who help me; short breaks; things that are difficult to do; and general happiness. Drawing was used as a tool to support the conversations in some cases, either by the child drawing on large sheets of paper or the researcher documenting the conversation.

Ethics

Children and young people were sent a pictorial leaflet/consent form to explain about the research and to seek consent. This contained a photograph of the researcher who would visit. A parent or carer was also present during most interviews to act as an interpreter or proxy during the session.

Main findings

The children reported how they coped well, in general, with relating to the many professionals in their lives. These relationships were stronger with those professionals who made an effort to communicate directly with the children. Several of the children did not know who their key worker was. The children's aspirations were similar to other children of their own age: the desire for friends, opportunities to interact with their contemporaries, and to be treated with respect and dignity.

Living with autism

Rachel and Ben have three children aged 13, 10 and 8. The two younger children are autistic, with severe learning disabilities. Ben gave up his job when their second child was diagnosed seven years ago as the children needed 24-hour care: *'I had a really good job me. I was earning £500/600 a week, good pay. Good bonus, really good pension scheme and I just had to give it all up. I had been there 21 years.'*

The family home was repossessed and they had to move into a council house and are totally reliant on benefits. Daily life is a struggle due mainly to the extra costs of their children's disabilities. The family receives £383.75 a week in benefits, including disability benefits, so technically they are above the government's poverty line of £345 – but this does not take account of the extra costs of disability. The family needs a large house because one of the children does not sleep properly and disturbs everyone, but this makes heating costs very high: the house has 13 or 14 radiators. The food bill is also high, as one of the children has coeliac disease and one of the parents is also diabetic; this frequently means having to prepare different meals for different family members, which increases the cost. They say that the only reason they get by is because of the children's disability living allowance (DLA). They do not go out as a family as short breaks are expensive: *'We were offered £29 (through direct payments) to get someone to look after Barbara for 6 hours, no one's going to do that … we couldn't afford that.'*

Ben and Rachel would like more money so that they can pay for care: *'I know of a child who went into respite care for one week and it cost £900.'* They say that they feel like prisoners in their own home. Although the family has managed to stay together (the move to a larger house helped), the stress is clear, as Rachel points out: *'We were constantly arguing all the time. You're tired; you're on top of each other, shouting at each other. There's definitely no way we would be together now if we hadn't moved.'*

For Ben the future is not hopeful: *'I'm 43 … I've not got anything. I probably won't have any skills to go back to work; I'll probably be too old.'*

Source: Sharma, 2007: 36

Refugee and asylum-seeking children

There are approximately 3,000 unaccompanied children who seek asylum in the UK each year and many more who come as part of families (Nandy, 2007). In 2006, there were 3,800 children in asylum-seeking families and 3,245 who were unaccompanied (Bennet et al., 2007). They can only gain refugee status if their asylum applications are granted and this requires proof of a real risk of persecution in the state they have left. Only 6% of applications are successful. Children of asylum seekers are excluded from the government's pledge to halve the number of children in poverty by 2010–11 and eradicate child poverty altogether by 2020 because it lodged a reservation to the article of the UNCRC which advocates this. There is an active campaign to try and reverse this, which, as yet, has been unsuccessful:

> The UK Government has entered a reservation to the UN Convention on the Rights of the Child, so that it does not apply to children subject to immigration control in the UK. All the UK Children's Commissioners and major children's voluntary organisations in the UK, including Barnardo's, urge the Government to withdraw this shameful reservation. The Westminster Government strap line 'Every Child Matters' is a deceit while such a reservation exists. (Reacroft, 2008: 7)

This makes asylum-seeking children, arguably, the most vulnerable and disadvantaged group. Moreover, Section 9 of the Asylum and Immigration (Treatment of Claimants) Act 2004 allows the withdrawal of asylum support from failed asylum-seeking families, which can result in children being taken into care because their parents can no longer support them. Unaccompanied children who fail in their asylum application are not granted refugee status but are permitted to stay in the UK until the age of seventeen and a half. However, their parents are not and families about to be deported face agonizing decisions of whether to return as a family or leave their children in the UK to be taken into care until they reach the age of seventeen and a half when they will then be deported also.

In the UK, the main legislation driving child refugee policy is the Education Act 1996, Immigration and Asylum Act 1999, the Nationality, Immigration and Asylum Act 2002, the Asylum and Immigration Act 2004, the Immigration Asylum and Nationality Act 2006 and the UK Borders Act 2007. The lived experiences of refugee and asylum-seeking children are much underresearched. What literature there is tends to be preoccupied with the mismatch of legislation with children's rights and/or the 'plight' of their 'victim' status (Crawley and Lester, 2005). Other authors highlight the relative lack of support for unaccompanied children and young people (for example Rutter, 2003). Much of the existing literature relies heavily on obtaining the views of adult professionals in the field and, while this serves a valuable purpose, it lacks the participation of children and young people themselves in the research process. Relatively few empirical studies have engaged specifically with children and young people:

It is noteworthy that the attention given to children and young people in legislation and policy is negligible. Refugee children and young people have little or no voice in decision making processes and asylum policies that impact upon both their everyday lives and their longer term prospects. (Maegusuku-Hewett et al., 2007: 310)

The asylum-seeking application process is lengthy and harrowing, during which time families were housed in detention-like quarters until very recently. An early initiative of the coalition government was an outright ban on asylum-seeking children being held in detention centres. The wisdom of that decision is evident from some children's experiences captured below.

" Children's Perspectives

Unaccompanied children's experiences of asylum-seeking application processes

Children find the experience very frightening. They have to wait a long time to be seen, sometimes all day, and the waiting room does not have any bright colours, toys, books or comfy chairs. Younger children find it hard to sit still on the hard chairs with no food or water for a long time. Older children find the experience scary. There are posters which say you must tell the truth or you may go to prison. Sometimes there are no interpreters available so they are not sure they have answered the questions properly … Before some children can claim asylum they have to prove they are really a child. This is because the Home Office believes they are an adult … While they are waiting to be assessed they are treated as adults and can be locked up with adults in detention centres so they do not have any support. Sometimes children are so traumatised by detention that they become mute.

The Government limits the amount of help given so lawyers can usually only see children once to talk to them about their asylum claim before they are interviewed by the Home Office. The child is usually very scared and does not want to talk about experiences of rape, torture and killings to a stranger. There is a big shortage of lawyers who are skilled in both immigration and children's law and can talk to children sensitively.

"I met my solicitor two times. She told me my case is hard but I don't understand why. Then she wouldn't work for free. I don't know if it's my fault, or something else … I live here alone. I have no family. I need someone to help me. I know I can't do it on my own" – Jason, child asylum seeker.

"They made me feel like I didn't have any rights" – Frankie, child asylum seeker.

Children in families are not interviewed about their asylum claim, but because there are no crèche facilities they are sometimes present when their parents have to recount details of torture, rape, loss and fear. This can be very upsetting for children and their parents.

Source: Nandy, 2007: 3–5

Experiences of children in asylum-seeking families

Olivia came to the UK from Malawi in 2005 with her husband and six-year-old son, Michael. Extracts from her story (Reacroft, 2008: 57–9) highlight the harrowing traumas that many children go through during the asylum-seeking process. Olivia is HIV-positive, has TB and suffers with epilepsy.

They came in at half past five in the morning. We were all in bed. … My little boy was crying and screaming. They told him 'Don't scream, we're not here to arrest your mum and dad, we're just taking them for questioning'. They told my little boy 'Go and pack your clothes'. He was only six. They wouldn't let me change my clothes or take my medication with me. I was in my pyjamas, so they just saw a dressing gown somewhere and put it on me. I was walking with the crutch, but they took it off me. They said 'Maybe there are bullets in this crutch'.

… We were kept in detention for a week and I was without medication for three days. My little boy was so frightened. He is still frightened now. While we were in detention, he couldn't sleep during the night; he couldn't eat during the day. He was so scared. When they came to take us to Heathrow they handcuffed me and my husband in front of my little boy. He was screaming, but they didn't bother about him. They put me in one van and my husband and my little boy in another van. But then they said they were no tickets for us. They told us we were not going and they took the handcuffs off us.

… They took us back into detention, but after four days our lawyer got an injunction against the Home Office and they released us. When they released us they just took us to a big gate and said 'You're released, you can go home'. They told us we had to find our own means to get home.

… When my son hears a bang at the door he runs screaming from the room. If we ask him, 'Why are you screaming?', he says it's the police at the door. All the time he's disturbed. Even at school teachers say 'Your son has been acting like he doesn't want to stay close to some other children, he's got a spirit of fear'. Now he's going through some sessions, just to make his mind forget all about those things. It's something like counselling. Even at home sometimes when you are upstairs and he is downstairs, he will bring something upstairs. You ask him why he can't stay downstairs and he says he's scared.

Conclusion

While it has not been possible to examine wide-ranging examples of disadvantaged and marginalized children, a sense of this has been conveyed through the overarching theme of child poverty, showing how children living in poverty are the most unlikely to achieve the intended five ECM outcomes. Various policies to address child poverty and disadvantage have been discussed, exposing the magnitude of this task and limited achievements to date. Central to the discourse has been the important part played by Sure Start children's centres in breaking the cycle of deprivation and of early interventions to improve the marginalized quality of childhood. Children's perspectives have been presented through the life stories and aspirations of children with learning difficulties and those seeking asylum. Their experiences persuade us that ECM outcomes are little more than wish lists for vulnerable groups. Eradicating child poverty is crucial to improving their life chances.

Reflection exercises

1. For all readers

Drawing on your own experience, consider what specific issues contribute to child poverty under each of the following headings:

- Level of family income
- Quality of housing
- Hidden costs of 'free' education
- School choice.

2. For staff working with children in multidisciplinary teams

Find a friend or colleague willing to help with this or perhaps make it an exercise during a staff development workshop. Try and communicate something important to that other person without using speech, for example you might want to convey that you have a food allergy, what kind of music you like to listen to, or what you thought about your recent visit to the dentist. Take no more than a minute or two and then reflect on what the difficulties are.

3. Children's perspectives

Read through Olivia's story again but on this occasion try and see it entirely through her six-year-old son's eyes. How would the events unfold for him? As you do this, remember he is only six years old and has no English whatsoever.

Suggested further reading

1. Griffin, S. (2008) *Inclusion, Equality and Diversity in Working with Children*, London: Heinemann

   No-nonsense text that gives simple explanations of terms and issues related to inclusion. Provides a helpful historical context, a non-technical summary of inclusion legislation and a holistic approach to critical issues about inclusive practice with children.

2. Ahmad. S., Akbar, H., Akbar, A. et al. (2009) *East Meets West: South Asian Young People and Identity Issues*, http://childrens'research-centre.open.ac.uk

   Small piece of research undertaken by young people, looks at the tensions and dilemmas they face in trying to balance respect for their race and cultural heritage with a desire to 'fit in' with their peers.

3. Glover, J. (2009) *Every Night You Cry: The Realities of Having a Parent in Prison*, Ilford: Barnardo's

   An estimated 160,000 children have a parent in prison. This research report on the poor outcomes for these children highlights findings from an audit of children's plans that too many local authorities are failing to address their needs. Calls for better identification of children affected, and more timely intervention.

4. Platt, L. (2009) *Ethnicity and Child Poverty,* DWP Research Report 576, http://research.dwp.gov.uk

   Focused report on poverty and children from minority ethnic communities based around major risk factors. Provides a good overview as well as a discrete exploration of critical issues for different ethnic and religious groups.

5. Voice for the Child in Care (2004) *The Care Experience Through Black Eyes*, London: National Children's Bureau

   Short, readable report from a group of black care leavers about their experiences of their time in care as children. Illustrates well how ethnicity and culture are central to identity.

6. Lewis, V. (2003) *Development and Disability*, Oxford: Blackwell

   Seminal text with excellent coverage of a range of disabilities, including children with visual and hearing impairments, autism, spina bifida, cerebral palsy, Down's syndrome and development coordination disorders. Provides explanations of the nature of each disability and how this impacts on children's development and their lives.

7. Myers, M. and Bhopal, K. (2009) 'Gypsy, Roma and Traveller children in schools: understandings of community and safety'. *British Journal of Educational Studies*, 57(4), 417–34

   Examines understandings of community and safety for Gypsy, Roma and Traveller groups in schools in a metropolitan borough of the UK. Identifies one school in particular as demonstrating good practice in the inclusion of Traveller children. Examines children's perspectives of their engagement with the education process and how the strong Traveller community played an important part in their understandings of safety and belonging.

8. *The SLD Experience*

   Particularly accessible and down-to-earth UK journal. Dedicated to promoting good practice with children of school age who have severe learning disabilities. Written for practitioners and parents, each issue carries news and information on curriculum matters, research, and medical and legal issues. Also has a regular news section from Mencap, and features on conferences, books and resources. Published three times a year.

8 The Family

The changing nature of the family

The family is at the heart of Every Child Matters (ECM) and necessarily overlaps with content in other chapters (especially Chapters 4, 5, 7 and 10). To avoid duplication, this chapter is confined to societal frameworks of the family and the two main arenas where state and family interconnect: parenting jurisdiction, and provision of family services. An in-depth examination of Family Intervention Projects (FIPs) provides a practice example of how ECM and integrated children's services are seen through the family lens.

Family units have changed significantly in the past three decades. Some of this is attributed to a decline in fertility and mortality and greater life expectancy. Other factors are an increase in cohabitation, divorce and single parenthood, which are reconstituting the nature of family groups (Daly, 2005). Stereotypical labelling of families as two heterosexual parents with 2.4 offspring is long outdated. A family of five might as easily relate to four parents and one child as to one parent with four children. More same-sex couples are choosing to have children, and families are no longer 'nuclear' in the sense that classical sociologists originally constructed them (Morrow, 2009). Cultural diversity has considerably enriched the family landscape. The extended family, especially grandparents, plays an increasingly important role (Lane, 2002). Indeed, Scotland has introduced a charter for grandchildren to acknowledge the importance of this (Scottish Executive, 2006). In the UK, 70% of mothers with children over nine months old do some paid employment compared to 25% a quarter of a century ago (Layard and Dunn, 2009). Such rapid changes have prompted a growth in family studies, although most have been concerned with issues of parenthood, marriage and divorce and very few have been grounded in *children's* family experiences:

> Until the late 1990s, there was remarkably little research into how children make sense of contemporary patterns of family life. For a long time, most knowledge of children's experiences of their families came from adults, from parents, from professionals such as social workers, lawyers or psychologists, or from adults' recollections of their own difficult childhood experiences. Much quantitative research focused on 'family structure effects' … which fed powerful popular debates about the harmful effect of family breakdown on children, generating a discourse that portrayed children in the 'wrong' kinds of family as being damaged, and leading to political rhetoric about the 'parenting deficit'. (Morrow, 2009: 63)

Even though parenting is regarded as gender neutral, the reality is that the vast majority of childcare is undertaken by women. One of the hottest current debates in family social policy is the evolving role of fathers, particularly around the importance of the emotional bonding of fathers, their nurturing role and issues of paternity leave. Children's centres, as flagships of ECM, are trying to address gender imbalances and recommend a range of measures in their practice guidance (Sure Start, 2006), for example fostering the development of father support networks, encouraging fathers to demonstrate their emotional attachment to their children, and helping fathers to understand their children's development needs. O'Brien's research (2005) points to the positive outcomes where fathers have more involvement in their children's upbringing – higher self-esteem, greater educational achievement, stronger friendships, more life satisfaction, and less likelihood of falling into crime. In 2007, the Department for Education and Skills issued guidelines on engaging with *all* fathers irrespective of their backgrounds (DfES, 2007a). The response from the organization Fathers Direct was: 'Staff are often good at engaging fathers if they are polite, articulate and middle class. But if they are young or from an ethnic minority, they are regarded as too much trouble' (Carvel, 2007, cited in Leverett, 2008: 77).

❝ Children's Perspectives

What does the concept of family mean to children? Mason and Tipper (2008) researched children's experiences of kinship. Their study was based on qualitative interviews with 49 children aged 7–12. Children were given disposable cameras prior to the interviews so that they could take photos of who mattered to them and the photos were used to stimulate discussion, a process known as 'photo-elicitation'. Children were also encouraged to draw pictures and family maps to show how close or otherwise connections were. Children expressed their ideas about who 'proper' kin was, who 'like-family kin' was and how all the different elements of kinship worked in their childhoods, for example how care, love and support influenced the quality and nomenclature of kinship. Mason and Tipper (2008: 444–55) argued that complexity of kinship was the norm and that conventional genealogical definitions based on heterosexual marriage, nuclear families or single cultural models were outdated:

Many [children] had close relatives who were separated or divorced. Some had half-siblings through a parent's previous relationship; most had half- and step-kin; many had relatives with cohabiting partners, or non-cohabiting partners, or ex-cohabiting partners, and in some cases these partners and ex-partners had children together; a few children had kin in same-sex relationships; some had kinship groups that included individuals from different religious and ethnic backgrounds; and some had kin they rarely saw because of geographical distance, or with whom they had lost contact due to family conflicts.

One way for possible kin to earn 'proper' kinship status was *involvement in ritual, celebratory and routine aspects of family life*. Children spoke of whether or not potential kin attended family 'dos' and *how* they behaved at such events, particularly whether they were friendly and involved … Being *friendly, nice, informal*, and perhaps most significantly *respecting children's orientations and interests*, was important to the children in our study when weighing up whether someone who was possible kin could be counted as 'proper' kin. This was especially significant when meeting new partners of 'proper' kin – such occasions being quite formative in children's judgement about whether or not they could be included as family. Children wanted to feel *physically* comfortable with potential kin, and indeed physicality – for example the freedom to touch or be cheeky with that person – was a significant part of many children's relationships.

However, kinship for children is not all about 'proper' relatives. Thirty-two (65 percent) of the children in our study specifically mentioned a special relationship that *seemed like family* with someone who was, genealogically speaking, unrelated to them. In all cases, this was clearly a conscious practice of drawing specific people close, by claiming them to be like family and this practice was always used by children to signify good or close relationships.

In our study, children's like-family kinship did not exclusively involve human relationships. In addition to their *own* household's pets, children frequently drew in 'proper' kin's pets (both living and dead) to their definitions of relatedness. When asked if there was anyone who he thought of as 'like family', Jake responded:

Jake: Milly … because she is gran's rabbit and …

Interviewer: She is kind of part of the family?

Jake: Yes and so is Alf [gran's rabbit] and Bert [Jake's hamster] and my old rabbit Bonnie and my old guinea pig, what was it called … Bonnie and what?

Sister: Clyde.

Jake: Clyde. Well basically all my pets are like family. And all the family that has had pets have been really like family.

Political dimensions

More than any other institution, the family has the power to undermine and subvert state governance, because its primary function as a private, self-serving unit puts it at odds with governance agendas to control society for the common good (Mount, 1982). Thus, successive governments have all grappled with finding the right balance between support and control. During the Thatcher years, the state adopted a minimalist (sometimes referred to as laissez-faire) approach to family matters, being content to leave parenting to parents and only interfering in crisis situations, where children were at risk or 'in need' of services, for example children with disabilities. The Children Act 1989 affirmed the fundamental concept of parental responsibility.

New Labour took a more proactive approach, espousing that state intervention can improve children's life chances. This resulted in a raft of legislation encroaching into traditional parenting territory such as standards of behaviour, physical chastisement and healthy living. While children's interests are touted as being paramount, the overriding interest is, nevertheless, located in their parents, as it is through them that children can be controlled: 'Our future depends upon [families'] success in bringing up children. That is why we are committed to strengthening family life' (Home Office, 1998: 4).

Parenting capacity can be limited by one or more sets of circumstances, for example substance abuse, mental health problems and poverty can lead to parental inadequacy. Quinton (2004) argues that services to parents in the community are the most disconnected and have the least effective interagency structures. Support for families is often locally driven and is more vulnerable to the vagaries of funding. Targeting families in need of support is not always easy because of the individual nature of need and the undesirability of any form of national screening. Therefore resources tend to be targeted towards 'groups of need' rather than 'families in need' such as disadvantaged neighbourhoods or single parents. The advancement of integrated children's services, notably the rollout of children's centres and extended schools, has enabled more 'universal' services to be offered to families, thus avoiding some of the stigma that accompanies 'targeted' support.

Chapter 3 outlined four conceptualizations of capital (economic, human, social and cultural) and showed how each of these connected to the family. Here, social capital is considered in more depth. According to Woolcock (2001), social capital can be broken down into three categories: bonding, bridging and linking. Social capital that comes from *bonding* is rich in the sense of identity and belonging that it creates and the superior understanding that comes with resource sharing and family interconnectivity. On its own, this kind of social capital is too insular, so there is a need for *bridging* mechanisms to build interactions with other families and mutual support groups within a community. *Linking* social capital takes bridging a stage further in making connections outside the immediate community and linking into regional/national groups and support structures. Social capital tends to be reflected in the areas in which families are located. Thus, areas of disadvantage, where need is greatest, often have the weakest capacity for social capital (Jack, 2006). Children play an important part. Their capacity to build social capital through their own social networking is serially underestimated. Integrated services, with the emphasis on multi-agency working, are crucial to families accessing social capital, since the potential for bridging and linking is far more extensive for multidisciplinary teams than single departments.

Children's contributions to family life

From the earliest anthropological archives we know that children have made substantial contributions to family life (Montgomery, 2009). Contributions typically include doing household chores and looking after younger siblings. In some cultures, children have an important economic role in supplying income through the paid labour they do outside the home. One of the less visible contributions children make is when they take on roles as young carers. Numerous studies highlight how important a 'sense of family' is to young carers including those by children themselves (see, for example, Tarapdar, 2007). Some children choose not to identify themselves as carers, either because they regard the caring tasks they undertake as a normal part of family life or because they want to avoid drawing attention to their situation and potential care proceedings that might ensue.

Children from disadvantaged backgrounds are most likely to take on responsibilities as carers and their role is made that much harder by financial disempowerment, which Bibby and Becker (2000: 40) refer to as 'being burdened by poverty as well as caring responsibility'. Unlike adult carers, where 66% are female, there is a fairly even distribution of gender in young carers, 57% being female and 43% male (Dearden and Becker, 2004: 3). In the past couple of years, attention has been focused on the importance of ensuring young carers achieve all five ECM outcomes. Manchester City Council (2008), in producing its Children and Young People's Plan, involved young carers and their families as key partners in a needs analysis to deliver better ECM outcomes for young carers. The identified objectives of the needs analysis were:

- To assess young carers' capacity to achieve the five outcomes set out in the ECM agenda.
- To identify the barriers that exist which prevent young carers from achieving the five outcomes.
- To identify young carers' (and their families') needs in terms of the five principles in ECM.

Children's own experiences, described in the following accounts, illuminate some of these young carer issues.

> **Children's Perspectives**

Gemma's story

I help care for my dad who has multiple sclerosis. Multiple sclerosis is an illness that affects the nervous system. This means that he can't do much for himself – he can't feed himself or pick up a cup. I've been helping to care for my dad for a while now. I've been giving him drinks and food ever since I was little and I started to help move him when I was about eight or nine-years-old. On a typical day I help my mum to get my dad out of bed and put him in his chair. I tidy up, give him drinks and help feed him. If it's a day when he's having a shower, I help shower him too. I wasn't taught how to do any of this – I just got on with it and copied my mum. I think this has meant that I've had to grow up faster because I've had a lot of responsibility from a young age. I don't get particularly fed-up that I have to do it or find it difficult – it's normal to me. I can't imagine not looking after my dad now.

Some people at school know that my dad's disabled. It's hard for them to understand the responsibility I've got though – I do stuff they wouldn't normally be doing. They don't really understand it until they come around to my house and see for themselves. If my dad is ill overnight I get the next day off school because I've had to spend the night in hospital. The teachers understand but sometimes other pupils don't. In the past I've been accused of skiving, which made me feel worse.

I usually go shopping with a friend rather than my mum because we can't leave dad. We don't go out as a family that much - we can't really go to the cinema and in restaurants people sometimes stare. It's also rare that we go on holidays.

Source: www.youngcarers.net

Olu's story

Olu is 10 and lives with his mother who has a mental health problem. Sometimes she's fine, but when she's ill she becomes very depressed and hardly gets out of bed. At these times, Olu has to look after the flat, get food for himself and his mum, get to school and back on his own and deal with the things his mother can't do, such as collecting her money and paying the rent and the bills. Olu is never sure when his mum will become ill again, so he worries about it even when she seems to be coping.

Source: www.youngcarers.net

Andre's message

This is to make things clearer
How it is to be a young carer
Stereotypes assume dat we're weirder
You think you're rare, but we're rarer
Here today, show no fear
We want you to know that we are here
For those who haven't heard us
I'm gonna tell you about our service
Some days we talk and chat

Other days we do more than that
We're all one big family,
you got Amy and you got Anthony
At home I do things carefully, taking on responsibility
I care for my family
YC cares for me
We are RBKC YC!

Source: www.rbkc.gov.uk

Family problems or 'problem families'?

Services that support children need to work in partnership with parents and a 'whole family' strategy is likely to produce a more successful outcome. Partnership working with parents can be challenging, particularly where power dynamics are acute between parents and social care professionals. Successive governments have, at various times, attempted to deal with what is commonly termed 'problem families'. In response to growing public concern about anti-social behaviour (ASB), Blair launched the Respect Task Force in 2006. While much of this was concerned with social control and the curtailment of perceived antisocial behaviour, it did acknowledge that sanctions would have to be accompanied by support measures if sustainable solutions were to be found. It drew on the work of the Dundee Families Project, 1996–2000 (Dillane et al., 2001) run by NCH (now Action for Children) Scotland, which provided intensive support to families at risk of becoming homeless as a result of antisocial behaviour. The Respect Task Force invested in a national network of 50 Family Intervention Projects (FIPs). These were run by local authorities, housing associations and family charities to 'rehabilitate' problem families.

The principal goal of FIPs was to stop the antisocial behaviour of a small number of 'problem families' in local neighbourhoods. A key practitioner worked intensively with families to address the underlying causes of their perceived poor behaviour. Professionals used a combination of resources, surveillance, sanctions and parenting contracts to bring about changes of attitude and lifestyle. If parents failed to comply with the terms of a voluntary parenting contract, parenting orders (Box 8.1) could be invoked.

Box 8.1	What are parenting orders?

- Parenting orders can be made for children up to 17 years old
- Parenting orders are imposed by a criminal court (youth, magistrate or crown court acting under civil jurisdiction) or a family court or a county court
- Parenting orders last up to a maximum of one year and any course or programme specified in the order can last up to three months

- Parents may be required to attend a parenting programme
- Parents may be prescribed specific parenting duties, for example accompanying children to school every day to ensure their attendance
- The courts may require parents to attend a residential parenting course

FIPs were a cross-department initiative originally under the remit of the Office of the Deputy Prime Minister, which were subsequently taken over by the Department of Children, Schools and Families when it was created. The majority of projects were funded through Supporting People grants and awarded to authorities on an annual basis. There were different types of delivery models:

- outreach support to families in their own home
- support in a non-secure tenancy located in the community
- 24-hour support in a supervised residential unit where the family live with project staff.

FIPs can help children achieve the five ECM outcomes, as they focus particularly on:

- Improving children and young people's attendance and behaviour at school, reducing the level of truancy and exclusion.
- Reducing the prevalence of teenage pregnancy and tackling broader sexual health issues.
- Reducing alcohol, drug and volatile substance abuse of children and their parents as well as a focus on other key public health areas such as obesity and smoking.
- Reducing the number of young people not in education, employment or training.
- Helping to deliver the Government's priority of halving Child Poverty by 2011, as a milestone towards eliminating it by 2020 and improving child support (DCSF, 2007c: 6).

In 2006, Nixon et al. carried out an evaluation of six FIPs based in the north of England (Sheffield, Manchester, Bolton, Salford, Oldham and Blackburn with Darwen). Their research provides insight into a number of integrated service issues affecting families. Service users were characterized as having long-standing, multiple and interrelated support needs. Problems connected with children's schooling affected just under half of all families and in a quarter of families, one or more child was reported as having special educational needs; 80% of referrals were female single parents. Ill health further compounded many of these difficulties, with a fifth of families having at least one member affected by a chronic condition. In 39% of families, one or more members of the household had mental health problems – most commonly depression. Substance abuse, drug and alcohol-related problems were identified in 27% of families. In 28% of cases, violence was a serious issue and researchers found that perpetrators of antisocial behaviour were also frequently victims of it themselves. Only 18% of adults were in full-time work and almost half were in debt.

Professionals provided a wide range of support services, some of them interventionist, to help families to find ways of ending negative spirals and enable them to return to their homes without risk of impending eviction. Families generally stayed in contact with the FIPs for an average of six months. The range of methods employed illustrates the array of professionals that were needed and the importance of interagency liaison (Box 8.2).

Box 8.2   **Range of methods employed by social care professionals in FIPs**

Mediation and liaison: One of the key forms of support offered by project workers involved mediating and liaising with other agencies on behalf of family members. For example, working with social landlords to provide assistance in resolving neighbour disputes, address complaints about behaviour and develop long term housing plans.

Development of financial and practical life skills: Central to many support plans was the development of financial and budgeting skills, help in clearing debts, accessing pre payment meters and in claiming benefits etc.

Addressing health needs: Given the very high levels of ill health amongst family members accessing appropriate health services, including alcohol and substance misuse services, was a core activity for project workers.

Addressing children's needs: Action to improve children's access to education was the most common form of support being provided to families with project workers liaising with schools either to secure a place for a child or to help in dealing with behavioural or attendance issues. It was also common for children to have their own individual support plans which included a wide range of interventions from helping them access out of school activities, through to one to one sessions to help them manage their behaviour.

Development of parenting skills and support in the home: The provision of practical day to day support in developing routines and managing the home was one of the elements of the project work that was most valued by service users. Many adults also welcomed help in developing their parenting skills and in improving family relationships. Further research is necessary to establish the different models of parenting support being employed by the projects.

Interpersonal work and the development of trust: Linked to the provision of practical support was the opportunity to develop relationships of trust with family members. For many adult family members having someone to talk to and if necessary to turn to for help was the single most important aspect of the support offered by the project.

Source: Nixon et al., 2006: 45–6

There were mixed responses from families to FIPs. Most appreciated the help with financial management, health and education support and organized activities to keep children from becoming bored and resorting to anti-social behaviour (Nixon et al., 2006; White et al., 2008), but resented any measures that suggested they were bad parents, particularly recommendations to attend parenting classes. The projects were effective in achieving other outcomes, such as preventing eviction and homelessness and improving school attendance. However, FIPs were costly and not without their critics, who felt that targeted families were being rewarded for bad behaviour when there were other deserving cases going without help:

> The continuing focus upon the domestic sphere of the family risks limiting the support provided to homeless individuals or couples without children, as is evident in both family intervention projects and housing benefit sanction schemes. Providing support primarily through addressing antisocial behaviour also risks denying access to this support for marginalised individuals who are not classified as being engaged in such conduct. (Flint, 2009: 248)

According to government statistics (DCLG, 2006), the average project cost £8,000 per family per year for those receiving outreach help in their homes or managed properties, and up to £15,000 per family per year for those placed in residential core units. Even so, the government of the day claimed that FIPs were good value for money, as the cost of inaction was higher and that prevention is ultimately the cheaper option:

> Society as a whole benefits through reduced spending on problems that can be avoided and through maximizing the contribution to society of all citizens. For instance, a child with a conduct disorder at age 10 will cost the public purse around £70,000 by age 28. (DfES, 2003: 14)

The Nixon et al. (2006) evaluation reported that the proportion of families involved in antisocial behaviour and criminal activities declined from 61% to 7%, those subject to ASB orders reduced from 45% to 23%, and the number of those at risk of eviction was cut by two-thirds, from 60% to 18%. Educational issues such as truancy or exclusion also fell from 37% to 21%.

Referrals came from a wide range of service providers (see Box 8.3) and FIPs required particularly good multi-agency collaboration to be successful.

FIP key workers acted as professional go-betweens brokering transactions with, for example, schools, health providers and counselling organizations. Part of their role was to advocate and negotiate for the families, who regularly complained of their powerlessness when dealing with professionals, a situation readily aggravated by poor health and/or the number of agencies they had to engage with. Thus, a vital element of the key worker's interagency communication involved putting across the family's perspective to the agencies involved and then clarifying with the family what action plans were being proposed. Families found this particularly valuable where any legal processes were concerned.

Box 8.3	Examples of key agencies and individuals that refer families and/ or co-work with FIPs

Housing: local authority housing departments; housing associations; private landlords and homeless prevention services

Police: including Police Officers, Police Community Support Officers and Neighbourhood Wardens

Antisocial behaviour: Community Safety enforcement officers

Social care: social services

Education: education welfare, educational psychology and Pupil Referral Units

Youth Offending Service: Youth Offending Teams, Preventing Youth Offending Project, Youth Inclusion Project, Youth Inclusion and Support Panel

Health: GPs, Child, Adolescent and Adult Mental Health Services, school nurses, health visitors alcohol and drug support and advisory services, teenage pregnancy interventions, counselling, family therapy, behavioural psychology and anger management

Parenting providers

JobCentre Plus

Connexions

Probation service

Domestic violence support services

Fire service

Providers of leisure/recreational activities

Childcare providers

Environmental health

Citizens Advice Bureau

Source: White et al., 2008: 28

Evaluations of FIPs (Nixon et al., 2006; White et al., 2008; Pawson et al., 2009) exposed the best and worst of multi-agency practices and their find-ings provide much food for thought. White et al. (2008) reported that the strongest interagency relationships were with schools, housing officers, the police, ASB teams and the youth offending service. Relationships with health and social care emerged as the weakest, although there were some pockets of good practice, particularly staff working in mental health and substance misuse. There were also reports of some good relationships with individual health workers, especially GPs, health visitors and school nurses. More engaged liaison appeared to be linked to those professionals who viewed the work of FIPs as directly relevant to them:

A number of contextual factors influenced the extent to which FIPs were able to establish good working relationships with other agencies. These included the quality of multi-agency relationships locally, the time and resources other professionals had to work with the FIP, and the extent to which links at a strategic level 'filtered down' to frontline workers. Attitudinal factors also influenced the extent to which other professionals had 'bought in' to FIPs. For example, they may have questioned the role, ethos or expertise of the FIP, or seen it as 'treading on the toes' of the professionals already involved. A lack of 'buy in' to FIPs could be manifested in other professionals' behaviour in a range of ways, including a lack of referrals, inappropriate referrals, or a reluctance to share information or work together. Local agency partners and FIP staff reported three types of impacts on other services: breaking down the barriers between families and services; reducing the burden on services; and improving multi-agency working. (White et al., 2008: 6)

Effective co-working was characterized by frequent contact and transactional information exchanges. The most difficult relationships were with social services and this was attributed to tensions arising from social workers seeing much of the work as encroaching on their territory and resenting the lack of comparable professional qualifications of many appointed key workers.

A significant achievement of FIPs was in rebuilding shattered relationships between families and service providers where disillusionment had set in. Once families saw that key workers were delivering on their promises, they became more willing to trust other services again. Three different levels of impact were identified (White et al., 2008: 116):

- **The FIP makes little or no impact on multi-agency working** when there were already good pre-existing links with other services. YOS-based FIPs presented a good example of where multi-agency links were already in existence and so the FIP was seen as 'joining the table' rather than improving the way agencies worked together.
- **The FIP helped to formalise multi-agency partnerships by giving them a structure**. In these circumstances the FIP was reported as having 'built up' partnerships with other agencies through formalising contact procedures and information sharing.
- The FIP was said to have **improved the way agencies were working together** by, for example, improving communication between agencies, set up procedures for information sharing and convened multi-agency meetings, including steering groups, referral panels and support plan meetings.

Some duplication of work was avoided where FIPs improved multi-agency working practices and better interagency communication led to a better understanding of the families' perspectives:

We had a meeting here, where I think that some of the professionals didn't want to involve one of the beat officers, because his view of the family was extremely negative. My view was, and luckily, the key workers here view was, well, if they have got a negative view of the family, let's bring them in so that we can actually get them to understand some of the issues. And work with us as opposed to excluding them ... and I believe it was a success that cut down the chances of the family and the kids being arrested. And, gave that police officer an understanding of the case ... oh, they are the kids we spoke about who are doing x, y and z because of their mum and dad. And they approached them in a very different way that I think was quite successful. (local service provider, cited in Nixon et al., 2006: 116)

Eight critical features were identified as contributing to the success of FIPs (White et al., 2008):

■ recruitment and retention of high-quality staff
■ small caseloads
■ dedicated key worker who manages a family and works intensively with them
■ whole family approach
■ staying involved with a family for as long as necessary
■ scope to use resources flexibly
■ combination of sanctions and support
■ effective multi-agency relationships.

Children living in single-parent families

The number of children living in single-parent families has increased significantly to around 3 million in the UK (Gingerbread, 2010). Since single parents score highly on the child poverty predictor index, based on working status, household structure, ethnicity, ill health, disability and housing tenure (Flaherty et al., 2004), children of single parents are more vulnerable to social exclusion and more likely to be users of integrated services. Research about children living in single-parent families is almost entirely adult based and adult defined. Walker et al. (2008: 431) alert us to the paucity of knowledge about children's perspectives, particularly the impact on their capacity for participation and inclusion:

Little is known, if anything, about how children living in single-parent families experience and perceive their lives as members of these families. Much of the existing research (for example, Millar & Ridge 2001, Sunderland 2002, Rowlingson & McKay 2005) carried out with single-parent families has focused on the problems and challenges they face, but the voices of the children that belong to these families have largely remained silent.

> **Children's Perspectives**

One of the principal research questions in Walker et al.'s (2008) study was how children perceive the support and services available to them. Their data included interviews with 40 children. Extended family and friends proved to be very important especially if the single parent was working, when grandparents' roles were frequently pivotal (both quotes cited in Walker et al., 2008: 431):

> *At the weekends, I go to Nanas. I sleep Saturday and Sunday night ... so my mum can get some peace. [Annie, girl, 8 years, urban interviewee]*

> *I talk to my cousin as we're still very close or my auntie ... It does take all the stuff off your chest, you just let it out. [Leon, boy, 12 years, urban interviewee]*

Children talked about their parental relationship as being very close but also time poor because of the pressures on busy single parents juggling work commitments. Grandparents provided emotional sounding boards as well as gifting them things their parent could not afford. A significant issue identified by the children was the limitations for play due to a lack of space at home, few parks or play areas and limited opportunities for organized leisure activities such as youth clubs. Transport costs were especially problematic for children living in rural areas.

Children considered themselves to be healthy and have good awareness of what was needed for a healthy lifestyle. Nevertheless, this was severely limited by the cost factor. Many single parents could only afford to buy cheaper, less healthy food. Poor quality social housing aggravated any underlying health issues. Healthy living is not just physical, it incorporates a capacity for happiness and emotional wellbeing. The interdependency of children's lives with that of their single parent, who, as a group, have a higher incidence of mental health problems, inevitably rubbed off on children's own experiences. Achieving the five ECM outcomes certainly appears to be more challenging for many children living in single-parent families. While children acknowledge these negatives, they also highlighted some benefits of being in a single-parent family, such as freedom from domestic violence and arguments they had experienced in earlier two-parent family existences. They wanted more quality time with their parent. This does raise questions about some of the 'welfare to work' policies and a need to adopt a more holistic approach:

> These issues are rarely addressed by policy-makers ... The implication taken in policy-making is that the two-parent family is a better family institution, when many families are more harmonious when they become a single-parent family. Those that use discriminatory discourses for popular effect and as a grounding for policy-making do not reflect public opinion or children's opinion of family life. The recent resurgence in political discourse and policy development of the two-parent family as a 'better' family institution will make life much harder for children in single-parent families. (Walker et al., 2008: 434)

Heather's story

Heather is a single parent with three children living on income support. She receives no maintenance payments. Her income from benefit is £210.44 a week – £40.56 below the government's poverty line. She is constantly in debt, and particularly struggles in holiday time to pay for social activities and school uniforms. *'It's when they all need the same clothes at the same time, especially school uniform – that's what I find really difficult ... the children have never been on holiday ... it was a case of do I take them on holiday for a week or pay the bills?'* She has suffered from depression because of financial pressure – she began training as a teaching assistant but found she could not cope; although she volunteers at Barnardo's, she feels unable to return to work. Heather has been to see a personal adviser under the New Deal for Lone Parents – childcare costs are an anxiety and she feels that she will be worse off in work. She also feels that there are no jobs that offer the flexibility that would enable her to care for her children. *'They are trying to make the workforce more flexible for working mothers and this, and that and the other but at the end of the day when you go back to work they want someone reliable, they don't want someone coming in and saying sorry I've got to go because I've had a phone call and my child's ill at school.'* For Heather, concerns over childcare costs and work flexibility are symptomatic of her general fear of returning to work after a long period of being a full-time parent. *'You don't expect life to get any better you just struggle all the time, you think this is life.'*

Source: Sharma, 2007: 29

Conclusion

This chapter began by considering how the nature of the family has changed over the past three decades and the importance of policy and service provision in keeping abreast of the changes, particularly the extended family and inter-pretations of kinship. The family plays a pivotal role in the provision of chil-dren's services, occupying the private space and autonomous jurisdiction to which policy makers have to negotiate access. Successive governments have grappled with finding the right balance between support and control as demonstrated in the different political approaches described here. The integra-tion of children's services has certainly helped in constructing a more holistic, whole family approach to ECM and once again best practice has been identi-fied in multi-agency teams. However, the substantial and enduring message, strengthened by children's own accounts, is that ECM is not an equal prospect for all children. Children living in poverty, whether this is as a result of single parenthood, family ill health or being located in socioeconomic areas of disad-vantage, are much less likely to achieve the five ECM outcomes, some may not achieve any. Initiatives such as FIPs, albeit controversial because of the control measures they invoke, have had some positive benefits. In the end, funding (or lack of it) is always going to be critical to what might be achieved.

Reflection exercises

1. For all readers
Imagine you are a key worker on a Family Intervention Project. You have been allocated a single female parent with three children aged nine, five

and two. The parent is depressed and feels she cannot cope. She has fallen behind with her rent and has other debts. The nine-year-old girl is exhibiting bad behaviour at school and is on the verge of exclusion. Neighbours have complained to the police about her damaging their properties. The five-year-old boy has chronic asthma and the mother's depression means she often fails to get him to school or takes him late. What agencies would you need to involve in supporting this family? Where would you start? Create a draft action plan.

2. For staff working with children and young people in multidisciplinary teams

Reflect on the discussion in this chapter on the role of fathers. What do you do in your services to encourage more involvement of fathers? Make a list of any good practice you or your colleagues engage in. Think about what else you might do and add these to the list. Consider running a staff workshop to raise awareness about gender issues.

3. Children's perspectives

Read Gemma's story again and reflect on the picture of family life she is painting. Jot down the five ECM outcomes and consider the extent to which Gemma is able to achieve them. List anything that gets in the way. What more could be done to help Gemma?

Suggested further reading

1. Aldridge, J. and Sharpe, D. (2007) Pictures of young caring, www.lboro. ac.uk/departments/ss/centres/YCRG/youngCarersDownload/Pictures

   Collection of pictures and photos of children in their role as carers put together by a team of researchers at Loughborough University, excellent for think prompts or visual aids for staff development sessions.

2. Layard, R. and Dunn, J. (2009) *A Good Childhood*, London: Penguin

   Sponsored by the Children's Society, touted as the biggest inquiry into childhood in the UK of the decade. While it contains some useful data about contemporary family life, it needs to be read with critical engagement, as it does take a value position on the family which not all academics and child professionals agree with.

3. Scottish Executive (2006) *Family Matters: Charter for Grandchildren*, www.scotland.gov.uk/Resource/Doc/112493/0027333

   Useful document if you are interested in learning more about the role of grandparents in family life.

4. *Child and Family Social Work*

Academic journal that takes a sociological perspective on the family and provides a forum to exchange knowledge between researchers, practitioners and policy makers. Although focused specifically on social work, makes good contributions to wider practice. A rich vein to explore for anyone who wants to do more in-depth study about the family. Available electronically in most academic libraries.

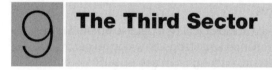

9 The Third Sector

A value-driven sector

The third sector is a collective term that relates to voluntary and community organizations, charities, social enterprises, mutuals and cooperatives. In the domain of children's services, there are a vast number of these of varying sizes from small local groups staffed entirely by volunteers to large global charities. Their independent status enables them to be flexible, responsive and use local community knowledge effectively. A definitive characteristic is that they are not for profit and are driven by values. In their comprehensive review of the third sector, Blake et al. (2007) defined these shared values as:

- Empowering people
- Pursuing equality
- Making voices heard
- Transforming lives
- Being responsible
- Finding fulfillment
- Doing a good job
- Generating public wealth.

This does not mean that all these values are not present separately and/or jointly in the public and private sectors, but what makes the third sector different is the way in which it prioritizes and fuses all these values in its operations.

New Labour's policy in setting out to transform public services was to involve more third sector bodies. This has resulted in new third sector territory such as foundation hospitals and school academies and a consequent shift towards organizing the activity of the third sector around the commissioning and purchasing of services. This poses some risks and threats to the way the third sector has traditionally functioned: 'the relationship becomes characterised by prescription and targets set by central government departments' (Blake et al., 2007: 26). There has been a reduction in grant funding and a rise in short-term contracts. A survey of 3,800 charities found that over two-thirds of all funding agreements for public service delivery are for one year only (Charity Commission, 2007). Some are concerned that collectively these circumstances are compromising the value base of the third sector and encouraging resource-led rather than needs-led processes (for example Blakemore, 2006; Kelly, 2007).

The following is a statement from Joanna Holmes, the chief executive of Barton Hill Settlement, which appeared on the Barton Hill Settlement website (www.bartonhillsettlement.org.uk) in 2006.

" **Children's Perspectives**

Barton Hill Settlement is a voluntary organisation in East Bristol and one of the services it provides is a Kids Club in an area of high deprivation. There have been constant differences of opinion between Barton Hill Settlement and the two different groups who fund this project about the number of workers that should be employed to run the activities. One of the funding groups argues that the art session for eight to eleven year olds should be run with two workers. Barton Hill thinks it takes three workers to provide the quality of service that is consistent with its values. The organisation's Trustees and staff feel so strongly that children in Barton Hill deserve a good quality service that they have decided that they can no longer compromise this value and will close the club if they are not able to run the service with the staff ratios required.

The third sector contributes to children's integrated services at a number of levels. One is the running of projects which directly benefit children, another is producing valuable resources which can be used to address children's needs and a third is consultation and evaluation processes, particularly those related to how Every Child Matters (ECM) is impacting on children's lives. Voluntary organizations often have a better understanding of local community needs and are sometimes more trusted because they are well known in a neighbourhood and are perceived to be independent of government, although this is only partially true, since some organizations do receive a portion of their funding from government bodies or are directly commissioned by local authorities to provide a service. Some would argue that the independence of third sector organizations is its greatest strength and that this is most at risk because of funding constraints which threaten not just their independence but also their advocacy role (for example Hardy,

2007). However, it is also important not to view this through rose-tinted glasses. Just because a service is delivered by a voluntary body does not necessarily mean it is any better or worse than a statutory body. There are different strengths and weaknesses and a key strategy in the provision of optimal integrated services for children is that local authorities draw on a diversity of provision and match need to the best provider, whatever sector (or indeed multiple sectors) this may come from:

> The Government is clear that it is not looking for evidence that a third sector organisation, simply because it is from the third sector, is necessarily more effective at delivering public services than other organisations from the private or public sector. It recognises that there are certain characteristics which make any service deliverer effective (being close to communities, an ability to be flexible, able to respond to the needs of users etc), and therefore is keen that commissioners commission from these kinds of effective organisations, in whatever sector they may be found. (Contaldo, 2007: 8)

Multi-agency working and the third sector

We have already seen in earlier chapters that one of the challenges of ECM has been getting the three previous autonomous departments of education, social services and health to work together. An even bigger challenge is to ensure that third sector workers are fully integrated into multi-agency working. This has been a particular issue for the training of staff to new ECM standards, as large tranches of transition funding, such as that ring-fenced to upskill the early years workforce, have been attached to local authorities, distributed through children's trusts and, en route, excluded many third sector bodies.

Other difficulties in multi-agency working with the third sector are lodged in issues around partnerships, commissions and contracts. A local authority or children's trust will sometimes devolve responsibility for delivery of a service partly or wholly to a voluntary organization. Relationships can become strained if, for example, there is arbitrary withdrawal of funding or a lack of clear communication – including feedback – on tendering and contract bids. Also, it may not be a level playing field when third sector organizations are bidding for contracts, since they have to cover all their costs and some of these are not recognized in local authority pricing structures. The Charity Commission (2007) found that only 12% recovered all their costs from the funder for the services they deliver. Short-term contracts, which are on the increase, destabilize the workforce and can further heighten tensions.

In Chapter 8, I talked about the importance of building human and social capital in the armoury against poverty. Third sector organizations are particularly skilled at this because of their extensive local knowledge which supports families to develop social capital networks. They also stimulate human capital through the diversity of voluntary input, ranging from one-off assistance to sustained support and long-term mentoring schemes. The growth of systems such as Employer Supported Volunteering, whereby companies invest staff time in community projects and local schools, is testament to the potent community spirit which the third sector is well placed to nurture. Another advantage of the third sector is its ability to foster social enterprise which provides additional funding streams for social care projects.

Third sector organizations are rarely full members of children's trusts (National Council for Voluntary Youth Services, 2007), so have little opportunity to shape the delivery of integrated children's services. They may be involved in consultation processes and service evaluations but these activities are reactive and do not influence change at the grass roots, ironically when grass-roots activity is precisely their core strength. This suggests that a centralized approach to integration is the best way to secure an effective third sector partnership and better ECM outcomes for children. Local authorities could be directed to ring-fence a proportion of funding for third sector organizations and ensure that there are sufficient incentives to involve them.

Third sector community projects

This section provides examples of some third sector community projects. The first, shown in Box 9.1, depicts a project partnered with, and funded by, a central government body – in this instance, the Home Office.

Box 9.1	Supporting Young Unaccompanied Asylum Seekers in School (SASS)

SASS aims to help raise the level of educational attainment and facilitate social inclusion of looked after children, particularly unaccompanied asylum seeking children. It was sponsored by the Home Office and awarded £154,000 from Treasury's Invest to Save Budget. The project provides mentoring support for looked after children and young asylum seekers, providing support in schools, allowing them access to statutory education and promoting their greater inclusion within the local community. SASS has been innovative in bringing together a charitable organisation with the Local Authority and individual schools, supporting the recent trend towards developing community partnerships to improve the delivery of public services. It provides an important and valuable additional resource that is well targeted to the particular needs of unaccompanied asylum seekers and refugees and other looked after children. The learning mentors have established excellent relationships with their designated pupils in schools, reflected in 100 per cent mentoring session attendance. The project has also led to mentees being more involved in the wider sphere of school activities. Mentees are receiving one-to-one support on a weekly basis and their feedback indicates this has been a vital part in their academic and social experience. SASS has produced a guidance handbook for refugee friendly schools and also a citizen teaching pack called 'Respecting our Differences'.

Source: HM Treasury, 2007: 10

By contrast, a second example illustrates a small project funded entirely by charitable donations but which makes a real difference in the lives of one group of disadvantaged children. Around 150,000 children every year suffer the trauma of the imprisonment of a parent. Seven per cent of all children will be affected in this way at some time during their primary school years. Storybook Dads is a charitable organization that helps to ease the pain of separation by enabling the imprisoned parent to record a bedtime story onto a CD or DVD which children can listen to whenever they need to hear their parent's voice. It was established in 2004 in Dartmoor Prison and has since helped over 6,000 prisoners in 70 prisons to stay connected with their children. Some prisoners also get involved in the production and editing process and thus have the opportunity to learn new skills.

" Children's Perspectives

"I miss my Dad so much. When I feel lonely I listen to my CD and hearing his voice makes me feel better".

"I took it to school and all my class listened to it and they all wished that they had one."

"It's daddy's special present for me. I listen to it every night."

"Daddy's done a CD for me which was The Frog Prince and he did Jack and the Beanstalk for my brother. They're both really good. He says he will do another one for us for Christmas."

"I like the three little pigs talking. It is Daddy talking but he talks squeaky and then it doesn't sound like him,"

"It's lovely to hear Mummy's voice whenever I want to."

Source: Quotes from children with an imprisoned parent, cited on www.storybookdads.co.uk

---

Other third sector organizations occupy a middle ground between service provision and advocacy, whereby a significant amount of their time and resources are spent on campaigning to improve children's lives. Their independence from the state enables them to take up strong positions that would not be possible for statutory service providers. The focus of their activity is often directly connected to statutory work and they may even be involved in multi-agency partnerships with local authorities to deliver services to children at the same time as running advocacy campaigns. This type of campaigning advocacy is sometimes termed 'lobbying' and is an important function of some third sector organizations. An example is Action for Children, a charitable organization working with and advocating for some of the most vulnerable and neglected children. It runs several campaigns to raise awareness about the vulnerability of neglected children and how the public can be proactive on their behalf and is also a major provider of services. For example, Islington council commissioned Action for Children to deliver children's centre services to families living in the area because the charity is well known in the community for its successful partnership working with parents on crisis interventionist projects. You can read Action for Children's mission statement and see an example of how it works in Box 9.2.

Box 9.2	Action for Children mission statement and case example

Mission statement

We run nearly 450 services and work with nearly 170,000 children, young people and their families across the UK. We are a leading provider of preventative and intensive support to families with vulnerable children, including those in care, in trouble with the law, who are disabled and who have mental health problems.

Action for Children meets the needs of the children and young people who are most in need of support, helping them to achieve their full potential. Through our work and through speaking out, we seek to break the cycle of deprivation. We challenge injustice and empower children and families to overcome the obstacles in their lives that hold them back. We tailor our work to local circumstances, in partnership with local authorities, health providers, communities and local organisations. We design our services around the specific needs of not only the child, but where appropriate the whole family (p. 2).

Phoenix (London) case example

In Merton, Action for Children works with the local authority to prevent children coming into care. When such children are identified, Action for Children intervenes and works to strengthen the family unit and enable them to see the positives in their lives.

The service works with families in crisis using a solution-focused brief therapy model of work. Support is offered for a period of three months, with all interventions regularly reviewed. When the work is completed, families are tracked after six months to see if the progress they made has been maintained and, in some cases, to offer a 'one-off' review session if this is considered useful.

The project consists of a rapid response team, adolescent resource team and family group meetings. The rapid response team offers crisis intervention by responding within 24 hours and providing intensive intervention with the family during their crisis. The adolescent resource team (ART) offers direct work with children and young people aged 9–19, using different methods to engage young people through play, activity and leisure. Family group conferences are used to ensure that children remain within extended families wherever possible.

Other services include group work for parents with teenagers and for young people. These help young people to gain confidence and raise their self esteem in order to develop healthier peer relationships.

The Action for Children Phoenix service operates in a multi-agency context, working in partnership with CAMHS, YOT, education, health and other voluntary agencies (p. 4).

Source: Action for Children, 2008

A final illustration shows how the third sector can bolster existing services for children provided by the state that fall short of meeting children's specific needs. Third sector organizations provide many specialized services to hard-to-reach groups and fill gaps left by the public and/or private sectors. There are many instances of this with children who have a disability (see text on child wheelchair users in Chapter 6).

Third sector resources that support integrated children's services

In addition to the many excellent resources and websites for children and families, the third sector produces particularly good resources to support childcare professionals and to develop practice more widely. Since voluntary bodies are close to their client groups, it enables them to stay in touch with client needs and to produce appropriate and accessible resources. Some resources are specific to particular needs and others can be used generically and educationally. An example of the former is a resource developed by the National Blind Children's Society to support children with a visual impairment to read a range of books that they could not otherwise read in commercially available print. Children with a visual impairment have the same desire to read popular fiction and non-fiction as their sighted peers. However, it is more difficult for them to find books that are suitable. The National Blind Children's Society has produced a resource known as CustomEyes, wherein books are tailor-made to suit a child's individual requirements. For example, some children have difficulty reading black print on a white background and yellow paper can sometimes make a big difference, as can font size – often a font as large as 24 is needed. The service has over 1,000 titles and is still expanding, including producing revision guides for Key Stage 2 statutory assessments (11-year-olds national tests), so that children with a visual impairment have the same advantages when preparing for national tests as their sighted peers.

An example of the latter is the National Children's Bureau's Cards for Little Lives scheme which was funded by the Equitable Charitable Trust. The scheme designed a collection of 'cards' for use as PowerPoint slides with interactive whiteboard technology. The cards present scenarios and dilemmas based on the five ECM outcomes for teachers and other adults working with primary school children. The intention is that they will stimulate discussion about issues that are important to children's health and well-being and their social development.

The bigger worldwide children's charities such as UNICEF and Save the Children are well known for the high-quality resources they produce such as UNICEF's children's version of the UNCRC (see Chapter 2). Other UNICEF resources which develop children's awareness of rights and citizenship include free downloadable games such as Wants and Needs (Midwinter, n.d.), a set of cards depicting a commodity which children have to decide is a 'want' or a 'need'. Each commodity is linked to an article from the UNCRC (see Box 9.3).

Box 9.3	UNICEF Wants and Needs cards

Needs

Clean air (Article 24 – health), clean water (Article 24 – health), decent shelter (Article 27 – standard of living), education (Articles 28 and 29), express your opinion (Article 12), medical care (Article 24), nutritious food (Article 24), play (Article 31), practise beliefs, culture and language (Article 30), protection from abuse and neglect (Article 19), protection from discrimination (Article 2)

Wants

Bicycle, fashionable clothes, fast food, holiday trips, money to spend, personal computer, mobile phone, television

Source: Midwinter, n.d.

Spotlight on a leading children's charity: Barnardo's

Origin

Thomas Barnardo (1845–1905) founded his children's charity in 1867 after an outbreak of cholera in London killed more than 3,000 people and left thousands of children destitute and sleeping on the streets. In that year, he set up the first Barnardo's school where poor children could get a basic education. This was followed by the first residential home for boys in 1870 and soon after the first girls' home. Barnardo believed that every child deserved the best possible start in life, whatever their background – a philosophy that still inspires the charity today. By the time children left Barnardo's, they were capable of living independently, girls having acquired a range of domestic skills and the boys a craft or trade.

When Barnardo died in 1905, the charity had 96 children's homes caring for more than 8,500 children. In many ways, the history of Barnardo's parallels the evolution of state children's services as described in Chapter 2. Similarly, it was the aftermath of the Second World War that brought about the biggest changes in children's social care. The disruption of war and the impact of the evacuation policy underlined the centrality of the family and Barnardo's postwar work in the 1950s with families reflected this. Barnardo's helped families stay together, whatever the circumstances of their destitution, even if this was due to unemployment or crime, via family grants and housing schemes.

As single parenthood became more acceptable and contraception and abortion reduced the number of unwanted children, Barnardo's reduced its residential homes and focused more on fostering and adoption services and family work with children who had emotional and behavioural difficulties. Much of its work involved helping families with social challenges such as unemployment, poor health, bad housing and poverty, and was aimed at defusing stresses and tensions before they led to family breakdown and/or child abuse.

In the 1990s, Barnardo's pioneered schemes for young juveniles and disabled children and developed new areas of work with child victims of sexual abuse, homelessness and those affected by HIV/AIDS. Over 140 years after it was founded, Barnardo's is still a leading children's charity working directly with more than a million children every year. Today, it runs 415 projects across the UK. Its mission is to bring out the best in every child and it believes that all children deserve the chance to fulfil their potential. Beyond its many community projects, it uses its influence to champion children's rights and to campaign for better care for all children.

Example of a Barnardo's community project: Hamara Family Project

Based in East London, the Hamara Family Project has been running for 20 years (Hamara means 'our' in Urdu/Hindi). It has been very successful in working with the area's black and minority ethnic communities and has developed expertise in training on a wide range of disability and short break issues. It provides a comprehensive range of services to local children including:

- *HIPHOP* (Hamara Inclusive Play & Holiday Opportunities Project): provides support staff to enable a disabled child to access mainstream after-school clubs, play schemes and leisure activities
- *Swimming Club:* held weekly
- *Stay and Play:* provides play activities to children with life-limiting/life-threatening conditions, in their own homes during school holidays
- *Early Bird and Early Bird Plus:* regularly runs the National Autistic Society 12-week programme for children aged up to five (and five–eight for Plus) who are newly diagnosed with autistic spectrum disorder
- *Baby Band:* a music therapy service for children aged five and under with social communication difficulties
- *Dad's Group:* meets one evening monthly during school term time for fathers of disabled children
- *The Me, Myself and I Club:* a group for mothers of disabled children which meets once monthly for lunch
- *Lifeline:* in partnership with a local children's centre, Hamara offers 12-week crisis intervention to vulnerable families of very young children, and a counselling service for parents
- *Siblings Group:* provides leisure activities and trips for siblings aged 5–13.

> **Children's Perspectives**

Barnardo's (www.barnardos.org.uk/) does much to advocate children's perspectives and to disseminate these views in free information resource sheets for practitioners. This is an example of what children and young people have to say:

Treat us individually, not as children as a whole.

When we make a complaint – sort it, not just report it.

Ask us what we think on our own and listen to what we say.

We want to be looked after by adults we can trust.

Don't always believe an adult over a child – ask for evidence and decide for yourself.

Keeping us busy keeps us out of trouble.

Even troublemakers may have a point or need to be protected.

We have a right not to be bullied.

Leah's story

Leah is a lone parent with one daughter Emily, who is 14 months old. Leah is of mixed race and her daughter has a white father. She is a recovered drug addict: *'There was a lot of drugs around in the area when I was growing up. I took it to make myself feel better because I'd been abused by a family friend and I was bullied all the time at school about race – it's mostly white around here. I wouldn't like my daughter to go through the same as me.'*

Leah does not work – her previous drug addiction has resulted in her losing all confidence – but she would like to work when Emily goes to school. Due to the previous abuse she cannot trust anyone but her mum to take care of Emily. Leah lives on benefits of £119.28 a week and she borrows from her mum and step dad. Leah describes the impact of living on a low income: *'We only have a basic living. I can't afford to do anything else. We don't struggle for food because my mum helps us out. I don't ever save any money – there is nothing left to save. I wish I could. Emily misses out on lots of things. I can't take her swimming or to playgroups or any activity as they will have to be paid for and I can't afford it. I can't take her out to parks and things like that as there are people doing drugs around here and I don't want to get caught up with them.'*

Leah would like to be able to attend social activities for her and her child but generally cannot afford them. She says: *'Priory is the only place around where I can go and be like the other mums. We don't have to pay to come here'.*

Source: Sharma, 2007: 18

Conclusion

The third sector plays an important part in children's integrated services. It is a not-for-profit, value-driven sector that is independent of the state. Its strengths lie in the expertise accumulated in local communities, flexibility of operating and independence. New Labour sought to harness these strengths and involve third sector organizations more directly in the ECM agenda by sharing the delivery of services with them. However, tensions have arisen in funding and commissioning processes and some are concerned that too sharp a move towards government-funded projects will erode their independence and threaten their traditional ethos. The third sector often operates at the margins of disadvantage and fills gaps in services that local authorities are failing to meet. Its work is invaluable. The enduring challenge is to integrate the third sector into the provision of children's services without compromising its value base.

Reflection exercises

1. For all readers

Divide a sheet of paper in half and list all the public and private children's services you are aware of that operate in your own community, public ones on the left side of the paper and private ones on the right. Now think of all the voluntary children's organizations you know about in your locality and put these in the middle of the paper. Draw connecting lines from each organization to any others they have contact with in any of the other sectors. Where are the lines busiest? Reflect on what this tells you about the integration of the three sectors in your area.

2. For staff working with children and young people in multidisciplinary teams

Reflect on the third sector organizations you are currently involved with. Can you identify any different approaches in the way third sector staff work with children and families? Do these differences lead to interagency tensions? Think about how these might be resolved.

3. Children's perspectives

Third sector organizations play a major role in child advocacy and have a wealth of expertise in running campaigns, for example Mencap's 'Don't stick it, stop it!' anti-bullying initiative. Reflect on why you think they are successful. What are they doing that we could do more of?

Suggested further reading

1. Blake, G., Robinson, D. and Smerdon, M. (2006) *Living Values: A Pocket Guide for Trustees,* London, Community Links/Esmée Fairbairn Foundation

   If you are interested in the value base of the third sector, you will enjoy reading this small booklet (only 30 pages), which encourages reflection

on values in the third sector, how to realize them in voluntary organizations, and how to measure them.

2. HM Treasury (2007) *Building the Evidence Base: Third Sector Values in
   the Delivery of Public Services*, London: Correspondence and Enquiry
   Unit, HM Treasury

   Provides a useful overview of where and how the third sector sits
   alongside public and private service providers.

3. Websites of third sector organizations

   The best way to get an insight into the workings of third sector
   organizations is to browse their websites. Here are a few examples
   of the hundreds of children's voluntary organizations, big and small,
   that you might like to research for yourselves, or spend some time
   investigating what organizations are active in your own locality: Save
   the Children, The Children's Society, National Children's Bureau,
   Prince's Trust, National Blind Children's Society, NSPCC, Over The
   Wall, Witness Confidence, Dyspraxia Foundation, Diana Award, Deaf
   Children's Society, and Mencap.

10 Safeguarding Children

What do we mean by safeguarding children?

It is necessary to impose some limitations on the scope of the chapter content and therefore I only refer to the child safeguarding processes in England. Readers can find resources relating to the other nation states in Suggested further reading. At the outset, we need to appreciate that what constitutes child abuse changes over time and across cultures. In the nineteenth century, small children were sent up chimneys and slow learners were brutally thrashed, activities which would clearly be deemed abusive in modern times. Equally, we might look back in years to come and wonder how physical chastisement of children by parents remained lawful well into the twenty-first century.

Before Every Child Matters (ECM), the term 'child protection' was in common usage among professionals. A change of terminology to 'safeguarding children' reflects the wider ECM ethos of promoting welfare through proactive intervention and support rather than reactive crisis management, such as when abuse occurs. This approach is reflected in the replacement of child protection area committees, which were non-statutory, by statutory safeguarding children boards. These boards have a much broader remit, as set out in *Working Together to Safeguard Children* (DfES, 2006c). In this document, the single precept of child protection is extended to encompass three others:

- Prevention from maltreatment (existing)

- Preventing impairment of children's health or development (new)
- Ensuring that children are growing up in circumstances consistent with the provision of safe and effective care (new)
- Professionals undertaking their role to enable children to have optimum life chances and to enter adulthood successfully (new).

See Suggested further reading for specific legislation relating to Northern Ireland, Scotland and Wales.

There are those who argue that this was a step too far and that subsuming child protection into only one of four prevention facets risks losing the sharp professional focus on child abuse (for example Walker, 2008):

> Professionals, when faced with complex family problems which may or do include child abuse, may focus on the other three elements of 'safeguarding' in the belief that these together override the one element concerned with 'protection'. If they feel encouraged to take a 'safeguarding' approach rather than a narrower 'protection' approach, they will have to make decisions, for instance about how to separate any harm they encounter from 'impairment of health or development' (which is not serious enough to warrant statutory intervention) or about what constitutes care that is not 'safe and effective', or indeed whether the harm is merely preventing children having 'optimum life chances ... to enter adulthood successfully' or is more significant and therefore requiring of immediate protective action. (Walker, 2008: 69)

To some extent, however, the death of Baby Peter in 2009 has had the effect of swinging the pendulum back the other way, prompting a renewed emphasis on protection from abuse and a dramatic rise in the number of children being taken into care. If a child is identified as being at risk of harm, they become the subject of a child protection plan. A 'core group' of professionals is involved in this, with a social worker coordinating the process. A core group is likely to be made up of social work staff, parents and professionals with direct involvement with the child such as teachers or health visitors. Practice guidelines recommend that this core group should be convened within ten days of a referral. A larger number of professionals, for example police, CAMHS and so on, are then involved in a wider group that convene for child protection review conferences. The first of these has to be scheduled within three months and thereafter usually every six months.

Four types of abuse are categorized in *Working Together to Safeguard Children* (DfES, 2006c): physical abuse, sexual abuse, emotional abuse, and neglect.

Physical abuse

Physical abuse now includes everything except 'reasonable' chastisement by a parent. This remains a contested area, as there is no legal definition of what constitutes 'reasonable' other than a requirement that punishment should not leave a mark, reddening or bruising of the skin. This renders children with dark skin more vulnerable as their skin type does not redden in the same way as white skin. It also fails to protect children from parents who hit children round the skull area where it is less likely to show a mark (and may even further encourage). NSPCC (2007) data, gathered in extensive interviews with young adults recounting their experiences of abuse, suggest that a quarter of all abused children suffer at the hands of a parent or carer (see Box 10.1). Despite compelling evidence that a high proportion of abuse happens in the home (see also Cawson et al., 2000), the government still resists imposing an outright ban on physical chastisement. A further concern is the reference, in *Working Together to Safeguard Children*, to children needing to be protected from *significant* harm. This puts added responsibility onto the role of the professional who has to judge what is reasonable or not. As Walker (2008: 71) points out:

How hard does the hit have to be to count as abuse? Is it more about the frequency of the hitting than about how hard it is? If a parent hits their child occasionally (even quite hard) but otherwise is warm and supportive towards them, is this better than the child never being hit, but also not receiving very much warmth and support?

Box 10.1	**Prevalence of child abuse**

These data have been compiled from interviews with young adults about their childhood experiences.

- 6% of children experienced frequent and severe emotional maltreatment during childhood
- 6% of children experienced serious absence of care at home during childhood
- 31% of children experienced bullying by their peers during childhood, a further 7% were discriminated against and 14% were made to feel different or 'like an outsider'; 43% experienced at least one of these things during childhood
- 72% of sexually abused children did not tell anyone about the abuse at the time, 27% told someone later, and 31% still had not told anyone about their experience(s) by early adulthood
- 25% of children experienced one or more forms of physical violence during childhood. This includes being hit with an implement, being hit with a fist, kicked, shaken, thrown or knocked down, beaten up, choked, burned or scalded on purpose, or threatened with a knife or gun. The majority of these children had experienced 'some degree of physical abuse' by parents or carers.

Source: NSPCC, 2007

> ## ❝ Children's Perspectives
>
> According to Home Office research (2005), children living with parents who have a poor marital relationship are almost five times more likely to be hit than children whose parents have a stable relationship. Many children tell ChildLine (NSPCC, 2006) that the physical abuse they suffer is often triggered by how their parents feel rather than a specific action:
>
> > 'Mum has been really stressed for the last few months – I don't know why. But she's started hitting me' (10-year-old boy).
>
> There is a strong correlation between physical abuse and alcohol abuse. Of the 3,442 children who expressed concerns to ChildLine in 2004/05 about a family member's alcohol use, nearly half also spoke of physical abuse:
>
> > 'I'm so unhappy. Dad's been drinking a lot. He's always arguing with me, and usually he hits me, too' (11-year-old girl).
>
> > 'I'm sick of Mum beating me, so I've run away, but I don't know where to go. I can't go to my dad's – he'll just hit me and send me back to Mum' (12-year-old boy).
>
> 'I've had children who have spoken of very severe abuse,' says a counsellor, 'but then said to me, "Well, I deserved it." They've come to believe that they deserve to be abused.'
>
> *Source:* NSPCC, 2006: 3–6

Emotional abuse

The category of emotional abuse now includes any behaviour intended to make a child feel worthless or unloved. Bullying is included, specifically, and general acknowledgement is made of situations that lead to overprotection and/or limitation of a child's exploration and learning. A significant step forward in safeguarding children has been the inclusion in this category of the emotional harm that might be caused to a child by witnessing ill-treatment to another. Stanley et al.'s (2010) research into children and families' experiences of domestic violence examined 460 case reports and found almost half of children were present during violent family incidents. Of these, approximately 80% were ten years of age or younger.

> ## ❝ Children's Perspectives
>
> Daniel's research (2008: 98) points to the importance of recognizing and valuing children's expertise in situations where they are at risk. Professionals sometimes focus too closely on protecting and shielding children as a victim and overlooking their expertise and desire to be agentic:

> Six year old Josefa, who was referred to a CAMHS service for bed-wetting, sleep disturbance and school difficulties, moved between the households of her mother and father who had separated acrimoniously two years previously. Since then, there had been several violent incidents between the parents witnessed by Josefa who also had countless experiences of hearing each parent criticise and 'bad-mouth' the other, behaviour she described as 'naughty'. A therapist met with Josefa alone, and, on hearing about this, kept saying to Josefa how hard this was for her and it must be too much because she is only six years old. Josefa was having none of this and kept insisting 'I can manage'. The therapist, understandably, didn't believe her and persisted in the line that it was too hard for her, receiving more of the same response. The therapist changed tack and asked Josefa to describe the ways in which she **did** manage. Josefa talked about how she told each of her parents off when they were 'naughty'. She thought that this sometimes worked. What did she do if they didn't listen? If they didn't listen, she went off to her room. In the middle of the discussion about her heroic attempts to have an effect on her parents, she turned to the therapist and said spontaneously 'but sometimes I can't manage'.

Other examples of children's expertise are described by Stanley et al. (2010):

> A male hit his partner in the face with a child's boot, verbally abused her and threatened to kill the children, and slammed the door in her face. Within the police log it was reported that their five-year-old daughter had been able to provide more details about the incident than the mother. (p. 103)

> A male broke the front door of his ex-partner's home in order to gain access. During this attack, their nine-year-old son tried to barricade his bedroom door to prevent his father from reaching his mother. (p. 102)

We can learn much from these perspectives. Principally, we need to appreciate the importance of listening to children and understand that they often see and hear more than we give them credit for. Crucially, when we listen to children, we should afford them the respect of being experts on their own lives and receive what they have to tell us as valuable.

Neglect

The third category, neglect, has seen two main additions. The first is the inclusion of neglect caused to an unborn child. The second is neglect occasioned by failure to adequately supervise a child, including when this duty is devolved to others such as babysitters. Neglect is a difficult concept to delineate as there are borderline areas where professionals have to use their expertise to determine whether something is systematic and harmful neglect or occasional lapses. It may be more harmful to remove a child, who is underfed and poorly clothed, from an otherwise loving family, although a child who is seriously malnourished and at risk of hypothermia is at immediate risk. Neglect can be a serious form of child abuse and is the highest incidence on the child protection register (DfES, 2006d). According to Bovarnick (2007: 2):

> Neglect is a complex phenomenon that is difficult to define. In the face of pluralistic notions of what constitutes adequate care, defining children's needs and determining what constitutes neglect has been problematic. The lack of clarity around what child neglect means and includes has practical implications. As most neglectful families have complex needs, interventions frequently entail responses from different service providers. Practitioners' understandings of neglect, however, are often shaped by different professional backgrounds and can vary within and across different services. This can contribute to vital pieces of information in neglect cases not being picked up, information being lost or not being effectively communicated across different agencies. An effective interagency approach is indispensable for successfully intervening in cases of child neglect and in safeguarding children.

Chronic neglect has far-reaching consequences for children and may be manifested in physical and mental health problems, attachment and relationship difficulties, and poor educational attainment (Taylor and Daniel, 2005). Sometimes it leads to death, such as the widely reported death of Tiffany Wright in 2008 (Levy and Scott-Clark, 2010).

Research has shown that some groups of children are particularly vulnerable to neglect (Taylor and Daniel, 2005). These include children born prematurely, children with disabilities, adolescents, children in care, runaways, asylum-seeking children and children from black and minority ethnic communities. The category of neglect is an area where early intervention, a cornerstone of the ECM, is clearly beneficial. Supporting families where children are at risk of neglect has been shown to be effective (see the section on Family Intervention Projects in Chapter 8). Child neglect is sometimes the result of parents who are struggling to cope, perhaps because of mental health issues or poverty (Cawson, 2002). Where it is a wilful act, it is frequently accompanied by other types of abuse such as emotional and physical (Daniel, 2005). The role of integrated services and multi-agency working could not be more crucial in preventing children from suffering neglect.

Sexual abuse

The rapid rise of internet and mobile phone paedophilia and the growth in trafficking of children for prostitution present additional perils for children today. Legislation has been slow to catch up with modern-day risks. It was not until the Sex Offenders Act 1997 that it became a requirement for known sex offenders to be registered through a police notification system. The Sex Offenders Act 2003 closed further loopholes, making sex with a child under 13 an automatic rape conviction, thus preventing any offender from using consent as a defence. It also brought in new laws on internet sex crimes and 'grooming', along with bestiality, voyeurism and necrophilia (Metcalf, 2008). Possession of images of child sexual abuse became a crime, whereas previously this related only to the making of images of child sexual abuse. The high-profile murder of eight-year-old Sarah Payne spearheaded a lengthy campaign by her mother to give parents the right to know when previously convicted sex offenders were being released into their communities. This became known as 'Sarah's Law' and enables parents to check with the police if anyone who has regular contact with their child has any paedophile convictions. After piloting, Sarah's Law was rolled out across all police forces in England and Wales in 2010.

The prevalence and consequences of child sexual abuse are far-reaching. Cawson et al.'s (2000) research with young adults in the UK found that 16% (11% of males and 21% of females) reported experiences of sexual abuse in childhood. Sexual abuse may be only one manifestation of other types of violence or neglect against a child, what Finkelhor et al. (2007) refer to as 'poly-victims'. Research also suggests that individuals with a history of sexual abuse and victimization are at a greater risk of revictimization (Roodman and Clum, 2001).

 Children's Perspectives

Imogen's story

'It's really hard to talk out about girls being trafficked in this country; no one wants to believe it.'

Born into a family who found it difficult to cope, Imogen was taken into care shortly after her 12th birthday.

'The girls in the home were all a bit older than me and were going out with older men. At first I just tagged along,' Imogen says.

Isolated and lonely, she soon became dependent on her new friends. The group would regularly go missing – running away to the boyfriends' flats and houses. To a 12-year-old it all seemed very exciting.

'They gave me drink and smokes – it was a laugh. Then one man started to take a special interest in me. He was much older, he was protective – I felt looked after, wanted, loved even. He gave me everything I wanted and when I was 13 he handed over the keys to a flat and said "It's yours, use it when you need it".'

For a young girl with no family support and little self-esteem it seemed like a dream come true, but before long it was 'payback' time. Imogen suspected that her 'boyfriend' was involved with other girls, but one night he asked her to dress up because they were going to a party.

Imogen was taken to London, miles away from her home. She was told to have sex with different 'friends'. It was a pattern that would soon become all too familiar.

'I didn't have any choice – I felt so guilty. Eventually, he'd take me all over the country: Leeds, Bradford, Manchester, London. He'd take me to hotels, some nights two or three.

I never saw any money change hands. Some men asked 'How old is she?' Some asked 'Have you got any younger?' They were really sick ... I wanted to escape, but he just controlled me. It was a mental thing – I was terrified,' she said.

Source: Barnardo's, 2009: 11

"My dad comes into my room, pulls his clothes down, takes out 'sausage' and rubs it against me. I don't like it." (Girl, aged seven)
   "Last night when I was in the toilet, my mum's new boyfriend came in and abused me. I don't want to tell Mum. I think she won't believe me." (Girl, aged eight)
   "My mum tried to rape me last night. I am upset. My mum came in from the pub drunk, asked me to take my clothes off and tried to put a rubber thing inside me. My mum is drinking a lot since Dad had broken up with her. Mum is in the pub now. I have not talked to her since last night." (Boy, aged 11)
   "I am being sexually abused by my brother. My mum and dad don't believe me. My parents think it is my fault and I must have led him on or come on to him. I am told to keep this a secret and I am struggling to cope with this." (Girl, aged 12)

Source: NSPCC, 2009

Child abuse in institutional and religious settings

At the time of writing, the media is awash with revelations of sexual abuse of children by Roman Catholic priests in the wake of the Irish Commission's (2009) *Inquiry into Child Abuse*, which took nine years to complete. It revealed that rape and sexual molestation were 'endemic' in Irish Catholic church-run industrial schools and orphanages where thousands of children were subjected to chronic beatings, rape and humiliation by priests and nuns (McDonald, 2009). It sparked a series of inquiries in Catholic churches in other countries, which exposed similar levels of systemic abuse that had been covered up for decades because of the secrecy and powerful autonomy of the church. Many offending clergy were protected by being moved to other areas rather than reported to the police and then went on to abuse more children. This raises issues about the vulnerability of children in institutional and religious settings more generally. Denial by religious leaders that their ministers, in positions of trust, could perpetrate such acts has hampered progress with child protection for decades. Power relations are more accentuated in religious organizations, as parents are frequently in awe of the perceived status of religious personnel. An innate belief in the goodness of ministers can make parents incredulous of their own children's reports of abuse.

   Siddique (2006) drew attention to similar problems happening with Muslim children worshipping at mosques. In some African cultures, children with disabilities are believed to be witches and brutal exorcisms are practised. *The Guardian* (Ward, 2005) recounted the case of a girl accused of being a witch who was beaten, cut more than 40 times and had chilli peppers rubbed in her eyes. Parents' misfortunes might be blamed on their children being 'possessed' by evil spirits. In extreme cases, the abuse can lead to ritual killings, such as the death of the Nigerian boy whose mutilated torso was found in the River Thames in London in 2001 (Kennison, 2008). Steps are being taken to better understand the cultural and religious issues involved in child protection. Project Violet, for example, was set up by the Metropolitan Police to work with African church leaders to stem the increase in faith-related abuse. Stobart's (2006: 19) report of Project Violet researched 38 cases and found that accusations of 'possession' or 'witchcraft' could include 'rationalising misfortune, a change of circumstances for the worse, a child with a "difference" and a weak bond of affection between the carer and the child'. Fourteen of the child cases were found to have some degree of disability or imperfection, ranging from a stammer to a severe mental or physical disability.

 Children's Perspectives

Harrowing testimony collected for the Irish Commission's inquiry (2009) into abuses in Roman Catholic institutions reveals that all forms of abuse were prevalent and children were the epitome of Finkelhor et al.'s (2007) 'poly-victims':

'Hunger was extreme, we stole cattle nuts and mangels and the hosts from the altar because we were so hungry.'

'They told me that my mother was dead and that it was no wonder as I was a bad boy, that it was my fault. I grew up thinking I had killed her somehow. Recently I discovered that she only died ... [a few years previously] ... and that for most of our lives we lived quite near each other.'

'You'd be more thirsty than anything else, we'd drink water out of the toilets, there would be little worms in the water, the older girls would show us how to spit them out like that ... demonstrated ... But you weren't afeared [afraid] ... It was the nuns you feared.'

Source: Irish Commission, 2009, vol. III, sections 7 and 9

Bullying

The widening of child protection to encompass safeguarding and to embrace ECM wellbeing outcomes brings additional types of abuse into the child safeguarding frame, including acts perpetrated by other children, such as bullying. This has become an important element of the safeguarding agenda. One of the outcomes of ECM is to raise awareness that bullying is not confined to school environments. This has given rise to a number of initiatives to tackle bullying in other circumstances and a suite of government guidance documents covering play and leisure, youth activities, extended services in and around schools, public transport, children's homes, and gender bullying:

Bullying includes: name-calling; taunting; mocking; making offensive comments; kicking; hitting; pushing; taking belongings; inappropriate touching; producing offensive graffiti; spreading hurtful and untruthful rumours; or always leaving someone out of groups. It is also bullying when a young person is pressured to act against their will by others. (DCSF, 2009: 5)

The emphasis in government guidance is on preventing bullying and, where it cannot be prevented, on responding appropriately. If bullying incidents are not responded to, it gives a message to perpetrators that bullying is acceptable. One strategy in tackling bullying is to remove the audience factor. O'Connell et al.'s research (1999) shows that 85% of bullying occurs in front of an audience of bystanders. Bystanders actively and passively reinforce bullying. Getting professionals to adopt strategies that will encourage bystanders to walk away or even better go and tell an adult is an important part of the training guidance. It is equally important that practitioners model appropriate behaviour that demonstrates respect, absence of prejudice and fairness. Other measures include developing anti-bullying policies – ideally involving children in the process – and behaviour charters.

> ** ❝   Children's Experiences**
>
> **Robbie's story**
>
> 'At swimming they would hold me under the water until I thought I was going to drown, I couldn't breathe, they just let me go as I was going limp. The bullying happened everywhere – on the way to the pool there was a dark path with a ditch – they used to knock me into the ditch so I got all wet and muddy. They said I was gay after I accidentally picked up someone else's rucksack. It looked like mine. That made everyone move away from me in the changing room. The swimming teacher did not seem to notice. It went on for ages. It was the worst year of my life.'
>
> *Source:* DCSF, 2009: 17

The pervasiveness of multimedia technology in contemporary society has created a new form of abusive behaviour commonly termed 'cyberbullying'. The incidence of cyberbullying is increasing rapidly, especially through mobile phones and social networking websites where hurtful messages, humiliating photos or malicious material are posted. Conditional friendship is also a form of bullying, where children are allowed to become part of a gang on condition they perpetrate some act – the most extreme being membership of gangs that is conditional upon a child committing an offence or hurting someone.

> ## " Children's Perspectives
>
> When consulted by the children's commissioner for England, children identified bullying as one of their main priorities and when asked what would improve their lives the most, reducing bullying came up repeatedly. In many cases, children and young people said that bullying was either their main concern, or one of the most important concerns. For children and young people, bullying was:
>
> - Stopping them enjoying school
> - Making them afraid to go to school
> - Making them worried about transition to secondary school
> - Preventing their learning
> - Making them unhappy even in pre-school settings
> - Causing them worries about staying safe
> - Hampering their ability to make a positive contribution
> - Making them feel unsafe on the way to school on buses (11 Million, 2006).
>
> Children are often unsure and confused about why they are being bullied. In a consultation exercise undertaken by Leicestershire County Council (2003), these were some of the reasons given:
>
> - 'My curly hair.'
> - 'My strange name.'
> - 'Because I have glasses.'
> - 'I was rubbish at football.'
> - 'Because I am different.'
> - 'He didn't like me.'
> - 'Because I was new in the school.'
> - 'Because of clothes and the property that I owned.'
> - 'I don't really know because I didn't do anything to them.'

Once again, the importance of prevention strategies is highlighted. ECM has done much to raise awareness about bullying and to prompt some innovative intervention practice. All primary schools now have bullying policies. Examples of good practice include the construction of bullying training programmes across the primary age (see Table 10.1) and many mentoring and 'buddy' schemes run by children themselves, for example the Young Anti-Bullying Alliance (www.anti-bullyingalliance.org. uk/young_anti-bullying_alliance.aspx).

Table 10.1	Primary school learning objectives for bullying		

Foundation stage	Years 1 and 2 (age 5–7)	Years 3 and 4 (age 7–9)	Years 5 and 6 (age 9–11)
I know I belong in my classroom.	I can tell you what bullying is.	I know what it means to be a witness to bullying.	I understand how rumour spreading and name calling can be bullying behaviours.
I like the ways we are all different and can tell you something special about me.	I can tell you some ways in which I am the same and different from my friends.	I know that witnesses can make the situation better or worse by what they do.	I can explain the difference between direct and indirect types of bullying.
I can tell you some ways in which children can be unkind and bully others.	I am proud of the ways in which I am different.	I know how it might feel to be a witness to and a target of bullying.	I can explain some of the ways in which one person (or group of people) can have power over another.
I can tell you how it feels when someone bullies you.	I can tell you how someone who is bullied feels.	I can tell you why witnesses sometimes join in with bullying or don't tell.	I know some of the reasons why people use bullying behaviours.
I can be kind to children who are bullied.	I can be kind to children who have been bullied.	I can tell you some ways of helping to make someone who is being bullied feel better.	I know some ways to encourage children who use bullying behaviours to make other choices.
I know who I could talk to in school if I was feeling unhappy or being bullied.	I know that when you feel sad, it affects the way you behave and how you think.	I know that sometimes bullying is hard to spot, and I know what to do if I thin it is going on but I am not sure.	I can tell you a range of strategies which I have for managing my feelings in bullying situations, and for problem solving when I am part of one.
I know what to do if I am bullied.	I know some people in and out of school who I could talk to if I was feeling unhappy or being bullied.	I can problem solve a bullying situation with others.	
	I know what to do if I am bullied.		

Source: DfES, 2005a: 4

Interagency working

The whole process of safeguarding children is crucially dependent on different agencies working together, so it is all the more poignant that of all children's services, those involved in child protection have come in for the greatest criticism for poor interagency liaison, leading to catastrophic mistakes. Some of these have been detailed in earlier chapters. Despite tragedies such as Victoria Climbié, lessons were still not learned. The notorious Soham murders in 2002, in which Holly Wells and Jessica Chapman, two ten-year-old girls, lost their lives, revealed the extent of this. It was discovered that Ian Huntley, the murderer, had secured a job as a caretaker in a local school despite having been investigated by the police for several sexual offences and one burglary. Huntley had been cleared for work with children through the Criminal Records Bureau disclosure process. It transpired that Humberside police had destroyed records of Huntley's charges because they had not led to convictions. Among other reforms, the Birchard Inquiry into the Soham murders led to the setting up of the Independent Safeguarding Authority, which overhauled screening processes and proposed introducing a new vetting and barring system to replace List 99 (Protection of Children Act 1999) from 2009. This would have substantially widened the net for the vetting of individuals whose work or voluntary activity brings them into contact with children. The proposed new system attracted criticism for lack of clarity and guidance through complex arrangements, such as whether adults bringing children on school trips from overseas are required to register (Palmer, 2009). This led to Sir Roger Singleton authoring *Drawing the Line* (2009), a series of recommendations to clarify confusions and anomalies with the vetting and barring scheme. The first phase of registration was due to commence on 26 July 2010. However, the scheme was halted when the coalition government took office and a review is under way to scale back activity to what the government describes as commonsense levels, such as not requiring grandparents caring for grandchildren to be brought into the net.

Research by Stanley et al. (2010) shows that interagency working is still beset by communication difficulties and inadequate resources, despite a heightened focus on professional liaison required by the Laming Report (2003) and several subsequent inquiries. In particular, Stanley et al. (2010) recommend regular interprofessional training to ensure that staff in all organizations are aware of the impact of domestic violence on children and have knowledge of other professionals' roles and procedures.

With the new emphasis on broader safeguarding replacing protection, effective interagency working has to extend beyond protecting children from abuse. The new directives to prevent impairment of children's health and ensure optimum life chances require tighter liaison between health, social care and education professionals, especially in the early years. The introduction of multi-agency children's trust boards, the statutory duty to cooperate, and the requirement for jointly produced children's plans have done much to move forward organizational safeguarding liaison. Annual reporting on the twin approach to safeguard *and* promote wellbeing has been established, accountable to the joint chief inspectors. The DCSF document *Safeguarding the Young and Vulnerable* (2009a) details actions taken to implement the recommendations of the joint chief inspectors on progress against more effective multi-agency safeguarding.

" Children's Perspectives

When it comes to improving child safeguarding services and developing interagency working, children themselves have some advice to offer. Mullender et al. (2002) interviewed 1,400 children about their experiences of domestic violence and found that children wanted to be listened to, have their views taken seriously, play an active part in making decisions and in helping to find solutions. Gopfert et al. (2004, cited in Daniel, 2008: 101–2) concur with this. The young carers' group in their research offered the following recommendations to mental health professionals:

Introduce yourself, tell us who you are and what your job is.

Tell us what is going to happen next.

Give us as much information as you can.

Remember to talk to us: we have first hand experience of what is going on.

Keep on talking to us and keep us informed. Tell us it's not our fault.

Tell us if there is anyone we can contact.

Conclusion

High-profile child abuse cases such as Victoria Climbié prompted sweeping changes in child protection. Indeed, the ECM agenda itself emanated from this. Improved interagency working was singled out as a critical priority, although achieving this goal is still very much a work in progress. The shift of emphasis from child protection to safeguarding children added three dimensions to the previously named child protection: impairment of health or development; safe and effective care; and the promoting of optimum life chances. This had the result of blurring the boundaries between protection and wellbeing, and tensions emerged between professional bodies with different approaches to protection versus prevention. Concerns were voiced about the potential loss of specialist child protection expertise if this were subsumed into broader roles and responsibilities. Notwithstanding the horrific abuse that some children endure, an underpinning theme throughout the chapter has been children's expertise and agentic potential. This is undervalued. Adults rarely see beyond the victim roles they cast for children, which obscure the important part they can play in working with us to find solutions.

Reflection exercises

1. For all readers

Reading any text about child abuse, however academic or clinical, can be harrowing. Do not feel guilty or unprofessional if you have been emotionally affected by the content of this chapter. Take time to explore and understand your own feelings and to identify the whats and whys. Give yourself space to deal with your own emotions first and then you will be better placed to develop objective and critical engagement with the issues.

2. For staff working with children and young people in multidisciplinary teams

Reflect on how effective your team is at balancing the four aspects of child safeguarding (preventing maltreatment, preventing impairment of children's health and/or development, ensuring children are growing up in circumstances consistent with the provision of safe and effective care, enabling children to have optimum life chances and to enter adulthood successfully). Are there any tensions that need airing? Is some specialist expertise being smothered? Do you have a common and consistent approach to what *significant* harm is?

3. Children's perspectives

Bovarnick's (2007) research with children and young people about the incidence of neglect found that many of the participants did not like to categorize their circumstances as 'neglect', preferring to term this as 'not good care' even when they self-reported being persistently underfed and left unsupervised. Why do you think this might be? Can you try and put yourselves in their shoes? What cocktail of emotions might they be dealing with?

Suggested further reading

1. Metcalf, C. (2008) 'Making sense of sex offender risk and the internet', in P. Kennison and A. Goodman (eds) *Children as Victims*, Exeter: Learning Matters

   Presents the social constructions and political debates about child sex offender risk from the internet. Draws on the Soham murders to show how political agendas have been influenced.

2. Sayer, T. (2008) *Critical Practice in Working with Children*, Basingstoke: Palgrave Macmillan

   Has a strong practice focus and will be of particular interest to social workers. Several chapters cover protection and prevention and contain some detailed operational and legislative information. Chapter 4 includes a section on children in prison. Sayer is a very readable author and will take your thinking to new places.

3. Walker, G. (2008) *Working Together for Children: A Critical Introduction to Multi-agency Working*, London: Continuum

   Excellent book that is clearly written and particularly accessible. Two chapters devoted to child protection, the second of which explores issues pertinent to early years practice.

4. Nation states

   Department of Health, Social Services and Public Safety (2003) *Cooperating to Safeguard Children*, Belfast: Department of Health, Social Services and Public Safety

   Scottish Executive (2004) *Protecting Children and Young People: Framework for Standards*, Edinburgh: Scottish Executive

   Welsh Assembly Government (2007) *Safeguarding Children: Working Together under the Children Act 2004*, Cardiff: Welsh Assembly Government

Part III

Contemporary Issues

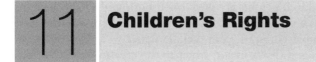

Children's Rights

In this chapter we discuss:

- ECM as a manifestation of children's rights
- Children's rights relating to physical assault
- Children's rights to 'active' citizenship
- Examples of children's active citizenship

ECM as a manifestation of children's rights

A dominant theme throughout this book is the consideration of children's own perspectives on the efficacy of an integrated approach to children's services and the extent to which their experiences of Every Child Matters (ECM) affect the quality of their childhoods. The rationale for this is based on a rights-constructed agenda. ECM amounts to little more than a mantra if it is not underpinned by a commitment to every child's rights. Every child has a right to a childhood free from poverty, neglect and abuse. The fact that many children get anything but such a childhood does not detract from their fundamental entitlement to one, just as the number of adults denied freedom of expression does not invalidate freedom of expression as a human right. The multiple definitions of childhood render conceptions of children's rights extremely complex. Within academic circles, children's rights are often discussed separately from human rights. However, this separation is itself a rights issue and there are calls for 'a re-integration of the isolated segments of the children's rights agenda within the frameworks of human rights' (Lenzer, 2002: 207). Others such as O'Byrne (2003) concur, maintaining that in so far as children are human, they are subjects of human rights standards and that age is irrelevant.

Freeman's (2009) distinction between the politics *for* children and politics *with* children is relevant here. In the former, children's rights are subsumed within a concept of childhood as being an integral part of family and therefore children as the possessions of parents. Hence rights, such as choice of schooling, are vested in the parents not the child: the only way children can exercise any right to school choice is by bringing influence to bear on their parents. In the latter, children's rights are positioned both within and beyond the family, with their own recognized status in society and access to the civil and human rights encompassed by modern welfare states.

It is widely acknowledged that a major driver in the creation of ECM was the UNCRC, and in particular the criticism of the Committee on the Rights of the Child of the UK government's failure to embed it in policy and practice (Freeman, 2009). The guiding principles of the UNCRC revolve around children's right to protection against violence, the right to an adequate standard of living, the right to education, to play and leisure and protection against all forms of exploitation (Tobin, 2006). Other rights documents have contributed, for example the European Convention on Human Rights and Fundamental Freedoms, 1950 and the European Social Charter, 1961, but ECM is now an important vehicle for change in the UK, and the integration of children's services gives added impetus to the fashioning of services around a rights-based agenda.

To consider children's services from a rights perspective requires a shift in thinking from a service-led to a needs-based approach. There is a tendency to provide for children according to what is available rather than what they need and, consequently, provision can fall short of what is required. Moreover, service provision decisions are in the adult domain and take little cognisance of children's views, commonly working through the proxy views of professionals and parents. This is a paternalistic perspective built on the premise that adults know best and always act in the best interest of children (see Chapter 2 for a fuller explanation). There are many who would challenge the assumption that intervention should be targeted at parents not children, not least children themselves. For children to be more involved in their service provision, effective listening mechanisms have to be put in place so that they can express their views and participate in decisions about their care. Importantly, children must be acquainted with the processes for making a complaint if they have a grievance about their service provision. A recent move towards direct payment schemes for adult service users, where they have control over what they buy with their service grant, is being extended to the parents of disabled children. This enables a system of personal budgets to be put in place that gives recipients of social care much more control over how they address their needs. Clients can receive direct payments, where all the allocated budget comes directly to them (in the case of disabled children, it will go directly to their parents or guardians) and they can employ their own care staff, arrange their own respite care, buy equipment they need, or decide to spend some of it on social activities to improve the quality of childhood.

Alternatively, an individual budget can be set up which is a mixture of direct payments and services that a local authority provides for the client on their instruction. This is a step in the right direction but there is a long way to go before all children using social care services are afforded the same rights and acknowledgement of entitlement to choice in the provision they receive.

The creation of a single government department (the former Department of Children, Schools and Families, now the Department for Education) to control children's services is a double-edged sword. On the one hand, a single department should be able to facilitate more closely integrated services, more robust child protection and better multi-agency working. On the other hand, it distils all the power into the hands of one secretary of state and one children's minister, whereas previous multiple government departments provided several key figures and, arguably, a more balanced governance. The danger of putting all the power into one department is that the focus will veer towards whatever the dominant party political primacies are at a given time. The fullness of time will reveal whether the coalition government's decision in 2010 to discontinue the DCSF in favour of a Department of Education (albeit one that includes children's services) is a signal that it intends education to dominate or whether this is just a new broom tactic to distance the coalition from New Labour.

There are many other aspects of children's everyday lives that we can look at from a rights' perspective. The right to fair and just treatment is a fundamental human right but one where children often draw the short straw. Sometimes it can be difficult to unpick what actions trigger events and whether original causes are inherent in children's behaviour or in the adult-dictated environments in which they are obliged to exist. In fact, it is not uncommon for children to take the blame for what is an adult-initiated problem. This is best explored through a concrete example. The number of school exclusions in Britain is increasing rapidly – and also the ages of exclusions are getting younger. Children in the UK start formal education much earlier than many of their European counterparts. Arguably, many children are not ready emotionally or in terms of their social maturity to cope with formal schooling. If they start school before they are ready and have to sit through formal instruction for long periods of time, they will likely become frustrated and disaffected. This can lead to the kinds of behaviours that ultimately result in school exclusions. How far back can the origins of exclusionary behaviour be traced and who is ultimately to blame – children or adults?

A rights issue that cuts across all three main providers of children's services – education, health and social services – is the control of children through powerful prescription medication. In years to come, history may judge this to have been one of the greatest forms of legalized child abuse to have scandalized the decades either side of the second millennium.

> **“ Children's Experiences**

Prescription rates for Ritalin and similar drugs used to treat attention deficit hyperactivity disorder (ADHD) have risen at an alarming rate. The greatest increase was in the 1990s. In 1991, prescription rates were around 2,000 and by 1999 had soared to 158,000, with the numbers still increasing into the 2000s. The administering of this drug is in the adult domain and children have no control over when and how it is used. Research highlights some disturbing findings:

> Since the indicators for ADHD cover behaviours that are ostensibly quite innocuous (such as fidgeting, being easily distracted, disliking schoolwork, talking excessively and interrupting) concerns have been expressed that the diagnostic criteria read more like a crime sheet of child and adolescent behaviours objected to by adults than any genuine disorder. (Coppock, 2002: 143)

The side effects from Ritalin and similar drugs can be extensive, with physical symptoms ranging from nausea, headaches and dizziness to mental health problems such as depression and psychotic episodes that lead to violent or bizarre behaviours (Rush and Baker, 2001). Thus the drug may, in some cases, be causing the very behaviours it is being prescribed to alleviate.

Ritalin is an amphetamine, which some adults try to get hold of for its psychotropic and performance-enhancing properties. On the street, it might be known as 'speed', 'kiddie coke' or 'poor man's cocaine'. Parents and teachers may agree to its use because it appears to alleviate the symptoms of ADHD. However, a study by Hechtman et al. (2005) at Montreal Children's Hospital found that after five years of continuous prescription, there was no hyperactivity behaviour difference between medicated and non-medicated children. This raises serious concerns and prompts me to question whether its practice is pursued more for the convenience of the children's carers than the wellbeing of the children.

I would suggest that before children are prescribed powerful drugs of this kind, other approaches are exhausted first. Simple dietary changes can sometimes be entirely effective without the need to resort to medication. Nutritional research has shown that the symptoms of ADHD can be reversed in 80% of children by eliminating processed foods and chemical food additives from their diets (www.naturalnews.com, n.d.). I would argue that, for many but not all children, the apparent 'disease' of ADHD may be no more than undesirable behaviour caused by extreme dietary imbalances. The popularity of physically interactive computer games consoles is also exploding the myth about ADHD. A child diagnosed with ADHD can sit for hours completely absorbed by and focused on a mentally and physically demanding game without resorting to deviant behaviour. This raises further questions about whether ADHD is a genuine medical hyperactive condition.

This takes us back to an argument, made repeatedly in this book, for more involvement of children in decisions that affect their lives. Only when children's rights are comprehensively addressed as fundamental human rights, their status as 'belongings' finally nullified, and their involvement in decision-making about their lives legitimated can they move to a position of genuine self-determination in society. Children are not in possession of economic assets and have little influence in economic planning or judicial deliberations: 'As we have learned from the history of non-represented groups, those in power are often able to ignore the interests of those who are absent from the table' (Kaufman and Rizzini, 2009: 432). The missing jigsaw piece, the elusive partner of integrated children's services would appear to be children themselves.

Children's rights relating to physical assault

The integration of children's services is having some beneficial effects in protecting children from legalized assault. The pulling together of services into one department has intensified the exposure of injustices in this respect. However, children are not afforded the same rights as other human beings. Physical chastisement can still be perpetrated against children, where this would be regarded as assault against an adult. Children as young as ten can be prosecuted for hitting another person but have no redress themselves against being 'smacked'. As we have seen in the previous section, children can be forced to take medication against their will, an act that would require a mental health section if the person were adult. These violations of human rights arise from historical standpoints about children being the 'property' of their parents and although significant inroads have been made towards restoring full human rights to children, the legislation in England and Wales still falls short of this. The Children Act 2004 was amended in 2005 with legislation to criminalize punishment of a child which caused visible bruising, grazes, scratches, minor swellings or cuts. The legislation was passed despite a revolt by 47 members of the sitting government who wanted a total ban on smacking. The new law is fundamentally flawed and impossible to police. As discussed in Chapter 10, it takes no account of the differences in children's skin types, such as those who bruise more easily than others, and implicitly affords more protection to fair-skinned white children than black children.

Other countries have gone further than England and Wales in legislating against physical chastisement. Scotland introduced an age limit to protect children under three from being smacked and was years ahead of England and Wales when, in 2003, it regulated exactly what kinds of punishments would be criminalized – shaking of the head, hitting the head and hitting with an implement – and the Scottish Executive regularly revisits the proposal for a total ban on physical chastisement. Many of our European partners already have full bans on smacking in place, with Sweden leading the way three decades ago in 1979. New Zealand became the sixteenth country to outlaw all forms of physical chastisement in 2007. All four of the UK's children's commissioners have called on the UK government to introduce legislation to ban the smacking of children. So far, governments have resisted the various pressures applied and have adhered to a position that 'reasonable chastisement' of children is a parental entitlement.

The UK position is at odds with international law and the United Nations. The UN Committee on the Rights of the Child publicly rebuked the UK in 2002 for persisting in retaining 'reasonable chastisement', which, in international law, is only a defence against common assault and therefore unjustifiable unless parents were defending themselves against common assault from their own children. The arguments for a total ban on smacking are mounting, with numerous pressure groups, including the UK-wide Children Are Unbeatable!

Alliance, mustering support, and more and more high-profile figures nailing their colours to the mast in public statements:

> Defining acceptable ways to hit children should become a thing of the past. It should be just as wrong to hit a child as it is to hit an adult. (Dame Mary Marsh, chief executive of NSPCC)

> There is no such think as 'a loving smack'. We want our children to grow up to be disciplined and to learn to handle their own angry feelings, and they do not learn that from being hit. (Baroness Helena Kennedy QC)

> All of us want to be around children who are considerate, well-behaved and who respect others, but physical punishment does not instil these values. Extensive data has shown that children who are frequently hit are more aggressive, and more prone to developing emotional and mental health problems, particularly depression. (Margaret McKay, chief executive of Children 1st)

References to the physical assault of children are frequently cloaked in terms such as smacking, tapping and slapping to disguise the violence occasioned. Reference to the physical assault of adults is more likely to use terms such as hitting, punching, thumping or beating. I fully expect that the UK will eventually support a total ban on physical chastisement of children, but how long this will be in coming is still unclear. My contention is that the integration of children's services into one department is more likely to bring this about than the previously fragmented structure, not least because the lobbying becomes more intense if it is focused on just one department. A counterargument is that power is now vested in one secretary of state rather than three so a particularly intransigent minister might more successfully employ stonewalling strategies.

There have been cases brought where parents see the curtailment of physical chastisement as an infringement of *their* rights. One such is the Williamson case (*R. (on the application of Williamson)* v *Secretary of State for Education and Employment*, UKHL 15 [2005] 2 AC 246). Here a group of parents and head teachers of fundamentalist Christian faith schools challenged the ruling on corporal punishment in schools on the basis that it went against their freedom of religion, claiming that corporal punishment was integral to their religion. Significantly, the views of the children did not feature at any stage of the proceedings – not only were their views not known, they were not even sought. In this particular case, they were being depicted as the property of their parents. I am encouraged by the fact that the case was ultimately lost.

Other examples serve to illustrate some adult attitudes towards children's rights. Freeman (2009: 378) cites the example of Julie Bindel, a freelance journalist, publishing an article entitled 'Six weeks of suffering', in which she argued for the six-week school summer holiday to be halved 'because the presence of children in her space – streets, parks, museums, public transport, restaurants – offends her':

> I live in an area where kids are routinely taken to proper restaurants for lunch, but I was here before it became Nappy Valley ... There seems to be no escape this summer. Ken Livingstone [the then Mayor of London] has made it easier for the little monsters to follow me around London by giving school children free bus travel ... There they are in the museums when you least expect them.

This article was not published in a tabloid newspaper but in *The Guardian* (18 August, 2006, p. 35). Freeman (2009: 379) does not hold back in his withering pillory:

> That it was written by the founder of 'Justice for Women' is all the more telling: that it was published in a leading liberal newspaper says much about how children are still perceived. If the article had focused on women or Muslims, there would have been an outcry ... Imagine The Guardian publishing an article which objected to black people in restaurants or gay people in museums!

Children's rights to 'active' citizenship

The changing views of childhood (as expounded in Chapter 3) have led to a re-evaluation of the concept of child citizenship. The so-called 'new sociology of childhood' (James et al., 1998), which outlawed the notion of children as becomings not beings, has placed greater emphasis on *active* citizenship for children rather than citizenship as a preparation for the responsibilities of adulthood. If children are no longer viewed as adults in waiting, then they can no longer be seen as citizens in waiting. It is widely acknowledged that children's citizenship status cannot be the same as adults because children do not enjoy the same civil rights or suffrage (Lister, 2007). Framing children's citizenship in these terms risks rendering it less equal and isolating it in what Cohen (2005) refers to as 'middle ground'. However, equality does not prohibit difference and it is this very sense of difference that we must prize if children's citizenship is ever to be anything other than rhetoric. As Waksler (1991) and Solberg (1996) remind us, children's competency is 'different' not lesser than adults. Should this not apply equally to citizenship? Children's citizenship can be different and still enjoy the same *status* as adult citizenship. This principle starts to unravel when children's citizenship is referenced to adult norms. Children's contribution to, and involvement in, society must be defined, enacted and evaluated from children's perspectives. For too long their participation has been in the gift of adults, an *allowing* of children's voice. This soft and fluffy end of listening to children is effective only where there is child compliance with adult agendas. It is a long way from the grittier realities of children choosing to use their participation rights to voice opposition to education and health policies, or oppose government decisions to wage war.

If child citizenship is to be active and consequential in children's everyday lives, then there have to be spaces created in which citizenship capacity can be developed and frameworks made available to accommodate this. Today, some of these processes do exist for older children, for example UK Youth Parliament, Funky Dragon in Wales, Scottish Youth Parliament and the Youth Forum in Northern Ireland, School Councils UK, and a number of youth forum groups and global organizations such as the First Children's Embassy, Macedonia, but this book is concerned with children aged 3–12, for whom active citizenship is still an evolving concept. The fact that youth citizenship is more advanced than children's citizenship should not detract from initiatives to build citizenship capacity for younger children. Indeed, one could argue that the stronger the roots of active child citizenship at an early age, the more effectively this will develop in youth.

In England, 11 Million is the name given to the English Office of the Children's Commissioner, the nomenclature reflecting the approximate number of children under 18 in England. Several initiatives to involve children, even very young children, in matters that affect them have been launched through 11 Million and specifically via its website (http://www. childrenscommissioner.gov.uk/). There is a designated area on the site for 0–4-year-olds ('Play and early years', via 'Have your say'), where young children can contribute their views by submitting drawings. In this area, short reports in plain English feature about consultation visits to children's centres to elicit young children's views about, for example, friendship, gender, equality and discrimination issues gathered via interactive games and activities. Any child of any age or ability can contribute to the 11 million website through 'Shape it' – an area of the website where children can create shapes to add to a dynamic jigsaw-like logo symbolic of child inclusivity. Significantly, the website invites children by means of multiple portals to have their say. Facilitations by 11 Million for children to express views and make contributions from early years onwards are important seeds of active child citizenship.

School councils have been a well-established component of secondary schools for many years now, less so in the primary sector. This is all changing and most primary schools now have a school council. When these work well, they are a good vehicle for active citizenship and provide opportunities for children to engage in decision-making, practise civil governance skills, develop responsibility, and stimulate agency.

The best models are those which have councils for every class in the school and representation from each of those class councils onto the main school council. In this way, all children can be involved at some level. This requires a commitment to regularly timetabled, formal meetings and systematic ways of feeding back. An effective school council is pupil led and concentrates on the core issues of the school, not adult-compliant topics that have been predetermined; innocuous examples that spring to mind are toilets, school lunches, recycling and pupil behaviour. It is somewhat concerning that the *School Council Handbook* (DfES, 2006e) is littered with these kinds of examples. Active child citizenship should encompass all school life. Teaching and learning, too often taboo territory for pupils, cannot be excluded.

" Children's Experiences

Some schools allow a school councillor to attend meetings of the governing body, others involve school councils in the appointment of staff. The following are some questions asked of a prospective deputy head teacher in an interview by primary pupils (Clay, 2005: 52):

Lauren: *Welcome to our school council meeting. My name is Lauren and I am the chairperson. This is Rachel and she is the secretary. We have taken a lot of time on these questions. John has the first question.*
John: **Why do you want to be a Deputy Headteacher?**
Lauren: *Charlie has the next question.*
Charlie: **What sorts of things will you do as a Deputy Headteacher?**
Lauren: *Maddie has the next question.*
Maddie: **Why do you really like this school?**
Lauren: *Jordan has the next question.*
Jordan: **What is the best thing in your classroom?**
Lauren: *Callum has the next question.*
Callum: **How do you tell people off?**
Lauren: *Joseph has the next question.*
Joseph: **Could you tell us about your rules in the classroom?**
Lauren: *Lauren has the next question.*
Lauren Cutler: **What sorts of subjects do you look after in your school?**

Lauren: *That's all of our questions.*
Do you want to ask us a question?
Thank you for coming.

Examples of children's active citizenship

First Children's Embassy

Between 1993 and 2007, the First Children's Embassy (FCE), based in Macedonia, ran children's rights workshops involving a total of 8,000 children. In 2003 it involved 60 children in a project called Civic Action through Theatre. A central rights issue for children in the Republic of Macedonia is access to education – 18,500 do not attend primary school. Among the adult population, 200,000 have never had any schooling. In 2009, as part of the Global Campaign for Education, FCE organized a silent march to show solidarity for all illiterate children. Four children were appointed as child ambassadors of the FCE and are lobbying the president to guarantee all children a primary education (First Children's Embassy, 2008/09).

Children's Parliament

Earlier, I alluded to organizations, such as Youth Parliament UK, as examples of civil governance initiatives for youth. So far, there have been few attempts to create similar opportunities for younger children. Scotland has led the way with the only major programme to date, with the Children's Parliament (CP) for children aged 9–14 (see www.childrensparliament.org.uk). Its core aim is 'to provide sustainable and meaningful opportunities for children of 14 and under to engage in local, national and international democratic processes'. An evaluation report highlighted many positives about the scheme but pointed to sustainable funding as being the main threat to its continuation (Britton et al., 2007). Two members of the CP were involved in a CP-commissioned research project called The Wee Democracy Project, which explored the extent to which children's rights could be embedded into family life. In earlier desk research conducted in 2005, Morrison and Fraser (2008: 3) reported finding little incidence of this:

> Despite some recognition of the UNCRC in the language of service providers, in policy and in legislation, for the most part when it comes to children's rights there has been little or no explicit or formal focus on children's rights in family life. It appears that the family has simply not been seen as a setting for implementation of the UNCRC or for the experience of rights. It would seem that for Government and for many agencies the family is still viewed as a private realm.

The Wee Democracy Project worked with children and parent family groups exploring rights issues within the family unit through an elaborate Arthurian quest that enabled contested issues to be addressed through fantasy role-playing and the artistic imagery of dragons, scrolls and magic. It was a successful project that raised awareness of UNCRC within families and had many positive outcomes for the enactment of democratic processes and the exercise of children's (and parents') rights within the family.

Children's Research Centre

The Children's Research Centre (CRC; http://childrens-research-centre.open.ac.uk) at the Open University focuses on optimal ways to develop children's research knowledge and skills and support children to undertake their own research. The CRC aims to minimize adult filters by shifting the balance to *supporting* rather than *managing* children's research. It offers diverse groups of children a taught programme of research process followed by assistance to carry out research projects about aspects of their lives that concern or interest them. The centre supports a variety of outreach programmes with links to schools and community organizations. Today, its website is host to over 100 research studies by children and young people. Some children undertake social research about issues that preoccupy adult researchers and policy makers, for example racial discrimination, poverty, bullying, social exclusion, educational attainment, knife crime and so on. Others research issues that impinge on their rights.

One such example is a study by Manasa Patil, aged 11 (Patil, 2006), who researched what it is like to be the child of a wheelchair user. Her research contended that such a childhood is blighted even though the child is not disabled. The failure of society to support a wheelchair-bound parent prevented the child from doing normal things children of that age enjoy (you can read Manasa's research in Chapter 3). Similar arguments have been made in research by young carers (see Tarapdar, 2007).

Children investigating their human rights

What Do They Know? (Davey, 2009), a research project undertaken by Children's Rights Alliance for England and funded by the national lottery, supported children and young people to investigate their human rights.

Around 1,362 children and young people completed an online survey and 346 children and young people took part in focus group interviews about what they knew of children's rights. The population sample was diverse in terms of age and geographical location and included Travellers, disabled young people, young people in care and those who are lesbian, gay, bisexual or transgendered. The research looked at six aspects of children's lives: respect and freedom; family and friends; health and safety; education; play and leisure; and crime and neighbourhood. Children and young people had strong ideas about what is important to them. These included:

- Knowing about and being able to exercise their rights
- Being part of a family, whatever that construction of family was
- Being respected and listened to
- The right to live in a good area with a sense of community.

Findings showed that very few children and young people knew about or understood their human rights. Even fewer knew how to seek redress if their rights were violated.

Conclusion

Freeman (2009: 388) regards the UNCRC as a beginning rather than the final word on children's rights:

> The Convention's scope is too narrow – there is, for example, too little attention to the girl child and to gay children or indigenous children or to citizenship rights. Its enforcement procedures are too weak. State parties are allowed to enter reservations and thus to opt out of important obligations ... The Convention is a convenient benchmark. Judged against it, the world continues to fail children.

There is a gap between the rhetoric of guaranteeing children's rights and the reality of those rights being violated on a daily basis all over the world (Kaufman and Rizzini, 2009). ECM is an important initiative in furthering children's rights but nevertheless encompasses those very gaps that Kaufman and Rizzini refer to. This is because the rhetoric does not translate into sufficient opportunities for children to build active citizenship capacity. Nor can a society which legitimates physical assault on children as a form of control demonstrate that it is serious about prioritizing their human rights. However, I remain hopeful that the intense discourse and gritty debates currently exercising professionals will eventually shift momentum within ECM closer to the reality rather than the rhetoric of children's rights.

Reflection exercises

1. For all readers

The Equality Act 2010 brings together all existing discrimination legislation and extends protection from unfair treatment. However, it explicitly excludes children and young people from legal protection from unfair discrimination on the grounds of age. Reflect on some of the likely consequences of this for children.

2. For staff working with children and young people in multidisciplinary teams

Rights 4 Me (www.rights4me.org) is the official website of the Office for the Children's Rights Director for England. It is written mainly to support children who are in a care situation. Spend some time exploring the website and then write an imaginary email (or a real one, if you wish) about your evaluation of the website.

3. Children's perspectives

Talk to some children about children's rights and listen to what they have to say, then ask them to prioritize the top five children's rights issues that they would implement if they had the power. Make a similar list from your own perspective, then compare how similar or different they are.

Suggested further reading

1. Alderson, P. (2008) *Young Children's Rights: Exploring Beliefs, Principles and Practice* (2nd edn), London, Jessica Kingsley

   An updated text and an excellent exploration, with rich examples, of rights issues for children under eight. Alderson is powerfully persuasive in her discussion of the competency and self-determination of young children. She urges much more active listening and consultation. The book is part of the Children in Charge edited series and has an interesting Forward written by Mary John.

2. Jones, P. and Welch, S. (2010) *Rethinking Children's Rights: Attitudes in Contemporary Society*, London: Continuum

   Part of the New Childhoods series. Takes a fresh look at some of the seminal children's rights debates and reviews how attitudes are changing in contemporary society. A particularly accessible text, with key questions articulated at the start of each chapter and helpful end of chapter summaries. It will challenge your thinking through, for example, exploration of how an understanding of negative responses to the rights agenda can be used to further children's rights.

3. Franklin, B. (ed.) (2001) *The New Handbook of Children's Rights: Comparative Policy and Practice*, Abingdon: Routledge

   Although published in 2001, it contains so many seminal debates that it is well worth dipping into. Organized in five parts, the first is an excellent overview of the developing rights agenda. Part 2 focuses on the legal aspects and Part 3 on some interesting case examples. Part 4 is organized around the listening agenda and Part 5 looks at the broader picture and comparative perspectives globally.

4. Freeman, M. (2005) 'Rethinking Gillick', *The International Journal of Children's Rights*, 13(1/2), 201–17

   An interesting article which re-examines the UK Gillick ruling of 1989 that upheld a child's right to make their own decision when of sufficient understanding and intelligence against parental wishes. Freeman describes this as a false dawn and discusses the retreat by English courts. He calls for a new Gillick, which puts goals and values in the forefront, and places less emphasis on knowledge and understanding.

12 Children's Participation and Voice

In this chapter we discuss:

■ Models of participation
■ The evolving participation agenda
■ What do we mean by voice?
■ How can integrated children's services best facilitate child voice?
■ Participation and voice as agency

Models of participation

Listening to children and encouraging their active participation in matters affecting them is a recent, increasingly prolific and arguably the most important dimension to integrated children's services. As alluded to in Chapter 2, the criticism by the UN Committee on the Rights of the Child of the UK's ineffectual attempts to deliver on Articles 3 and 13 of the UNCRC (listening to, and consulting with, children) was a prime driver of Every Child Matters (ECM) and the aspiration to make children's participation transparent and meaningful. Historically, children have been denied decision-making rights on the basis of moral and cognitive incompetence, as epitomized in the paternalist stance of so-called 'child savers' (Archard, 2004). This standpoint has been challenged by liberationists, who argue that even young children can make rational decisions (Hyder, 2002; Lansdown, 2004). It is worth noting that in Norway, where it is a legal requirement that children must be given the opportunity to express themselves, the age of participation has been lowered from twelve to seven. Although we are still some way from this position in the UK, the ECM agenda has kick-started a process through which meaningful participation of all children could become a reality.

The participation agenda evolved in three phases: listening, consulting and involving children in decision-making processes. Hart's (2002) much-cited 'ladder of participation' was the first real attempt to define participatory practices with children but has been criticized for its sequential nature (Reddy and Ratna, 2002) and its hierarchical value structure (Hart et al., 2004). Shier's model (2001) emphasizes collaborative activity between adults and children to optimize participation and builds a continuum, with children being listened to at one end and sharing power and responsibility for decision-making at the other. Treseder's model (1997) is less hierarchical and takes account of children's heterogeneity and levels of participation reflecting individual difference. His model focuses on degrees of involvement, with five non-hierarchical categories: consulted and informed; assigned but informed; adult-initiated, shared decision with children; child-initiated and directed; child-initiated, shared decisions with adults. Francis and Lorenzo (2002: 161) refer to seven 'realms' of children's participation, with a specific focus on environmental agendas (Table 12.1).

Table 12.1	Seven realms of children's participation			
Realm	**Theory**	**Objective**	**Audience**	**Limitations**
1. Romantic	Planning 'by' children. Children define and make their own future, often without adult involvement. Much of the 'rights' movement grew out of this approach	Child-defined cities	Schools, communities, architects and planners, futurists	Relies on children to envision and make their own communities, future environments, etc. Did not typically involve adults in process
2. Advocacy	Planning 'for' children with needs advocated by adult planners	Represent the interests of children by advocating their needs as adult professionals	Citizen groups, public planning bodies making decisions that affect the lives of children	Not holistic. Often creates separate plans and places. No attempt at consensus building with other interests outside those being 'advocated for'
3. Needs	Research-based approach that addresses children's needs	Define the spatial needs of children and incorporate them into design	Largely academic but has expanded to include design and policy makers	Sometimes does not recognize the importance of children's participation in advancing knowledge
4. Learning	Participation through environmental education and learning	Learning outcomes of participation are as important as physical changes. Architects teach children about architecture	Teachers, environmental educators	Designers and decision makers do not always use research knowledge; children are frequently not directly involved in research. Process changed perceptions and skills but not many physical places

5. Rights	Children have rights that need to be protected	Mandate children's participation in planning and city decision-making	City officials, international organizations	Tends to focus more on children's rights and less on their environmental needs
6. Institutionalization	Planning 'by' children but within institutional boundaries set by adults, authorities and clients	Mandated/ required child participation	Typically official city plans and programmes	Tends to create limited results or results counter to what children really want
7. Proactive	Planning 'with' children. Combines research, participation and action to engage children and adults in planning and design. Children are active participants in process but designers/planners play an important role	Develop participatory plans and designs with children that incorporate their ideas and needs. Plans should be focused on strong vision of empowering children and making substantive changes to the city environment	Children, community organizations, design professionals	Not always possible in every project; requires designers/planners with special training and skills

Source: Adapted from Francis and Lorenzo, 2002: 161–2

The evolving participation agenda

Despite the rhetoric surrounding the build–up to ECM, entrenched adult–child power relations meant that institutional change, brought about by meaningful child participation, was slow in coming. Various initiatives were set up to oil the wheels. One such was the children's fund. The children's fund is a preventive service for children aged 5–13 who are at risk of social exclusion. It was originally set up in three phases between 2000 and 2003 as a transitional fund, but proved to be highly successful and enjoyed a number of funding extensions. The funds are divided between local authorities who involve voluntary and community sector partners in the strategic planning and delivery of projects aimed at improving the life quality of vulnerable, isolated or disadvantaged children. Projects are commonly about children's home life, leisure, health and education, and children themselves are involved in planning and monitoring them (Leverett, 2008). In their national evaluation of the children's fund, Coad and Lewis (2004) drew attention to the development of research-based approaches to elicit the views of children and a mushrooming of child-friendly methods to generate evaluation data, such as photographs, videos, drama, mappings, role play, storytelling and diaries.

> ## Children's Perspectives

Headliners (formerly Children's Express, relaunched as Headliners in 2007) is a children and young people-led group. It facilitates journalism training for children and young people and then supports them to write stories on issues that are important to them for publication in national and local newspapers, magazines, television and radio. The group has produced over 1,200 stories for public dissemination since its foundation in 1994.

Jordan, 12

My name's Jordan and I've been a member of Headliners for roughly three years now. I first got involved with Headliners through another group known as the Children's Parliament. We went on a trip to the office because we were being interviewed for Loud 'n' Clear magazine. I really liked it there, so I joined at the following training session!

Since I joined, Headliners has enabled me to do the sorts of things I never thought I'd be able to do. I've been on the radio twice, and made a feature for the BBC on school dinners, which was really exciting.

This year I wrote a story after learning about what it means to become a <u>vegetarian</u> and trying it for a week. It got published in the Japanese Times! I also wrote for Children Now magazine about participation.

I like being able to go and do stories and ask questions. I also like that you can tell the staff how you want the organisation to run. I even got to do the interviews for some new members of staff.

Source: http://www.headliners.org/aboutus/whoweare/youngpeople/young_people

Headliners give children and young people a means of expressing their views. Sometimes children's views are in direct conflict with the adults who hold the power and make the decisions.

You've got to fight for your right to ... hug

Do you think hugging is a form of bullying? Well, the teachers at [name of academy] do. They have enforced a rule that says there will be no physical contact, which includes hugging and embracing. According to staff at the academy, hugging or any sort of physical contact could be classified as a form of bullying. Is the school going too far? And, if so, are they trying to bring back the severity of schooling from the olden days?

From our point of view, hugging is just a form of affection – but perhaps this is what they're scared of? However, even if it is, affection is still part of growing up and teenage life. It's as if they don't want us to grow up and become responsible young adults.

Hugging is like a greeting to us and, without it, we feel like we haven't said hello properly. It seems that many of the things that young people enjoy in school life are being banned, and it feels like the years that are said to be "the best years of our lives" are being limited and monitored closely.

There seems to be no freedom in school anymore, and soon there will be nothing left for the children.

By Crystal and Nyasha, both aged 13

Source: http://www.headliners.org/storylibrary/stories/2007/hugging

Mittler and May-Chahal (2004) carried out an evaluation of the St Helen's Children's Fund. Their report illustrates numerous examples of the kind of community projects initiated to support vulnerable children and nurture an ethos of participation. Many of the projects were set up as after-school and holiday clubs to enhance play and wellbeing opportunities. Others were set up to improve community services for vulnerable families. An example is Family Well Being, an early intervention service to support children and their families and enhance wellbeing. Another is the Keeping Children Safe service which includes a Junior Youth Inclusion programme of safety awareness for children. Bullying and transition are major sources of stress, and strategies for children to deal with them are addressed through workshops, drama and peer mentoring. Staff attend multi-agency family forums and other interdisciplinary groups. Indeed, the activities of many local children's funds might be viewed as a successful microcosm of effective multi-agency working more generally.

Other activities that feature in the evaluation report include a Children's Voices Group which acts as a consultation group for the St Helen's Children Fund activities and evaluation. The children also have the opportunity to have a say in what the fund is used for in St Helen's. They participate and comment on events, training, recruitment panels and evaluation. Sharon's story, below, is an example of a child's personal experience of involvement in the St Helen's Children Fund.

> ## " Children's Perspectives
>
> ### Sharon's story
>
> #### Background situation and concerns
>
> Sharon, aged 9 years, had frequent separations from her mother and had very little contact with her father from an early age. Both her parents were drug users. Sharon and her brothers and sisters were in alternative care, each with different relatives. When Sharon came to live with her relatives she also changed schools. She was withdrawn and unhappy and found it difficult to make friends. She was unused to boundaries and reacted with temper and moodiness. She lacked social skills and was awkward in social situations.
>
> #### Work done by Family Well Being
>
> Sharon was referred by her new head teacher to the After School Club. Staff encouraged her to:
>
> ■ participate in all the creative activities and games
> ■ interact and cooperate with the other children
> ■ express her feelings and views

However, staff noticed that Sharon became tearful at any mention of mothers. The worker for the Living Together in Families service (LIFT) designed for children who experience trauma, loss or bereavement or other major change offered individual sessions for Sharon to work with her in greater depth, including:

■ exploring her feelings and worries
■ story work relevant to her situation
■ discussion of how to express her anger/other negative feelings in a safe way
■ encouraged her to develop her creativity, including story writing
■ advocated for her to be directly involved in decision making re future care arrangements

Outcomes

Sharon is now:

■ settled in school and in the family
■ more accepting of boundaries
■ has made a good friend in whom she can confide
■ has greatly increased her confidence
■ using a diary to write down worries and concerns
■ in regular contact with her brothers and sisters and her mother
■ more caring towards others

Sharon says, "Now I am happier in groups. I can play with people and talk to adults. I get on OK with work at school. I've got more confidence. I've learned to be a lot calmer and to think about Mum with happy thoughts".

Source: Mittler and May-Chahal, 2004: 25

Fostering meaningful participation

The challenge for integrated children's services is to implement meaningful participation of children without tokenism and to avoid box-ticking initiatives that appear to give decision-making processes legitimacy but in reality have little substance or value. The token black child, wheelchair user and young person with learning disabilities regularly appear in adult-convened children's groups. However, there are some groups which foster meaningful participation by children. Participation Works is a consortium made up of six agencies: the British Youth Council, Children's Rights Alliance for England, National Children's Bureau, National Youth Agency, National Council for Voluntary Youth Services and Save the Children UK. Its primary purpose is to enable organizations to involve children effectively in the development, delivery and evaluation of services that affect their lives and to bring about positive change. Hear by Right (http://www.nya.org.uk/quality/hear-by-right; see also Badham and Wade, 2005) and the Young Researchers Network (http://www.nya.org.uk/integrated-youth-support-services/young-researcher-network) are both initiatives set up within the National Youth Agency. The former provides guidance for statutory and voluntary organizations to improve the ways in which they involve children and young people in decision-making. The latter supports children and young people who want to undertake their own research. The Children's Research Centre at the Open University (http://childrens-research-centre.open.ac.uk) is an organization which exists solely to support research *by* children about matters that concern them and features over 100 original research studies by children and young people.

There are demonstrable benefits of children's active participation on their personal and social development (Sinclair, 2004; Kellett, 2005) and their involvement has begun to impact on the growth in service user-led training for professionals in the children's workforce (Leverett, 2008). However, there is still a paucity of evidence about how children's participation impacts on service development (Cavet and Sloper, 2004). According to Leverett (2008: 195):

> The continued involvement of children can only be achieved, and
> sceptics (both children and adults) won over, if participation is shown
> to result in improvements to children's quality of life. If participation
> becomes an end in itself, there is an inherent danger that people will
> not be open and honest about what does and does not work.

Article 12 of the UNCRC refers to the right of every child 'capable of forming his or her own views' to participate, so age should not be a barrier to involving even very young children. One can argue that babies are capable of forming views which they express in non-adult language. Alderson (2008) maintains that participation for young children begins in the less observed and more private world of the family and develops over time. It is helpful to think of a continuum of participation that increases throughout childhood as children's competences, agency and skills develop. It is the responsibility of adults to support children and create spaces for them to develop participatory skills. Lansdown (2009) emphasizes the importance of these grassroots structures. Such has been the pressure from policy makers to ensure participation is seen to happen that the risk of tokenism replacing sustainability is very real and has been alluded to above. This brings us to a consideration of children's voice.

What do we mean by voice?

Participation is the act of doing and being involved. There is a danger that it becomes no more than this and children merely participate in participation. Voice, on the other hand, is the right to free expression of views that may or may not emanate from participation. Lundy (2007: 933) maintains that voice is constituted in four parts not one:

- *Space:* Children must be given the opportunity to express a view
- *Voice:* Children must be facilitated to express their views
- *Audience:* The view must be listened to
- *Influence:* The view must be acted upon as appropriate.

This is a helpful orientation and highlights the ineffectiveness of voice operating in a vacuum. Before children can exercise voice, there have to be the right conditions in place and mechanisms to carry that voice to an audience in a way that can influence society. Creating space for children to express their views is underpinned by the 'assurance' of this as cited in Article 12 of the UNCRC. This means that governments have to be proactive rather than passive in providing for, and encouraging, children to express their views in safe spaces without fear of reprisal. Again, we return to the importance of the role of integrated services in this process. Children, as end users, have the same need of voice across all their services and there is more chance of achieving this if all services adopt equivalent standards and points of reference. It is interesting to note attitudinal shifts in education policy, particularly the embracing of pupil voice, since the amalgamation of the three big children's departments. In November 2008, the government announced new legislation relating to the expression of pupil views in the form of the Education and Skills Act 2008 (DfES, 2008b: para. 199):

> *Section 157* inserts a new section 29B into the 2002 Act, the effect of
> which is to place duties on governing bodies of maintained schools
> in England and Wales to invite the views of registered pupils about
> prescribed matters, and consider any views on those matters expressed
> by pupils (whether or not in response to an invitation) in light of
> their age and understanding. The matters on which governing bodies
> must consult pupils are to be prescribed by regulations made by the
> Secretary of State for England and the Welsh Ministers for Wales (and
> paragraph 79 of Schedule 1 prescribes the procedure in the National
> Assembly for Wales for the latter).

In my view, schools have buttressed adult–child power relations long beyond other children's service providers who have accepted varying degrees of democratization. Outside youth offending institutions, schools are places where children are least able to exercise their human rights. Their time, use of space, mode of dress, times of eating and genre of social interaction are controlled by adults (Kellett, 2005a). The cross-fertilization of participatory agendas within the integrated framework of children's services can only help to diminish such autocracy and enable children to have more say in the educational decisions that affect them (see Chapter 5).

How can integrated children's services best facilitate child voice?

Voice is best developed through opportunities which reflect local needs, interests and children's preferred ways of engagement, so that children's voices do not simply reinforce adult perspectives and adult governance (Wyness, 2006). This can be facilitated by an integrated approach to the creation of child-friendly spaces in which to nurture voice which is fair and equitable to all and not a postcode lottery. Multi-agency working can support the construction of child-led infrastructures for the exercising of voice. Importantly, an integrated and universal approach to the training of adults in ways to overcome their resistance to child voice is called for (Bennett Woodhouse, 2003).

The requirement for audience means that adults have to *listen* to children and not just *hear* what they say. Many children do not express their views in words. For these children to be heard, adults need to know how to interpret their nonverbal cues. Ultimately, adults still have the power to decide how to listen. Indeed, they can listen and then choose not to act on anything they hear. Once voiced, children's views do not necessarily progress to a point of influence. A combination of circumstances is needed for child voice to have influence, not least a predisposition on the part of adults to value what children have to say and to appreciate the uniqueness of their perspective. Better understanding leads to better provision for children. Taking us a step nearer to realizing influential children's voice would be the introduction of a form of listening accountability, such as a requirement on the part of services to demonstrate *how* they provide opportunities for children to participate in decision-making, and a similar mandate to account for *how* they feedback to children after consultations would be prescient. There are some excellent examples of consultation activities and joint research projects where children's voices have influenced outcomes and policy, but these are still relatively sparse on the overall canvass.

" Children's Perspectives

The following extract is taken from a research project by Eleanor Frank (2005: 1–3), aged 11, about children's experiences of their local housing estates.

I wanted to find out what children from years 4 to 7 (8 years old to 13 years old) felt about Fishermead and Springfield. I used a questionnaire to find out in a very basic form what children felt of the two estates. The questionnaires were anonymous, so that the children would feel safe giving away their opinions ... I wanted to find out how children felt going outside on their own, or with someone else, and at what times they felt comfortable, and what they did on the estates. I also used in-depth interviews with a small group of children ...

I used a video to pinpoint what it really looked like in Fishermead and Springfield, to show the litter and graffiti, and in my video I had an unplanned interview with two girls who lived on Fishermead, and I got a chance to discover how it felt for other children who lived on the estate. There were places where I knew I was going to record, but also parts that just happened to be there at the time I was videoing. I used a storyboard to plan it. ...

So far my interviews have shown that children do not feel safe on the estates, other than when they are in their homes. Children have the right to feel safe wherever they go, and they also have the right to have fun, be it at the shop or not, and taking away these two rights is something that should never happen.

All of the children I interviewed thought that there should be more clubs on the estates and more things to do ... The younger children all seemed to want the same thing - a quiet club to go to, to feel safe and away from bullies. Sports club were also an issue. Emily in year 4 says that the youth club on Springfield starts too late, and the only clubs she does on Springfield are school based. The younger children wanted clubs that started straight after school.

There are parks to play on in Springfield and Fishermead, but the interviews proved that children feel unsafe going to them. Billy from year 4 says he only ever goes to the park if his mum is watching ... In my video, all the equipment at the park had been vandalized.

Participation and voice as agency

Although children in the UK are not, as yet, directly involved in the construction of legislation, there are examples of their voice influencing some local policy issues. Children making contributions to law reform already happens in some other countries.

Children's Perspectives

In South Africa, children from age 11 upwards were actively involved in the drafting of the Children's Act and its subsequent amendments between 2003 and 2007 (Jamieson and Mukoma, 2009). A group of 12 children, representing four provinces, participated in parliamentary hearings and public debates about the Children Bill. The Children's Institute at the University of Cape Town provided training and legal advice for the participating children as well as funding transport to public events. Workshops helped the children with the 300 clauses of complex legal text in the draft Bill. The children were able to make particularly pertinent contributions on behalf of vulnerable children affected by HIV/AIDS:

I've got six other siblings, four of which are HIV positive. I am taking care of my four siblings with my old grandmother and that doesn't mean my mother is not alive. She is very alive but the problem is that she doesn't stay at home with us and take care of us. She is always away and when she comes home she comes drunk and she abuses us emotionally. This affects me mentally. I cannot cope well with my school and I don't have enough time to rest. (child's words at one of the public hearings of the Children Bill, cited in Jamieson and Mukoma, 2009: 76)

Percy-Smith and Thomas (2009) remind us that a rights-based concept of participation, in so far as it represents an entitlement to have a say, is not enough. For them, the most effective participation is that where children work 'as members of a community where roles and responsibilities are shared, where "agency" rather than "voice" is the key concept' (Percy-Smith and Thomas, 2009: 359). Participation as agency is not solely about making a difference through measurable outcomes but is also about process and learning. Young children begin to participate through everyday family practices and this learning curve continues throughout childhood, as children gradually take up more and more opportunities in society to exercise agency. As Fitzgerald and Kay (2009) state, participation is about achieving inter-subjectivity and shared responsibility that deepen intergenerational relations.

The interface of social participation and community agency is potentially a more powerful form of child involvement than voice initiatives, many of which imitate adult governance structures such as youth parliaments and youth councils (Thomas, 2007). Local community participatory initiatives that start in relatively small ways are more likely to be sustainable and provide platforms on which more extensive political links can ultimately be built. Adult responsibilities lie in putting the empowering structures in place that will provide children with the right kinds of opportunities and in being willing to exchange some power and control for advocacy and facilitation. These enabling environments can be developed throughout childhood on a continuum that starts in the home and moves through school, community, and regional and national levels of intergenerational engagement.

Finally, the impact of children's participation should not be overlooked. This is not impact in the sense of measurable outcomes to satisfy a tick-box mindset, but impact as efficacy in relation to children's self-development, skill expansion and active citizenship. This broader realization of children's agency can be used to good effect across the full spectrum of integrated children's services.

Conclusion

This chapter has explored a range of models of participation and discussed how voice complements participation rather than being integral to it. A strong theme is the potential for participation and voice to be translated into agency and active citizenship, and how this can be harnessed to more meaningful participation, in the sense of children being involved in decision-making about matters that affect them. This has important ramifications for the involvement of children in the evaluating and shaping of children's services. A consequence of the increasingly political rhetoric about participation has been an increase in the numbers of children invited onto advisory groups and steering committees. The natural progression from meaningful participation is towards children leading initiatives such as evaluations and investigations. This takes us to the focus of the penultimate chapter which examines issues relating to children undertaking their own research.

Reflection exercises

1. For all readers
Reflect on what you consider to be the difference between participation and voice. Jot down some examples of each and consider why they might be different.

2. For staff working with children and young people in multidisciplinary teams
Reflect on where you are on the participation spectrum in your own multidisciplinary team. Are some in a different place than others? It can be a useful exercise in a staff development session to compare where each of you position yourself on the participation spectrum. Consider using masking tape to create a participation line down the middle of the room and each stand on it where you feel you are most comfortable in your practice.

3. Children's perspectives
Look again at Crystal and Nyasha's piece about adults viewing hugging as a form of bullying and children viewing it as a vital expression of affection. It is an example of how easily adult and children's perspectives can become polarized and their standpoints opaque to one other, when in fact the issue is much more complex, with well-made points on both sides. Presumably adults have taken this stance from a protectionist position which has not been explained to the children. How would you go about drawing the two positions closer together and reaching a better understanding about the pros and cons of hugging at this academy?

Suggested further reading

1. Lundy, L. (2007) 'Voice is not enough: conceptualizing Article 12 of the United Nations Convention on the Rights of the Child', *British Educational Research Journal*, 33(6), 927–42

   An interesting and much-cited article which sets voice out as four parts rather than a single whole: space, voice, audience and influence. It is useful to take Lundy's model and work through the four aspects in your own practice.

2. Sinclair, R. (2004) 'Participation in practice: making it meaningful, effective and sustainable', *Children & Society,* 18(2), 106–18

   Published soon after ECM, a powerful article that discusses the gap between rhetoric and reality. Illustrated with numerous examples of where participation is tokenistic.

3. Thomas, N. (2007) 'Towards a theory of children's participation', *International Journal of Children's Rights*, 15(2), 199–218

   If you are interested in a more in-depth discussion of the theoretical discourses on participation, this will extend your thinking. Drawn mainly from a sociological perspective, it draws on a range of international participation examples and posits some challenging views on political perspectives and where the application of participation theory is taking us. Not an introductory text – presupposes some prior knowledge of participation agendas.

4. Percy-Smith, B. and Thomas, N. (eds) (2009) *A Handbook of Children and Young People's Participation: Perspectives from Theory and Practice*, Abingdon: Routledge

   Presents the most comprehensive recent work in children's participation. An edited collection of chapters by experts in this field. Introduces key concepts and debates and presents a rich collection of accounts of the diverse ways in which children's participation is understood and enacted around the world, interspersed with reflective commentaries from adults and young people. Applies theoretical insights to challenge practice and enhance children's rights and citizenship.

Children as Researchers

A rationale for children as researchers

A book about integrated children's services, especially one with a focus on how children are experiencing Every Child Matters (ECM), would not be complete without a chapter devoted entirely to children's own research. Child-led research provides a valuable insider perspective on how ECM and integrated services are working for children. A corollary of the sharper focus on children's rights and an increased participation agenda, where children are more involved in issues that affect their lives, has been the empowerment of children as researchers in their own right. This parallels developments in other user settings such as disability emancipatory research, minority ethnic research and gendered research (Kellett, 2005a). As detailed in Chapter 2, the impetus of the UNCRC (1989) saw a shift from children as objects of research to subjects in research (James et al., 1998) and later to participant researchers (Lansdown, 2004). The realization that children could be agents in their own worlds provided momentum towards a gradual acceptance that children could be more than participants in research, they could be co-researchers (Nieuwenhuys, 2001; Jones, 2004). However, even though this was accompanied by greater consultation with children, criticism was still levelled at the tokenism and adult manipulation of children's co-participation (Sinclair, 2004). Unequal power relations persisted. Adults still framed the research questions, chose the methods and controlled the analysis. Children were partners only in the generation of data. It was increasingly common for adults to design a project and not involve children until the data collection phase. Equally common were situations where adults analysed children's data, rather than the children themselves, on the pretext that analysis is 'too difficult' for children. This imposes a layer of adult-mediated interpretation that significantly undermines the value of the child-generated data. Children must be involved in the analysis of their own data wherever possible because it is they who understand the context in which it has been collected.

Since the turn of the century, the political participation agenda has been heating up and more children have been invited onto steering committees and advisory groups. However, it required another step change to challenge the status quo. This came with a move to empower children to lead their own research (Kellett, 2003; Kellett et al., 2004a). Such an approach enables children to set their own research agendas and choose to investigate what they, rather than adults, identify as important. It offers a new paradigm in which children determine the focus of exploration, choose the methods of investigation, and actively disseminate their own findings. Hitherto, the missing link has been children's – especially primary-aged children's – research knowledge and skills. Scepticism still abounds as to the ability of this age group to engage with the research process. I hope the examples in this chapter and elsewhere in the book will go some way to countering some of that scepticism.

Age and competency issues

Perceived lack of competence has been a principal barrier to children undertaking their own research (Alderson and Morrow, 2004), and age in particular a common delineating factor. These perspectives have been widely challenged (Alderson, 2000; Kellett, 2005a; Woodhead and Faulkner, 2008) and supplanted by the principle that social experience, not age, is a more reliable marker of competence (Christensen and Prout, 2002). Moreover, children's competence should be regarded as different from, not less than, adults' competence (Solberg, 1996). Age and competency barriers have been further broken down by research such as Clark and Moss's (2001) 'mosaic' approach, in which very young children actively participate in data collection. Clark (2004) describes how she used a variety of different methods to explore what three- and four-year-olds felt about their early years environments. Children's centres are a crucial resource of ECM and accessing the perspectives of young children about these settings is highly informative. Clark cast herself in the guise of non-expert so that she could listen and learn from the young children. She adopted child-friendly participatory methodologies to elicit perceptions through young children's own eyes, such as children taking photographs of their early years environments, guiding adults on tours of their settings, drawing pictures and making maps. She combined this with her own observations and conversations with children in order to build a mosaic-style depiction of their worlds through their windows.

Another barrier commonly cited is the belief that children do not have sufficient knowledge and understanding to investigate subjects to the depth required by empirical research. Undoubtedly, adults have greater knowledge than children in many areas of life but with regard to childhood itself – in the sense of what it is like to be a child – it is children who have the expert knowledge (Mayall, 2000). If children are empowered to research issues that emanate directly from their own experiences, they can unlock inherent knowledge about their worlds and subcultures.

Reflecting on the skills needed to undertake research, it is apparent that these are not synonymous with being an adult, they are synonymous with being a researcher, and most researchers undergo some kind of training. A barrier to empowering children as researchers is not their age or adult status but their lack of research skills.

Empowerment

None of these barriers is insurmountable and it should be entirely possible to empower children and young people to lead their own research (Sinclair, 2004; Kellett, 2005). Empowerment goes beyond recognizing children's rights and expertise. It requires the provision of meaningful opportunities that enable children to build participation capacity in order to become more effective participators and ultimately more effective researchers. Other benefits, such as raised self-esteem, have also been linked to increased partici- pation (Lansdown, 2002).

Most adults cannot undertake quality research without some form of training and unless children are given similar opportunities, we will not discover what they are capable of. Until recently, the level of research training commonly afforded to children was either nonexistent or confined to a discrete element such as a pre-identified data collection method. Child participant researchers were not routinely taught about the rationale for research, the power of research or the ethics of research. I have argued persistently (Kellett, 2003, 2005a, 2009) that children need to be trained in a comprehensive range of research methods so that they can make informed choices about what might be the best methods to employ – or indeed whether they might need to design something new if traditional approaches do not fit the nature of their investigation. Interest in children's participation in research has spawned a growth in child-friendly methods of collecting and presenting research, for example storyboards, artwork, songs, drama, mapping, photography, interactive questionnaires and ranking activity games.

The Children's Research Centre (CRC) at the Open University offers children the opportunity to be trained by university research staff through a range of outreach projects. Several years of pilot work led to the construc- tion of a differentiated teaching programme (Kellett, 2005a). This 18-hour interactive programme introduces children to the nature of research, ethics, the refining of a research question, data collection techniques, data analysis approaches and dissemination skills. Once trained, children embark on a research study of their own choosing about aspects of their lives that concern or interest them. The CRC focuses on optimal ways to develop children's research knowledge and skills and supports them to undertake their own research. It aims to minimize adult filters by shifting the balance to *supporting* rather than *managing* children's research. Today, the website (http://childrens-research-centre.open.ac.uk) is host to over 100 original research studies by children and young people aged nine upwards.

Children as researchers and ECM

We established in Chapter 11 that children have a *right* to be involved in decisions that affect their lives. Some of that decision-making is informed by research. This suggests an imperative to engage with children at an active rather than a passive level, what Christensen and James (2000) refer to as 'cultures of communication'. ECM is about and for children, so it is entirely fitting that children's own research, sourced from their perspectives, should provide us with knowledge that can inform our understanding. Many children choose to research topics about their daily lives such as their school experiences, consumer incidence, or family matters. Others undertake social research about issues that overlap with adult agendas, for example political governance, racial discrimination, poverty, crime and social exclusion. All can provide us with valuable insights into children's lived experiences.

Research by children can and should inform policy since it generates new knowledge from children's perspectives which adults are unlikely to be able to access. However, influence brings responsibility. There is a responsibility that children, and the adults who support them, undertake reliable and valid research. Children, just as adults, must expect their findings to be critically scrutinized. This is why quality research training is so important. The scale and size of children's research is generally small and localized but even so there is the potential for these research 'snapshots' to influence policy. Small studies can raise awareness and lead to larger evidence-gathering projects. Equally, a series of small studies by different children in different locations about the same issue can create a powerful montage.

The remaining part of this chapter is devoted to examples of children's own research and how this relates to each of the five ECM outcomes: be healthy, stay safe, enjoy and achieve, make a positive contribution, and achieve economic wellbeing.

Be healthy

Examples of children's research influencing change at policy and practice levels in the health domain are more common with young people than with primary-aged children, so I have also included a research study by young people in this section. Investing in Children is a not-for-profit organization that encourages societal change and improved investment in children. The

Patient and Public Involvement Trust commissioned it to find out what young people thought about hospitals in County Durham. Part of that research was a study led by young people (Cole et al., 2009). The young people's investigation explored the potential benefits of a young person liaison officer acting in an intermediary role within the health service. Their research asked 'How effective are young people's health liaison officers and why are they needed in our local NHS trust?' It was a wide-ranging exploration that encompassed numerous data collection methods. These are set out in Box 13.1.

Box 13.1 | **Young researchers' data collection methods**

Agenda days: where young people are asked very open questions, and this in an adult free environment.

Questionnaires: to young people, health professionals and parents/carers.

Desk top research: to find out where liaison officers are based – through internet and phone.

Sample quota: by region of liaison officers: interviewing them and observation of the work they do and how they do it (if possible).

Interviewing staff: by spending a day in a hospital and asking staff if they think a liaison officer would be useful.

Interviewing young people from other areas: speaking to young people who have had experience of working with a liaison officer to find out [their] effectiveness.

Speak to adults in other areas of country: parents/carers/health professionals using questionnaires and asking in the clinics to find out how effective liaison officers are.

Surveying: going into youth centres and interviewing young people who are willing to speak to us using the format questions from our questionnaire.

Source: Cole et al., 2008: 6

Findings from their research confirmed a need for a young people's health liaison officer in County Durham. They were able to make a series of recommendations for how such a role would work optimally (see Box 13.2).

Box 13.2 | **Important characteristics for young people's health liaison officers**

■ They should be approachable and relaxed.
■ They need to understand health settings so they can give us advice and translate information for us.

- They MUST understand and keep confidentiality.
- They should give out information leaflets in language we understand.
- They need to be identifiable and there when you need them
- You need to know where to find them.
- They should be able to help with all aspects of health – both in hospital and in the community.
- Should be there for parents and children and young people
- There should be more than one than one officer so that there is one in each area of the county.

Source: Adapted from Cole et al., 2009: 15

Cole et al. put together a research report from their findings and presented it to the trust board for Children's Hospital Services in County Durham. It was received very favourably and the young people have been meeting regularly with the trust board since then.

Being healthy is just as much about mental and emotional wellbeing as physical health. Often the two are inextricably connected. A study by Shannon Davidson, aged 10, highlighted the social isolation factors and consequent impact on emotional wellbeing for children living with Graves' disease, a rare thyroid disorder.

Children's Perspectives

I have a thyroid disorder called Graves Disease. Medications stop my thyroid making too many hormones. Some children are born with no thyroid. Some children either have under-active or over-active thyroids. I wanted to find out what other children think about having a thyroid disorder because I've no one to talk to. Graves disease is most common in adults, so I feel quite lonely being the only person I know who has it. At the moment I can't find any research on what children think about having a thyroid disorder. The British Thyroid Foundation support groups are only for adults and they're local. There are not many children with thyroid disorders and they live all over the country so a local support group wouldn't do any good for children around the country. These are my research questions:

- How does having a thyroid disorder affect children's day to day lives?
- Do people treat them differently because they have a thyroid disorder?
- Do children think there should be a support group for children with thyroid disorders?

I wanted to give out questionnaires to other children with thyroid disorders but I didn't know anyone with one. Someone who works for the British Thyroid Foundation gives information to families and she had a list of addresses. She sent out my questionnaires on my behalf with a letter explaining what it was about with stamped envelopes for the questionnaires to be sent back to my school.

Source: Davidson, 2008

Among Shannon's findings was a strong consensus that children wanted to have access to a support group or, if a physical group was not possible, at least a web-based virtual support group. A theme of loneliness and social isolation emerged from Shannon's data, not least because Graves' disease is a rare condition and sufferers are spread thinly across the UK. Some of the participants in Shannon's research were linked to Great Ormond Street Hospital (GOSH), so she shared her research findings with members of the GOSH management board, who took it very seriously. She was invited to discuss with them how they could help establish better support for children with Graves' disease, and for sick children more generally, who suffer similar social isolation. This resulted in a regular page of the GOSH newsletter being allocated to the Graves' group of children and an invitation to Shannon to be the child editor.

There are many examples of research studies by children on diet, exercise and healthy living. One such is a study by a group of 12-year-old students at Worle Community School (2007), who compared their peers' diet and exercise habits during normal school term time and when on school vacation – with some surprising findings. The questionnaire they designed sought information about the types of food consumed and exercise undertaken. They analysed the data according to three participant groups: A = those who went abroad on holiday; B = those who holidayed in the UK; and C = those who stayed at home for their holiday. Figures 13.1–5 show some of the graphs they produced from their questionnaire data (pp. 4–10; see the full study for others).

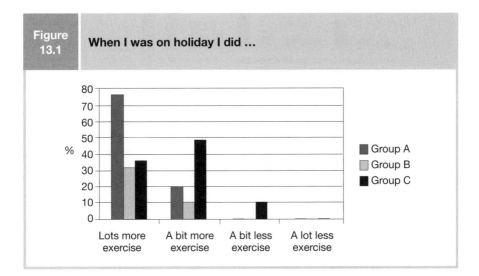

Figure 13.1 When I was on holiday I did ...

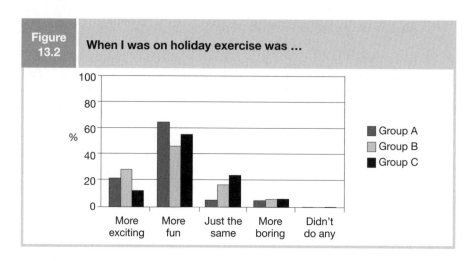

Figure 13.2 When I was on holiday exercise was …

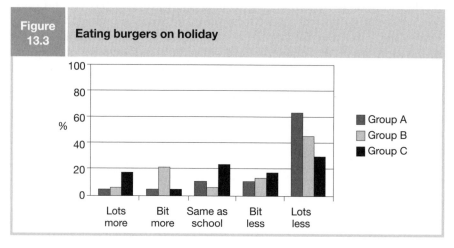

Figure 13.3 Eating burgers on holiday

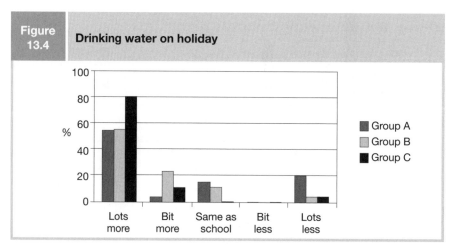

Figure 13.4 Drinking water on holiday

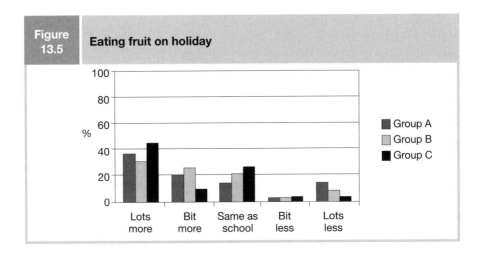

Figure 13.5 Eating fruit on holiday

Here is what the students at Worle Community School (2007) had to say in summary.

> **Children's Perspectives**

Discussion

There are some interesting summary points that can be drawn out from the findings. It would appear that young people of this age do want to eat healthily and take more exercise when on holiday. They like to do different kinds of exercise from school and want it to be fun. There is no notable difference in the amounts of sweets and ice cream they consume on holiday compared to a school week but there are some significant differences in the consumption of fast food and fizzy drinks. Surprisingly this tends to be less on holiday than in school weeks and it tends to be least in those young people holidaying abroad. This challenges some of the common perceptions of holidays being linked to fast food and ice cream. The only category where young people ate less healthily on holiday was the amount of vegetables they consumed. The least number of vegetables were eaten by those holidaying abroad. A striking finding was the very big difference in the quantity of water drunk on a holiday week compared to a school week.

Limitations of the study

This study is based on 55 students aged 12 years. Therefore it is limited in both the narrowness of the age band and the number of participants. However, the location of the school is in an average socio-economic area and a control questionnaire with a group of students one year younger (n=25) was also carried out with similar results.

Source: Worle Community School, 2008: 13

These 12-year-olds appeared to exercise more, drink more water and eat more healthily *away* from school. Their research gives us an insight into children's attitudes and goes some way to challenging the image young people are often saddled with as eating fast food and being couch potatoes. It also calls into question earlier policy decisions to sell off sports fields and reduce physical education lesson time to make way for more of the 'three Rs' in the primary curriculum.

Stay safe

As we saw from extracts from Eleanor Frank's (2005) research in Chapter 12, she had become increasingly aware that children did not play on the housing estate as much as they used to. Her findings highlighted the plight of children feeling unsafe on their own streets. Another research study by 11-year-old Simon Kirby investigated safety at bus stops and on bus journeys. Simon was about to move from primary to secondary school and would have to travel to school by bus on his own. He was very nervous about this as he had heard disturbing stories from friends about not feeling safe at bus stops. Many of the bus stops were located near pubs or had bushes nearby where people could hide if they wanted to spy on people or harm them. Simon collected data from his peers via questionnaires and interviews about their views and experiences of safety on buses. As part of the presentation of his data, Simon wrote a fictional story (and also acted it out in role play with friends) into which he wove findings from his research so as to create a realistic picture of how unsafe bus travel can sometimes be for children of his age. He called his story 'The ok bus journey'. No one was physically harmed, although anxiety levels ran high.

> ## " Children's Perspectives
>
> ### The ok bus journey
>
> [Lewis] was going to meet up with his friends Amir and Bob at the bus stop. They all lived in different areas but went to the same school.
>
> [Lewis] noticed a group of chavs huddled around an old rover metro, trying to fix the old banger as they called it. A few others were standing around chatting, Lewis couldn't help but feel a bit nervous as he walked past, because he noticed some were smoking. He looked up and saw one of them holding a screwdriver as if it was a dagger, gripping it with a clenched fist. He could smell petrol fumes. One of the boys was trying to start up his scooter, like you would start up a motor boat. He was unsuccessful ... [and] made a rude sign at the scooter. Lewis crossed over the road. They all seemed to be looking in his direction. He looked forward, quickened his pace and did not look back until he was safely around the corner.

The bus stop was near a Tesco Express. When he met his friends he showed the respect symbol. They had grown out of doing their secret handshake, that had involved banging their shoulders together, even though Lewis still practiced it in front of the mirror. They couldn't sit down because the plastic benches had been smashed a long time ago, so they just stood and waited for the bus. The windows had also been smashed and hundreds of bits of glass were scattered over the bus shelter's floor.

A man stopped at the bus stop. He had a strong smell of alcohol around him. He stopped and looked at the three of them. He walked of in the direction of the pub.

Even though the bus was on schedule, Lewis was a little nervous. But Amir started laughing when he saw a boy dressed as 'sponge Bob square pants'. He was walking on his own to what looked like a fancy dress party and the others giggled madly, out loud. The boy did not hear them, luckily, thought Lewis.

They saw the bus in the distance the bus was an old MK metro a 20 seater ... but it did not seem to be slowing down. Bob stuck his hand out but the driver did not slow. Amir ran into the road and waved his arms round, and the bus came to a screeching halt.

Source: Kirby, 2007: 3–4

Enjoy and achieve

The rationale for merging education, health and social services into one large, integrated department was to improve overall communication and raise standards. 'Education, education, education' was the mantra of New Labour on taking up the reins of office in 1997 and its focus was clearly on raising standards. There has been much criticism of the coupling of 'enjoy and achieve' in this ECM outcome, arguing that children have a right to enjoyment for enjoyment's sake and it should not be dependent on achievement. An interesting study by Sai Parapelli (2008), an 11-year-old girl, provides food for thought. Her research explores the effect of wearing school uniform on children's confidence, enjoyment and achievement levels. While children may be consulted about the colours and styles of uniform, they have no power over decisions about the compulsory wearing of uniform in their schools. Sai hypothesized that children work differently when they are free of school uniform. She compared the views of a Year 4 class (age 8–9) with a Year 8 class (age 12–13). The overwhelming majority in both age groups disagreed with having to wear school uniform. Interestingly, while neither group thought that the presence or absence of uniform affected how hard they worked, it did affect how confident they felt and how creatively they worked, as shown in Figures 13.6 and 13.7 (Parapelli, 2008; slides 14 and 20).

If children work more confidently and creatively, they are likely to achieve more but also more likely to enjoy the process that leads to their achievements.

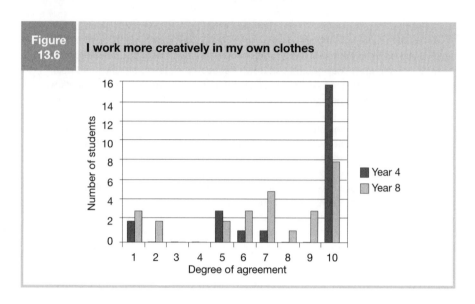

Figure 13.6 — I work more creatively in my own clothes

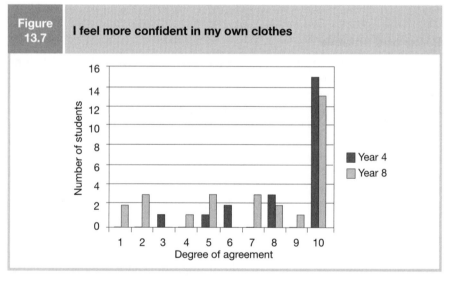

Figure 13.7 — I feel more confident in my own clothes

Are boys and girls treated differently?

We know from numerous sources (see, for example, Clark and Akerman, 2006) that girls currently outperform boys in the primary years. Professionals in any service area will always strive to eliminate personal bias in their practice, whether this is triggered by race, culture, gender, sexual persuasion or any other factor. Many practitioners are not aware of subconscious biases seeping into their practice.

❝❝   Children's Perspectives

Helen Dandridge, aged 10, conducted some research into whether girls and boys were treated differently by teachers at her school (Dandridge, 2008). After comprehensive training in the research process, she began her investigation by searching the internet for any opinions being expressed by children on this subject. On websites such as BBC Newsround, a children's topical news programme, she found some strong views being expressed that boys and girls are treated differently in school. So she decided to find out what the situation was in her own school. There were no significant gender differences in pupil numbers in the classes. She collected three complementary sets of data: a self-designed questionnaire for 9–11-year-olds in her school, lesson observations, and an analysis of the gender differences on the school's Golden Time chart (Golden Time was a free choice activity period on Friday afternoons which was prized by pupils but could be withdrawn by teachers for bad behaviour). Questionnaire results showed that the majority of pupils (86%) did not believe that teachers deliberately favoured one gender and 72% believed that teachers did not choose girls to answer more questions in class than boys. However, 80% of 11-year-olds thought that girls were chosen over boys to help with special jobs in the classroom, and 63% thought that teachers treated boys and girls differently as a response to their behaviour. The lesson observations – there were only three, so caution needs to be employed in making any inferences – generated some different data.

Lesson	Number of times girls picked to answer	Number of times boys picked to answer	Number of times girls told off	Number of times boys told off
English	9	3	4	19
Maths	18	5	5	14
Art	16	8	11	39

When Helen analysed the Golden Time chart, she found a similar picture of many more boys being denied Golden Time than girls. Her report concluded that boys and girls were treated differently at her school, although she did not think this was a deliberate act on the part of teachers. However, she did comment that the teachers were nearly all female and wondered whether this had any impact on the gender interaction.

Source: Adapted from Dandridge, 2008

Clearly, Helen's research cannot be generalized from. It is very small scale and merely provides a snapshot of the situation in one primary school. Nevertheless, children's research that privileges the child perspective can be influential at a local level. Helen presented her research to teachers and governors to raise awareness and succeeded in getting gender issues onto the school management radar.

Make a positive contribution

There are many examples of children's research which demonstrate their willingness to make a positive contribution to their families, schools, local communities and, more generally, to global society. Most children make ongoing, and frequently unacknowledged, positive contributions both economically and socially through the 'informal work' they do in family units. Looking after younger siblings, doing an array of domestic chores and finding paid work such as paper rounds to avoid drawing down pocket money all make positive contributions (Zelizer, 2005). There are also many examples of children making positive contributions at a global level in the concerns they express about the environment (see, for example, child researcher Watson, 2004). Roshni Reeves (2008), aged 10, carried out some research about children's attitude to water usage and water conservation. Roshni felt strongly that this was something where children could make a positive contribution and that it was not just the responsibility of adults. She tells us how she went about researching this in Figure 13.8.

Figure 13.8	My methods

❋ I kept a water diary for a week

❋ I designed a questionnaire for years 5 and 6 in my school

❋ This was to see what attitudes to water they have

❋ I also sent it out to parents to see if there was any difference

Source: Reeves, 2008: PowerPoint slide 5

From her findings, Roshni concluded that children could be doing more to conserve water. For example, her questionnaire data revealed that 83% of adults take a shower rather than a bath, as compared to 58% of children. However, Roshni was encouraged that children of her age (ten years old) demonstrated a surprising awareness about the scarcity of natural resources, more so than many of their parents.

Children can make a positive contribution at a number of levels: in the home, at school, in the local community, or as part of national groups. The perennial appeal of programmes like *Blue Peter*, which encourage children towards communitarian and humanitarian action, is legendary. Clearly, there is no shortage of goodwill for children to make a positive contribution. Achieving this ECM outcome is more about creating opportunities, raising awareness and documenting the evidence. Children's research can do all three.

Some children's research raises awareness of initiatives that children can join, for example anti-bullying groups or national schemes such as the Diana

Award for outstanding community contributions (see, for example, child researchers Howard, 2005; Cook, 2009). Others research opportunity issues. One such was ten-year-old Ellie Leather's study (2008) about the lack of opportunity for primary-age children to learn first aid skills. In her research, she cited a British Red Cross survey (2008) which asked 1,100 children from 20 schools throughout the UK questions about first aid:

- 60% of those aged 9 to 13 didn't know enough to help themselves or others at an accident
- Over half the children in the survey had never learnt first aid
- 94% of children thought it was important to learn first aid and most wanted to learn more (Leather, 2008: slide 3).

Currently, children can learn first aid at classes run by St John's Ambulance but Ellie's research showed that hardly any attended these, even though 94% thought it was important to learn first aid. Of the four classes (ages 7–11) she surveyed, only 5% attended first aid training either because they did not know about the existence of the classes or because no one could take them. However, she discovered that a large majority would attend first aid training if it were held at school. The preferred time for this would be an after-school rather than a lunchtime club. Her research led to some negotiations between her school and the local St John's Ambulance group to establish a school first aid club.

Achieve economic wellbeing

We cannot achieve economic wellbeing for all our children until child poverty is eradicated. The case for education as a route out of poverty has been powerfully argued (Machin and MacNally, 2006). Literacy is a key element of this since it is the platform on which much curricular endeavour is built. It is also an area of the curriculum which has been under a spotlight in the past decade, with a raft of government policy initiatives aimed at raising literacy standards. Poverty has long been linked to literacy underachievement (Haverman and Wolfe, 1995). If ECM is working for every child, then we should be seeing some educational benefits, particularly at the child poverty end of the spectrum.

Children's Perspectives

As part of the Joseph Rowntree Education and Poverty funded programme coordinated by Donald Hirsch (2007), two groups of 11-year-olds decided to investigate for themselves what literacy opportunities there were for their peers (Rhodes et al., 2007; Carter-Davies, 2007). The groups were drawn from contrasting areas of socioeconomic advantage and disadvantage (see Kellett, 2009).

The young researchers felt that their peers responded more openly and honestly to child–child data generation than they might have done to adult elicitations. Operating independently in their contrasting socioeconomic groups, the child researchers in both groups identified confidence as a significant factor in literacy achievement: 100% of the girls and 88% of the boys (n = 80) in the area of socioeconomic advantage rated their reading ability as high. These high levels of reading confidence and self-esteem were arrived at by ample opportunities for literacy confidence-building activities in private. They needed lots of opportunity to read by themselves or in safe, non-threatening environments such as reading to younger siblings. Children talked about building up what they termed their 'private confidence' by reading on their own, sometimes rehearsing pronunciation and expression in whispers. As they grew in 'private confidence', they became less afraid of being called upon to read in class or to talk about what they had read. It was the facilitation of these opportunities in the home – quiet reading environments, encouragement to read as a leisure activity, plenty of books readily available – which proved to be the biggest differentiator between the socioeconomically advantaged and disadvantaged schools. Child researchers in the area of socioeconomic disadvantage found few, if any, opportunities for their peers to practise similar private confidence-building activities. The children's research around literacy development also made a direct link between reading skills and speaking and listening skills, since private and public confidence in reading helps with the development of these, creating a virtuous circle.

The child researchers maintained that if adults had undertaken similar research, they would not have accessed the same findings, especially those relating to what children feel they need to do in their own private space. The children's research reveals much about the impact of poverty on educational achievement, but it is also worth reflecting on the extent to which their findings contradict current literacy practices in primary schools.

Other small-scale research by children highlighting links between poverty and educational achievement include a study by an 11-year-old researcher (Carter-Davies, 2007). This study looked at the difficulties for economically disadvantaged children in completing simple homework tasks. The participant children in this study (n = 17) were aged eight and nine and living in home environments classified as below the poverty threshold (Hirsch, 2007). The accommodation was typically overcrowded bedsits with nowhere to do homework, no resources to do it with, and no adult capable of helping them. For these children, homework clubs were a lifeline. Their educational achievement – and with it a better chance of achieving economic wellbeing – was greatly enhanced by having access to a quiet learning environment, a teacher and resources such as computers. Homework clubs are an integral feature of extended schools and Carter-Davies's research is a positive affirmation of how this particular policy is supporting ECM.

The five ECM strands taken as a whole aim to ensure a quality childhood. Knowing what makes children anxious and what they worry about can help our understanding of how such wellbeing can be better achieved. Isobel Sutherland (2007) has given us an insight, from her ten-year old perspective, into what children in her class worry about.

> **Children's Perspectives**
>
> While Isobel's research can only provide a small picture (n = 20), its child-to-child-generated data is, nevertheless, illuminating and a fitting way to conclude an exploration of children's research related to ECM. Isobel summarizes the principal anxieties that preoccupy her ten-year-old peers in Figure 13.9 (Sutherland, 2007: slide 7).
>
> Figure 13.9 **My results**

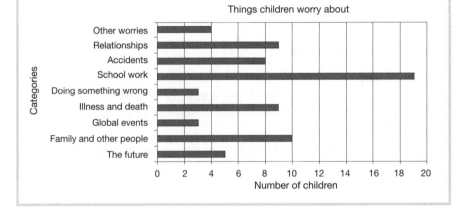

Conclusion

This chapter has focused on children's own research, the outlier on the spectrum of children's perspectives, but arguably the most important. It began with a rationale that demonstrated how child-led research has grown out of escalating participation and voice agendas and draws on parallel emancipatory advancements. Accepting children as researchers in their own right promotes their democratic involvement in all phases of decision-making. This led to a discussion of the barriers and challenges that impede children undertaking their own research, which were found to be centred mainly on age and competency issues. The remainder of the chapter was devoted to examples of children's original research and how these studies can illuminate and inform our understanding of their perspectives on ECM.

Perhaps the biggest impact of research by children is the contribution it makes to our knowledge and understanding of childhood and children's worlds. Research *by* children and young people – where they set the agendas, determine the foci for exploration, choose the methods of investigation, and actively disseminate the findings – has announced itself on the world stage and is here to stay. The adult community is tasked with accommodating this new body of knowledge and, crucially, valuing it. Wider issues of children's research influencing policy and practice were explored in the chapter and, notwithstanding caveats relating to small scale, the potential for this was acknowledged. But where does it all lead? How do we move from children's research having the potential to influence policy to a real and sustainable influence? It brings us full circle to the seismic shift in children's status in society described in Chapter 2. It requires a similar attitudinal shift to accept that children's perspectives, particularly those expressed from an evidence base of their own research, are an invaluable aide to optimizing our understanding of how children's services can best be provided. Reflecting on some of the catastrophic mistakes that have been made over time, our collective failure to listen to children is a poignantly recurring theme.

Reflection exercises

1. For all readers

How would you go about persuading a sceptic to support the concept of children undertaking their own research? Make a list of your main arguments.

2. For staff working with children and young people in multidisciplinary teams

Reflect on where you are in your own practice on the spectrum of children's involvement in research:

listening → consulting → inviting participation → co-researching → empowering children to research

What barriers and challenges currently exist in your multidisciplinary team to children undertaking their own research? How could they be overcome?

3. Children's perspectives

Reflect on how useful it is to have child–child data about what ten-year-olds worry about. Putting Isobel's findings aside for the moment, order the nine categories that she compiled in Figure 13.9 – the future, family and other people, global events, illness and death, doing something wrong, schoolwork, accidents, relationships, and other worries – according to what you, as an adult, think a ten-year-old would worry about the most and least. Compare yours with the graph in Figure 13.9. Do they differ? If so, what surprises you?

Suggested further reading

1. Greene, S. and Hogan, D. (2005) *Researching Children's Experiences: Approaches and Methods*, London: Sage

   Good volume to dip into for ideas of different methods in research involving children. In two parts, the first is a conceptual and ethical overview and the second has ten chapters, each depicting a different type of method for conducting research with children, from traditional methods such as interviews to narrative analysis of children and participatory approaches.

2. http://childrens-research-centre.open.ac.uk

   The Children's Research Centre is all about children by children. Its primary objective is to empower children and young people as active researchers. It recognizes children as experts on their own lives and values their perspectives. It actively promotes child voice by training and supporting children to carry out research on topics that are important to them. The website is host to more than 100 research studies by children from age nine upwards.

3. Christensen, P.M. and James, A. (eds) (2008) *Research with Children and Young People: Perspectives and Practice* (2nd edn), London: Routledge

   Excellent text comprising different chapters by leading writers in the field discussing critical aspects of theory and practice. Avoids giving 'recipes' for doing research with children or adopting any particular orthodoxy but encourages readers to use the chapters to find what is going to work best for them in different situations.

4. Kellett, M. (2005) *How to Develop Children as Researchers: A Step by Step Guide to Teaching Research Process.* London: Sage

   For anyone interested in supporting children to engage in their own research, provides step-by-step guidance to a differentiated training programme. All aspects of the research process are covered. Differentiated activities, games and photocopiable resources enable practitioners to set up their own children's research groups.

5. Kellett, M. (2005) 'Children as active researchers: a new research paradigm for the 21st century?', http://www.ncrm.ac.uk/research/outputs/publications/methodsreview/MethodsReviewPaperNCRM-003.pdf

   Theoretically based paper that sets out the rationale for a new paradigm of children as researchers in their own right. Draws parallels with the evolution of other new paradigms such as feminism and emancipatory research and discusses some of the critical issues involved.

14 Beyond Every Child Matters

In this chapter we discuss:

- What have we learned from ECM?
- Where is ECM leading us?
- Change of government
- The crucial importance of children's perspectives

What have we learned from ECM?

This final chapter briefly pulls together the main points that have been made in this book and looks beyond Every Child Matters (ECM) to next steps and new directions. There are several recurring themes traceable through the build-up to, and implementation of, ECM, from which we can learn how best to move forward with integrated services for children. I have summarized the main themes which have currency beyond ECM, as communication, holism, early intervention and listening.

Communication

Imperfect lessons learned from the Laming Report (2003) did not prevent further communication errors and tragedies occurring. Improved communication at all levels and across all agencies had to be a clear priority of ECM:

> Communicating effectively across these agencies has become essential to identifying the needs and planning the support for each child or young person ... [communication] is the ingredient that brings all of the agencies together, ensures that they become 'joined up' and allows integrated working to be carried out. (Dunhill et al., 2009: 18)

The roles of professionals working with, and for, children do not just involve communication, they *rely* on it. Thus it was fitting that communication was made the first skill in the Common Core of Knowledge and Skills for all the children's workforce (DfES, 2005: 19):

Have a general knowledge and understanding of the range of
organizations and individuals working with children, young
people and those caring for them, and be aware of the roles and
responsibilities of other professionals.

Improved communication is something that has to stay with us beyond
ECM. The systems and structures that support it, however, will inevitably
change, for example the new coalition government has already wound up
the ContactPoint database as part of its new agenda of 'power to the
people'. This will satisfy some of the misgivings that children have about
access to their personal data but care must be taken that this does not
impede important information being made available and clearly communicated between agencies when necessary. However, it is important not to get
distracted by the need for guarantees and certainties. No matter how expert
the professionals are and how good the systems, we are never going to be
able to guarantee to prevent some children being harmed in some situations
by some parents. A good way to prevent as many childcare tragedies as
possible is to continue to improve interagency working and address ongoing
training issues. I would suggest that searching for scapegoats and vilifying
professionals, as happened to Sharon Shoesmith, the director of children's
services for Haringey, at the time of the death of Baby Peter (Bennett, 2009),
is neither constructive nor helpful.

Holism

The shift to a focusing of services 'around the child' and the notion that
provision should 'follow the child' has had a major impact on efficacy. It has
ensured that services are needs driven rather than resource driven. A holistic
approach looks at all the care needs of a child and joins them up via a lead
professional. This avoids situations where children with multiple needs can
end up with dozens of professionals either duplicating work or passing the
buck. Interagency working is a natural corollary of holism and it would be a
retrograde step to lose this new focus and return to the silo states of mind
that reinforce lone practice, isolation and entrenched professional ideologies.
An approach that views the child as part of a larger family unit appreciates
the need that sometimes family needs have to be addressed in order to
provide for the child. As demonstrated repeatedly in this book, poverty is
very often a root cause.

Early intervention

A success story of ECM has been the transformation of the early years
workforce, the effective interagency working that has built up around the
child from birth through the cornerstone of children's centres, which have
brought provision *to* children within a local community. This has enabled
holistic approaches to be maintained. A beneficial outcome of this has been
the valuable early intervention work that has been achieved for innumerable

children and their families. A well-run Sure Start children's centre represents a microcosm of how the wider ECM programme could work to advantage. It is important to build on these solid foundations and to take heart from the positives that are being achieved. A major contributing factor has been the fusion of early childcare and early education, an embodiment of focusing on the needs of the whole child and, by association, the whole family. The coalition government recognizes the value of early intervention but is still cutting back the children's centres initiative, directing the majority of the reduced funds to those most in need. In my opinion, it is regrettable that what was originally intended to be a universal service will be diminished to a crisis service and this is likely to have a negative impact on the quality of early years provision.

Listening

Listening to children, and the participation momentum emanating from ECM, is possibly the most significant outcome of all. Early in Chapter 2, I spoke about the UNCRC as a major driver of ECM, rooted in the increased attention to children's rights. This has resulted in the fostering of a listening culture across the children's workforce, greater consultation, and the increased involvement of children in decision-making processes. Although still patchy in its implementation, there are some examples of good participation practice emerging. In some instances, this is leading to initiatives to empower children as researchers that have the potential to inform policy and practice. Effective listening to children underpins everything that ECM stands for. Moreover, ineffective listening is an acknowledged contributory cause at the heart of all the high-profile childcare tragedies in living memory. So, wherever we move to beyond ECM, it is imperative that we build on this listening platform.

Change of government

The issues and problems that professionals face in the delivery of children's integrated services have to be viewed within the cultural, economic and political context of the times (Parton, 2006). This is inextricably bound up with the sitting government of the day. This book is concerned with reviewing ECM up until the end of New Labour. May 2010 ushered in a new era in British politics, with a coalition government of the Conservative and Liberal Democrat parties. History has shown us that a change of government often brings intense policy swings as an incoming government seeks to assert itself, frequently doing so by reversing the policy initiatives of the outgoing government:

> In these changing times where politicians are pledging to rise above
> party politics in the best interests of the nation, we are urging the new

government to put the needs of the most vulnerable and neglected children first. As we enter into a new era, politicians must learn from the lessons of the past, where we know policies have too often been influenced by short term, headline driven gains ... This new government must implement long term policies, seeking cross party consensus to benefit the most vulnerable across the UK. (Dame Clare Tickell, chief executive of Action for Children)

Of concern is the close association of ECM as a flagship of New Labour and the temptation, for that very reason, for the coalition government to distance itself from it, risking throwing the baby out with the bath water. The immediate dismantling of the DCSF and the eradication of its rainbow children logo is an example of a desire to stamp out the trappings of an old government and to rebadge with a vision of the new. Replacing the DCSF in favour of a Department for Education, albeit one that will continue to include children's services, suggests a move towards a system that will be heavily dominated by an education agenda.

At the time of writing, it is only possible to speculate on how coalition policies will influence children's future experiences of ECM. It is clear that budget cuts will run deep and many initiatives of ECM are at risk. Early indicators suggest that the 'power to the people' mantra will bring more control of social care budgets directly to families and an expansion of citizenship agendas. More say for users over how to spend funding is all to the good as long as the funding itself does not disappear, otherwise what is given with one hand is taken away with the other. The serious economic situation inevitably means that there will be cuts to services. One has to hope that the axe will not fall too heavily on provision for children and stall much of the good work that ECM has brought about. The coalition government's commitment to restoring a central focus on the family suggests that a holistic style may prevail, albeit overlain with a more laissez-faire approach that may see an increase in family self-help measures. This will need to be tempered with an understanding that in an economic downturn, many families are likely to need more not less help.

ECM is not a golden solution and its flaws and shortcomings have been exposed in this book, not least the criticism that it is predicated on unconscious social and moral beliefs which reflect white, heterosexual, Christian ideals. However, there are many positives about ECM which are making real differences in many children's lives and it would be disappointing if the new government were to throw out the good with the bad. One hopes that the mantra of compromise politics and the rhetoric of coalition will temper this and that the promise to govern in the national interest ahead of individual party interests will prevail. Nomenclature, systems, processes and intricacies of funding may change but the ideology of ECM must endure. Every child has to matter, whatever government is in power, and our most vulnerable children can best be provided for by effective multi-agency practice.

The crucial importance of children's perspectives

This book has been written with children's perspectives as its propelling force. It documents how children are experiencing ECM in their daily lives and reviews issues of integrated services from the standpoint of how they are working (or not) for them. With a recent change of government, it is even more imperative that their views are heard. The illustrations and case studies cited in earlier chapters illustrate just how powerful children's voice can be in informing our knowledge and understanding and the directions we need to take to best serve their needs. This is particularly influential when informed by an evidence base of child-led research which has the potential to impact on policy and practice.

As part of Morgan's (2005: 22) research into the views of children aged 5–12 about ECM, he collected messages from them that they would like to give to adults. One of these resonates strongly with the thrust of the children's perspectives I have tried to give voice to in this book:

Please listen to us instead of ignoring us or just interrupting us.

There could not be a more important time to champion the voice of the child and to accommodate their perspectives. Beyond ECM lies another coalition, not just between political parties, but between adults and children. Politicians and children's workforce professionals can join forces with children to optimize the life chances of the next generation.

References

11 Million (2006) *Bullying Today*. London, Office of the Children's Commissioner.

11 Million (2007) *Pushed into the Shadows: Young People's Experiences of Mental Health Facilities*. London, Office of the Children's Commissioner.

11 Million (2008) *Making Children's Mental Health Matter*. London, Office of the Children's Commissioner.

11 Million (2008a) *Out of the Shadows?: A Review of the Responses to Recommendations Made in Pushed into the Shadows: Young People's Experience of Adult Mental Health Facilities*. London, Office of the Children's Commissioner.

Action for Children (2008) *Supporting Families: Children on the Edge of Care*, http://www.actionforchildren.org.uk/uploads/media/29/347.pdf [accessed 17/01/11].

Action for Children (2010) *Deprivation and Risk: The Case for Early Intervention*, www.actionforchildren.org.uk [accessed 09/09/2010].

Alderson, P. (2000) 'Children as researchers: the effects of participation rights on research methodology', in P. Christensen and A. James (eds) *Research with Children: Perspectives and Practices*. London, Falmer Press.

Alderson, P. (2008) *Young Children's Rights: Exploring Beliefs, Principles and Practice* (2nd edn). London, Jessica Kingsley.

Alderson, P. and Morrow, V. (2004) *Ethics and Social Research with Children and Young People*. Ilford, Barnardo's.

Alexander, R. (ed.) (2009) *Children, Their World, Their Education: Final Report of the Cambridge Primary Review Report* (Alexander Report). Cambridge, University of Cambridge/Esmée Fairburn Foundation.

Allen, K. (2009) Two million children now in homes with no working adult, *The Guardian*, 26 August.

Anning, A., Cottrell, D., Frost, N. et al. (2006) *Developing Multiprofessional Teamwork for Integrated Children's Services*. Maidenhead, Open University Press.

Appleby, L., Shaw, J., Sherratt J. et al. (2001) *Safety First: Report of the National Confidential Inquiry into Suicide and Homicide by People with Mental Illness*. London, TSO.

Archard, D. (2004) *Children: Rights and Childhood* (2nd edn). London, Routledge.

Badham, B. and Wade, H. (2005) *Hear by Right: Standards for the Active Involvement of Children and Young People*. Leicester, National Youth Agency/LGA.

Barker, R. (ed.) (2009) *Making Sense of Every Child Matters: Multi-professional Practice Guidance*. Bristol, Policy Press.

Barnardo's (2008) Barnardo's response to the CAMHS review: improving the mental health and psychological well-being of children and young people: call for evidence, http://www.barnardos.org.uk/barnardo_s_response_to_camhs_review_3rd_july_08.pdf [accessed 10/01/11].

Barnardo's (2009) Whose child now? Fifteen years of working to prevent sexual exploitation of children in the UK, http://www.barnardos.org.uk/whose_child_now.pdf [accessed 17/01/11].

Batty, D. (2003) BMA raises concerns over child databases, *The Guardian*, 29 October.

BBC News (2008) Rose denounces impact of testing, 20 October, www.news.bbc.co.uk/1/hi/education/7680895.stm [accessed 20/09/09].

BBC News (2009) One in six UK homes 'has no work', 26 August, http://news.bbc.co.uk/1/hi/8222145.stm [accessed 17/01/11].

Bennet, K., Heath, T. and Jeffries, R. (2007) *Home Office Statistical Bulletin 14/07: Asylum Statistics United Kingdom 2006* (2nd edn). London, Home Office.

Bennett, R. (2009) Baby P chief Sharon Shoesmith 'suicidal' after dismissal, *The Times*, 8 October.

Bennett Woodhouse, B. (2003) 'Enhancing children's participation in policy formulation'. *Arizona Law Review*, 45, 750–763.

Bibby, A. and Becker, S. (eds) (2000) *Young Carers in their Own Words*. London, Calouste Gulbenkian Foundation.

Bindel, J. (2006) Six weeks of suffering, *The Guardian*, 18 August.

Blackemore, A. (2006) *How Voluntary and Community Organisations Can Help Transform Public Services*. London, National Council for Voluntary Organisations.

Blake, G., Robinson, D. and Smerdon, M. (2007) *Living Values: A Report Encouraging Boldness in Third Sector Organisations*. London, Community Links/ Esmée Fairbairn Foundation.

Blom-Cooper, L. (1985) *'A Child in Trust': Report of the Panel of Inquiry into the Circumstances Surrounding the Death of Jasmine Beckford*. London, Brent Council.

Bourdieu, P. (1986) 'The forms of capital', in J. Richardson (ed.) *Handbook of Theory and Research for the Sociology of Education*. New York, Greenwood.

Bovarnick, S. (2007) *Child Neglect*. London, NSPCC.

Bradwell, J., Crawford, D., Crawford, J. et al. (2009) How looked after children are involved in their care review process, http://childrens-research-centre.open.ac.uk [accessed 16/04/10].

Bragg, S. (2001) 'Taking a joke: learning from the voices we don't want to hear'. *Forum*, 43(2), 70–3.

Brandon, M., Howe, A., Dagley, V. et al. (2006) *Evaluating the Common Assessment Framework and Lead Professional Guidance and Implementation in 2005-6*. London, DfES.

British Red Cross (2008) Research shows children lack first aid skills, www.redcross.org.uk/standard.asp?id=45878 [accessed 20/09/09].

Britton, A., Blee, H. and McMahon, M. (2007) *Evaluation of the Children's Parliament*. Education for Global Citizenship Unit, University of Glasgow.

CAMHS (Children and Adolescent Mental Health Services) (2008) *CAMHS Review: Improving the Mental Health and Psychological Well-Being of Children and Young People*, CAMHS Review Interim Report, www.dcsf.gov.uk/CAMHSreview [accessed 16/04/10].

Carter-Davies, A. (2007) What environment do children like doing their homework in?, http://childrens-research-centre.open.ac.uk [accessed 16/04/10].

Carvel, J. (2001) Catalogue of errors in abuse case, *The Guardian*, 27 September.

Cavet, J. and Sloper, P. (2004) 'The participation of children and young people in decisions about UK service development'. *Child Care, Health and Development*, 30(6), 613–21.

Cawson, P. (2002) *Child Maltreatment in the Family: The Experience of a National Sample of Young People*. London, NSPCC.

Cawson, P., Wattam, C., Brooker, S. and Kelly, G. (2000) *Child Maltreatment in the United Kingdom: A Study of the Prevalence of Child Abuse and Neglect*. London, NSPCC.

Chandiramani, R. (2010) 'Outstanding challenge for Ofsted'. *Children & Young People Now*, 2 February.

Charity Commission (2007) *Stand and Deliver: The Future for Charities Providing Public Services*. London, Charity Commission.

Children, Schools and Families Committee (2008) *Testing and Assessment: Government and Ofsted Responses to the Committee's Third Report of the Session 2007–08, Fifth Special Report of Session 2007–08*, http://www.publications.parliament.uk/pa/cm200708/cmselect/cmchilsch/1003/1003.pdf [accessed 20/01/11].

Christensen, P. and James, A. (2000) 'Childhood diversity and commonality', in P. Christensen and A. James (eds) *Research with Children: Perspectives and Practices*. London, Falmer Press.

Christensen, P. and Prout, A. (2002) 'Working with ethical symmetry in social research with children'. *Childhood*, 9(4), 477–97.

Christensen, P. and Prout, A. (2005) 'Anthropological and sociological perspectives on the study of children', in S. Greene and D. Hogan (eds) *Researching Children's Experiences: Approaches and Methods*. London, Sage.

Clark, A. (2004) 'The mosaic approach and research with young children', in V. Lewis, V.M. Kellett, C. Robinson et al. (eds) *The Reality of Research with Children and Young People*. London, Sage.

Clark, A. and Moss, P. (2001) *Listening to Young Children: The Mosaic Approach*. London, National Children's Bureau.

Clark, C. and Akerman, R. (2006) *Social Inclusion and Reading: An Exploration*. London, National Literacy Trust.

Clay, D. (2005) *Participation and School Councils Toolkit: Taking Part and Helping our School*. London, School Councils UK.

Coad, J. and Lewis, A. (2004) *Engaging Children and Young People in Research: Literature Review for the National Evaluation of the Children's Fund*. Birmingham, Institute of Applied Social Studies.

Cohen, E. (2005) 'Neither seen nor heard: children's citizenship in contemporary democracies'. *Citizenship Studies*, 9(2), 221–40.

Cole, D. (2005) When can we have *our* say?, http://childrens-research-centre.open.ac.uk [accessed 16/04/10].

Cole, L., Davies, R., Fenwick, M. et al. (2009) How effective are young people's health liaison officers and why are they needed in our local NHS trust?, http://childrens-research-centre.open.ac.uk [accessed 16/04/10].

Contaldo, M. (2007) *Building the Evidence Base: Third Sector Values in the Delivery of Public Services*. London, Charity and Third Sector Finance Unit, HM Treasury.

Cook, A. (2009) Somerset youth volunteering, http://childrens-research-centre.open.ac.uk [accessed 16/04/10].

Cook, B. (2010) Sure Start dubbed 'a great achievement', http://www.cypnow.co.uk/bulletins/Daily-Bulletin/news/990635/?DCMP=EMC-DailyBulletin [accessed 16/01/11].

Coppock, V. (2002) 'Medicalising children's behaviour', in B. Franklin (ed.) *The New Handbook of Children's Rights: Comparative Policy and Practice*. New York, Routledge.

Coughlan, J. (2007) 'Values at risk in children's services'. *Community Care*, 21 June.

Coyne, I. (2006) 'Children's experiences of hospitalization'. *Journal of Health Care*, 10(4), 326–36.

Craft, A. and Killen, S. (2007) *Better Care: Better Lives*. London, DH.

Crawley, H. and Lester, T. (2005) *No Place for a Child: Children in Immigration Detention in the UK – Impacts, Alternatives and Safeguards*. London, Save the Children UK.

Curtis, P. (2008) We failed over Haringey – Ofsted head, *The Guardian*, 6 December, http://www.guardian.co.uk/education/2008/dec/06/ofsted-child-protection [accessed 20/01/11].

CWDC (Children's Workforce Development Council) (2007) *Briefing Note: Social Work with Children, Their Families and Carers*. London, CWDC/GSCC.

Dale, D. (1986) '"A child in trust": the report of the inquiry into the case of Jasmine Beckford'. British Journal of Criminology, 26(2), 173–8.

Daly, M. (2005) 'Changing family life in Europe: significance for state and society'. *European Societies*, 7(3), 379–98.

Dandridge, H. (2008) Are girls and boys treated differently in school?, http://childrens-research-centre.open.ac.uk [accessed 03/09/2010].

Daniel, B. (2005) 'Introduction to issues for health and social care in neglect', in J. Taylor and B. Daniel (eds) *Child Neglect: Practice Issues for Health and Social Care*. London, Jessica Kingsley.

Daniel, G. (2008) 'Talking with children: constructing victim-hood or agency?', in P. Kennison and A. Goodman (eds) *Children as Victims*. Exeter, Learning Matters.

Daniel, P. and Ivatts, J. (1998) *Children and Social Policy*. Basingstoke, Macmillan – now Palgrave Macmillan.

Davey, C. (2009) *What Do They Know? Investigating the Human Rights Concerns of Children and Young People Living in England*, http://www.getreadyforchange. org.uk/images/uploads/Compressed_What_do_they_know_FINAL.pdf [accessed 20/01/2011].

Davidson, S. (2008) What children think about having a thyroid disorder, http:// childrens-research-centre.open.ac.uk [accessed 16/04/10].

Daycare Trust (2010) *Childcare Costs Survey 2010*, www.daycaretrust.org.uk/pages/ childcare-costs-surveys.html [accessed 20/01/2011].

DCLG (Department for Communities and Local Government) (2006) *Anti-Social Behaviour Intensive Family Support Projects: An Evaluation of Six Pioneering Projects*. Oxford, Blackwell.

DCSF (Department for Children, Schools and Families) (2007) *The Children's Plan: Building Brighter Futures*. London, HMSO.

DCSF (2007a) *Care Matters: Time for Change*, White Paper. London, HMSO.

DCSF (2007b) *Aiming High for Disabled Children*. London, HMSO.

DCSF (2007c) *Family Intervention Projects: A Toolkit for Local Practitioners*. London, HMSO.

DCSF (2008) *Piloting the Social Work Practice Model: A Prospectus*. London, HMSO.

DCSF (2008a) Narrowing the gaps: pre and post 16 data, www.dcsf.gov.uk/14-19/ documents/ntg_pre_post16_data.ppt [accessed 27/01/2011].

DCSF (2008b) Education and Skills Act 2008. London, HMSO.

DCSF (2009) *Safe from Bullying in Play and Leisure Provision*. London, HMSO.

DCSF (2009a) *Safeguarding the Young and Vulnerable*. London, HMSO.

Dearden, C. and Becker, S. (2004) *Young Carers in the UK: The 2004 Report*. London, Carers UK/Children's Society.

Devine, D. (2002) 'Children's citizenship and the structuring of adult–child relationships in the primary school'. *Childhood,* 9(3), 303–20.

DfE (Department for Education) (2009) Parental experiences of services provided to disabled children 2009–10, http://www.education.gov.uk/rsgateway/DB/STR/d000846/index.shtml [accessed 16/01/11].

DfEE (Department for Education and Employment) (1998) *National Childcare Strategy.* London, HMSO.

DfES (Department for Education and Skills) (2002) *Birth to Three Matters: A Framework for Supporting Children in their Earliest Years.* London, HMSO.

DfES (2003) *Every Child Matters,* Green Paper. London, HMSO.

DfES (2003a) *Ministerial Foreword to Guide to Setting up a Children's Trust Pathfinder.* London, HMSO.

DfES (2003b) *National Standards for Under 8s Daycare and Childminding.* London, HMSO.

DfES (2004) *Every Child Matters: Change for Children.* London: HMSO.

DfES (2004a) *Every Child Matters: Next Steps.* London: HMSO.

DfES (2004b) *Working Together: Giving Children and Young People a Say.* London, HMSO.

DfES (2004c) *Removing Barriers to Achievement.* London, HMSO.

DfES (2005) *Common Core of Skills and Knowledge for the Children's Workforce.* London, HMSO.

DfES (2005a) *Social and Emotional Aspects of Learning (SEAL): Say No to Bullying, Overview.* London, HMSO.

DfES (2006) *Care Matters,* Green Paper. London, HMSO.

DfES (2006a) *Personalised Learning and Pupil Voice: The East Sussex Project.* London, DfES/Centre for British Teachers.

DfES (2006b) *Sure Start Children's Centres: Planning and Performance Management Guidance.* London, HMSO.

DfES (2006c) *Working Together to Safeguard Children.* London, HMSO.

DfES (2006d) *Statistics of Education. Referrals, Assessments and Children and Young People on the Child Protection Registers, England: Year Ending 31 March 2006.* London, HMSO.

DfES (2006e) *School Council Handbook.* London, HMSO.

DfES (2007) *Early Years Foundation Stage.* London, HMSO.

DfES (2007a) *Governance Guidance for Sure Start Children's Centres and Extended Schools.* Nottingham, DfES.

DH (Department of Health) (1999) *National Service Framework for Mental Health: Modern Standards and Service Models.* London, HMSO.

DH (2004) *Choosing Health: Making Healthy Choices Easier,* White Paper. London, HMSO.

DH (2004a) *National Service Framework for Children, Young People and Maternity Services.* London, HMSO.

DH (2008) *Tackling Health Inequalities: 2005–7 Policy and Data Update for the 2010 National Target.* London, HMSO.

Diamond, P. and Liddle, R. (2008) *Beyond New Labour: The Future of Social Democracy in Britain.* London, Politico's.

Dillane, J., Hill, M., Bannister, J. and Scott, S. (2001) *Evaluation of the Dundee Families Project.* Edinburgh, Scottish Executive.

Disability Alliance (2009) *Disability Manifesto 2009: Tackling Disability Poverty,* www.disabilityalliance.org/damanifesto [accessed 16/01/11].

Dunhill, A., Elliot, B. and Shaw, A. (eds) (2009) *Effective Communication and Engagement with Children and Young People, their Families and Carers.* Exeter, Learning Matters.

DWP (Department for Work and Pensions) (2009) *Households Below Average Income,* http://research.dwp.gov.uk/asd/hbai/hbai2008/pdf_files/full_hbai09.pdf [accessed 16/01/11].

Eaton N. (2008) '"I don't know how we coped before": a study of respite care for children in the home and hospice'. *Journal of Clinical Nursing,* 17, 3196–204.

EDCM (Every Disabled Child Matters) (2007) If I could change one thing … , http://www.ncb.org.uk/edcm/if_i_could_change_childrens.pdf [accessed 13/01/11].

Emerson, E. and Hatton, C. (2005) *The Socio-economic Circumstances of Families with Disabled Children.* Institute of Health Studies, University of Lancaster.

EOC (Equal Opportunities Commission) (2006) *Annual Report and Accounts 2005–2006,* http://www.official-documents.gov.uk/document/hc0506/hc14/1423/1423.pdf [accessed 20/01/11].

Finkelhor, D., Cuevas, C., Turner, H. and Omrod, R. (2007) 'Juvenile delinquency and victimization: a theoretical typology'. *Journal of Interpersonal Violence,* 22(12), 1581–1602.

First Children's Embassy (2008/09) *Newsletter of the First Children's Embassy in the World, Megjashi, Republic of Macedonia,* http://www.megjashi.org.mk/WBStorage/Files/Newsletter35.pdf [accessed 20/09/09].

Fitzgerald, D. and Kay, J. (2009) *Working Together in Children's Services.* London, David Fulton.

Flaherty, J., Veit-Wilson, J. and Dornan, P. (2004) *Poverty: The Facts.* London, Child Poverty Action Group.

Flint, J. (2009) 'Governing marginalised populations: the role of coercion, support and agency'. *European Journal of Homelessness,* 4, 247–60.

Fox-Harding, L. (1997) *Perspectives in Child Care Policy* (2nd edn). Harlow, Longman.

Francis, M. and Lorenzo, R. (2002) 'Seven realms of children's participation'. *Journal of Environmental Psychology,* 22(2), 157–69.

Frank, E. (2005) How children feel about their local housing estates, http://childrens-research-centre.open.ac.uk [accessed 16/04/10].

Freeman, M. (2009) 'Children's rights as human rights: reading the UNCRC', in J. Qvortrup, W. Corsaro and M.S. Honig (eds) *The Palgrave Handbook of Childhood Studies.* Basingstoke, Palgrave Macmillan.

Gallagher, M. (2006) Foucault, Power and Participation. Paper presented at the Theorising Children's Participation: International and Interdisciplinary Perspectives Conference, University of Edinburgh, 6 September.

Garret, P.M. (2009) *Transforming Children's Services? Social Work, Neoliberalism and the Modern World.* Maidenhead, Open University Press.

Giddens, A. (1995) *Sociology* (2nd edn). Cambridge, Polity Press.

Gill, T. (2007) *No Fear: Growing Up in Risk-averse Society.* London, Calouste Gulbenkian Foundation.

Gingerbread (2010) Gingerbread factfile, http://www.gingerbread.org.uk/content/365/Gingerbread-Factfile [accessed 13/09/2010].

Gopfert, M., Webster, J. and Seeman, M. (eds) (2004) *Parental Psychiatric Disorder.* Cambridge, Cambridge University Press.

Gray, D.E. and Denicolo, P. (1998) 'Research in special needs education: objectivity or ideology?' *British Journal of Special Education*, 25(3), 140–5.

Hall, D. (2002) *Paediatrics and Child Health Report to the Joint Committee of Human Rights*, www.publications.parliament.uk/pa/jt200102/jtselect/jtrights [accessed 16/04/2010].

Hardy, J. (2007) Forward to *Living Values: A Report Encouraging Boldness in Third Sector Organisations*. London, Community Links/Esmée Fairbairn Foundation.

Hart, J., Newman, J., Ackerman L. and Feeney, T. (2004) *Children Changing their World: Understanding and Evaluating Children's Participation in Development*. Woking, Plan International.

Hart, S. (2002) 'Making sure the child's voice is heard'. *International Review of Education*, 43(3/4), 251–8.

Haverman, R. and Wolfe, B. (1995) 'The determinants of children's attainments: a review of methods and findings'. *Journal of Economic Literature*, 33, 1829–78.

Hechtman, L., Abikoff, H. and Jensen, P. (2005) 'Methylphenidate and multimodal treatment in attention deficit hyperactive disorder', in P.S. Jensen and E.D. Hibbs (eds) *Psychosocial Treatment Research with Children and Adolescents*. Washington, APA Press.

Hilton, Z and Mills, C. (2006) *'I Think It's About Trust': The Views of Young People on Information Sharing*. London, NSPCC.

Hirsch, D. (2007) *Experiences of Poverty and Educational Disadvantage*. York, Joseph Rowntree Foundation.

HM Treasury (2007) *Supporting Young Unaccompanied Asylum Seekers in School*. London, HM Treasury.

Home Office (1945) Report by Sir William Monckton KCMG KCVO MC KC on the Circumstances which Led to the Boarding out of Dennis and Terence O'Neill at Bank Farm, Minsterly and the Steps Taken to Supervise Their Welfare. London, Home Office.

Home Office (1998) *Supporting Families*, Green Paper. London, Home Office.

Home Office (1998) *Fairer, Faster, Firmer*. London, Home Office.

Home Office (2005) *Crime in England and Wales*. London, Home Office.

Howard, J. (2005) Levels of awareness about the Diana Princess of Wales Award in my school and local community, http://childrens-research-centre.open.ac.uk [accessed 16/04/10].

Hoyle, D. (2008) *Problematizing Every Child Matters*, www.infed.org/socialwork/every_child_matters_a_critique.htm [accessed 16/04/10].

Hoyle, E. (2000) 'Micropolitics of educational organisations', in A. Westoby (ed.) *Culture and Power in Educational Organisations*. Milton Keynes, Open University Press.

Hudson, B. (2005) 'Not a cigarette paper between us: integrated inspection of children's services in England'. *Social Policy and Administration,* 39(5), 513–27.

Human Rights Nexus (n.d.) Children's rights, http://www.humanrightsnexus.org/index.php?option=com_content&task=view&id=64&Itemid=88 [accessed 24/01/11].

Hyder, T. (2002) 'Making it happen: young children's rights in action', in B. Franklin (ed.) *The New Handbook of Children's Rights: Comparative Policy and Practice*. London, Routledge.

Involver (2010) *Amazing Student Voice Case Study, Little Heath, Reading*, www.involver.org.uk/2010/02/amazing-student-voice-case-study-little-heath-reading.

Irish Commission (2009) *Inquiry into Child Abuse*. Dublin, Ireland.

Jack, G. (2006) 'The area and community components of children's wellbeing'. *Children & Society*, 20(5), 334–47.

James, A. and James, A. (2004) *Constructing Childhood: Theory, Policy and Social Practice.* Basingstoke, Palgrave Macmillan.

James, A., Jenks, C. and Prout, A. (1998) *Theorizing Childhood.* Cambridge, Polity Press.

Jamieson, L. and Mukoma, W. (2009) 'Dikwankwetla: children in action', in B. Percy-Smith and N. Thomas (eds) *A Handbook of Children and Young People's Participation: Perspectives from Theory and Practice.* Abingdon, Routledge.

Jones, A. (2004) 'Involving children and young people as researchers', in S. Fraser, V. Lewis, S. Ding et al. (eds) *Doing Research with Children and Young People.* London, Sage/Open University Press.

Kahan, B. (1994) *Growing up in Groups.* London, National Institute of Social Work/ HMSO.

Kapasi, H. and Gleave, J. (2009) *Because It's Freedom: Children's Views on their Time to Play,* http://www.playday.org.uk/pdf/Because-its-freedom-Childrens-views-on-their-time-to-play.pdf [accessed 12/01/2011].

Kaufman, N.H. and Rizzini, I. (2009) 'Closing the gap between rights and the realities of children's lives', in J. Qvortrup, W. Corsaro and M.S. Honig (eds) *The Palgrave Handbook of Childhood Studies.* Basingstoke, Palgrave Macmillan.

Kelleher, K.J., McInerny, T., Gardner W. et al. (2000) 'Increasing identification of psychological problems 1979-1996'. *Pediatrics*, 5(6), 1313–22.

Kellett, M. (2003) Empowering Ten-year-olds as Active Researchers. Paper presented at the British Educational Research Association Annual Conference, 11–13 September, Heriot-Watt University, Edinburgh.

Kellett, M. (2005) *How to Develop Children as Researchers: A Step by Step Guide to Teaching the Research Process.* London, Sage.

Kellett, M. (2005a) Children as active researchers: a new research paradigm for the 21st century?, http://www.ncrm.ac.uk/research/outputs/publications/methodsreview/MethodsReviewPaperNCRM-003.pdf [accessed 16/04/10].

Kellett, M. (2009) 'Windows on links between education and poverty: what we can learn from 11-year-olds researching children's literacy?' *International Journal of Inclusive Education*, 13(4), 395–408.

Kellett, M., Robinson, C. and Burr, R. (2004) 'Images of childhood', in S. Fraser, V. Lewis, S. Ding et al. (eds) *Doing Research with Children and Young People.* London, Sage/Open University Press.

Kellett, M., Forrest, R., Dent, N. and Ward, S. (2004a) 'Just teach us the skills please, we'll do the rest: empowering ten-year-olds as active researchers'. *Children & Society*, 18(5), 1–15.

Kelly, J. (2007) 'Reforming public services in the UK: bringing in the third sector'. *Public Administration*, 85(4), 1003–22.

Kennison, P. (2008) 'Child abuse in the religious context: the abuse of trust', in P. Kennison and A. Goodman (eds) *Children as Victims.* Exeter, Learning Matters.

Kirby, S. (2007) Safety at bus stops from children's point of view, http://childrens-research-centre.open.ac.uk [accessed 03/09/2010].

Kirkwood, A. (1993) *The Leicestershire Inquiry 1992.* Leicester, Leicestershire County Council.

Laming, H. (2003) *The Victoria Climbié Inquiry.* London, HMSO.

Lane, D. (2002) Review of Dunn, J. and Deater-Deckard, K.'s (2001)'Children's views of their changing families'. *British Journal of Social Work*, 32(5), 521–3.

Langerman, C. and Worral, E. (2005) *Ordinary Lives: Disabled Children and their Families*. London, New Philanthropy Capital.

Lansdown, G. (2002) 'The participation of children', in H. Montgomery, R. Burr and M. Woodhead (eds) *Changing Childhoods*. Milton Keynes: Open University Press.

Lansdown, G. (2004) *Evolving Capacities and Participation*, http://www.acdicida. gc.ca/INET/IMAGES.NSF/vLUImages/Childprotection [accessed 08/07/09].

Lansdown, G. (2005) *The Evolving Capacities of the Child*. Florence, UNICEF.

Lansdown, G. (2009) 'The realisation of children's participation rights: critical reflections', in B. Percy-Smith and N. Thomas (eds) *A Handbook of Children and Young People's Participation: Perspectives from Theory and Practice*. Abingdon, Routledge.

Layard, R. and Dunn, J. (2009) *A Good Childhood Guide: Searching for Values in a Competitive Age*. London, Penguin.

Leather, E. (2008) What children in my school think about first aid, http://childrens-research-centre.open.ac.uk [accessed 16/04/10].

Le Grand, J. (2007) 'The politics of choice and competition in public services'. *The Political Quarterly*, 78(2), 207–13.

Leicestershire County Council (2003) *Preliminary Findings of Primary Questionnaire, Spring/Summer 2003*. Leicestershire County Council Educational Psychology Service.

Leitch, R. and Mitchell, S. (2007) 'Caged birds and cloning machines: how student imagery "speaks" to us about cultures of schooling and student participation'. *Improving Schools*, 10(1), 53–71.

Lenzer, G. (2002) 'Children's studies and the human rights of children: toward a unified approach', in K. Alaimo and B. Klug Lanham (eds) Children as Equals: *Exploring the Rights of the Child*. Lanham, MD, University Press of America.

Leverett, S. (2008) 'Children's participation', in P. Foley and S. Leverett (eds) *Connecting with Children: Developing Working Relationships*. Bristol, Policy Press.

Levy, A. and Scott-Clark, C. (2010) Death of a child, *The Guardian,* 6 February, www.guardian.co.uk/society/2010/feb/06/child-neglect-adrian-levy-cathy-scott-clark [accessed 03/09/2010].

Lister, R. (2007) 'Inclusive citizenship: realizing the potential'. *Citizenship Studies*, 11(1), 49–61.

London Borough of Newham (2009) *Joint Strategic Needs Assessment*, http://www. newham.gov.uk/HealthAndSocialCare/JointStrategicNeedsAssessment.htm [accessed 6/1/11].

Lundy, L. (2007) 'Voice is not enough: conceptualising Article 12 of the United Nations Convention on the Rights of the Child'. *British Educational Research Journal*, 33(6), 927–42.

McDonald, H. (2009) 'Endemic' rape and abuse of Irish children in Catholic care, *The Guardian*, 20 May.

Machin, S. and McNally, S. (2006) *Education and Child Poverty: A Literature Review*. York, Joseph Rowntree Foundation.

Maegusuku-Hewett, T., Dunkerley, D., Scourfield, J. and Smalley, N. (2007) 'Refugee children in Wales: coping and adaptation in the face of adversity'. *Children and Society*, 21(4) 309–21.

Manchester City Council (2008) *Manchester's Children and Young People's Strategic Plan, 2010–2012*. Manchester City Council.

Marchant, P. and Hall, K. (2003) 'Explaining differences in key stage 2 pupil attainments: a multilevel analysis'. *London Review of Education*, 1(2), 142–51.

Mason, J. and Tipper, R. (2008) 'Being related: how children define and create kinship'. *Childhood*, 15(4), 441–60.

Matosevic, T., Knapp, M., Kendall, J. et al. (2007) 'Care home providers as professionals: understanding the motivations of care home providers in England'. *Ageing and Society*, 27(1), 103–26.

Mayall, B. (2000) *Negotiating Childhoods: Children 5–16*, Research Briefing no.13. Swindon, ESRC.

Mayall, B. and Zeiher, H. (eds) (2003) *Childhood in Generational Perspective*. London, Institute of Education.

Mencap (2007) Don't stick it, stop it!, http://www.mencap.org.uk/case.asp?id=377 [accessed 20/01/11].

Metcalf, J. (2008) 'Making sense of sex offender risk and the internet', in P. Kennison and A. Goodman (eds) *Children as Victims*. Exeter, Learning Matters.

Midwinter, C. (n.d.) Children's rights and citizenship, www.teachingcitizenship.org.uk/.../primary_citizenship_and_rights.doc [accessed 20/01/11].

Mittler, H. and May-Chahal, C. (2004) *Evaluation of St Helen's Children's Fund: Final Report 2002-04*, www.lancs.ac.uk/fass/apsocsci/research/.../shcffinalreport2002-04.doc [accessed 20/01/11].

Montgomery, H. (2009) *An Introduction to Childhood: Anthropological Perspectives on Children's Lives*. Oxford, Blackwell.

Morgan, R. (2005) *Younger Children's Views on Every Child Matters*. London, CSCI.

Morgan, R. (2007) *Making ContactPoint Work*. London, HMSO.

Morrison, C. and Fraser, Y. (2008) *Building a Nation of Wee Democracies*, http://www.childrensparliament.org.uk/assets/new/pdfs/wee_democracy_report.pdf [accessed 14/01/11].

Morrow, V. (2009) 'Children, young people and their families in the UK', in H. Montgomery and M. Kellett (eds) *Children and Young Peoples' Lives: Developing Frameworks for Integrated Practice*. Bristol, Polity Press.

Mount, F. (1982) *The Subversive Family: An Alternative History of Love and Marriage*. London, Jonathan Cape.

Mullender, A., Hagues, G., Imam, U. et al. (2000) *Children's Perspectives on Domestic Violence*. London, Sage.

Nandy, L. (2007) *Going it Alone: Children in the Asylum Process*. London, Children's Society.

NaturalNews.com (n.d.) Ritalin stunts growth of children; long-term risk to children's health unknown, http://www.naturalnews.com/021944.html [accessed 14/01/11].

NCVYS (National Council for Voluntary Youth Services) (2007) *Talking Trusts: Recommendations for Children's Trusts Working with Voluntary and Community Organisations*. London, NCVYS.

Nieuwenhuys, O. (2001) 'By the sweat of their brow? Street children, NGOs and children's rights in Addis Ababa'. *Africa*, 71(4), 539–57.

Nixon, J., Hunter, C., Parr, S. et al. (2006) *Anti-Social Behaviour Intensive Family Support Projects : An Evaluation of Six Pioneering Projects*. London, Office of the Deputy Prime Minister.

NSPCC (National Society for the Prevention of Cruelty to Children) (2006) ChildLine casenotes: what children and young people tell ChildLine about physical abuse, http://www.nspcc.org.uk/Inform/publications/casenotes/clcasenotes-physicalabuse_wdf48114.pdf [accessed 17/01/11].

NSPCC (2007) *Prevalence and Incidence of Child Abuse and Neglect: Key Child Protection Statistics*. London, NSPCC.

NSPCC (2009) ChildLine casenotes: children talking to ChildLine about sexual abuse, http://www.nspcc.org.uk/Inform/publications/casenotes/clcasenotessexualabuse2_wdf69493.pdf [accessed 17/01/11].

O'Brien, M. (2005) *Shared Caring: Bringing Fathers into the Frame*. Manchester, Equal Opportunities Commission.

O'Brien, M., Bachmann. M., Husbands, C. et al. (2006) 'Integrating children's services to promote children's welfare: early findings from the implementation of children's trusts in England'. *Child Abuse Review*, 15(6), 377–95.

O'Byrne, D. (2003) *Human Rights: An Introduction*. Harlow, Prentice Hall.

O'Connell, P., Pepler, D. and Craig, W. (1999) 'Peer involvement in bullying: insights and challenges of intervention'. *Journal of Adolescence*, 22, 437–52.

Office of the First Minister and Deputy First Minister (2006) *Our Children and Young People – Our Pledge*. Belfast, OFMDFM.

Ofsted (2009) *The Impact of Integrated Services on Children and Their Families in Sure Start Children's Centres*. London, HMSO.

O'Herlihy, A., Lelliott, P., Bannister, D. et al. (2007) 'Provision of child and adolescent mental health in-patient services in England between 1999 and 2006'. *Psychiatric Bulletin*, 31(12), 454–6.

Oliver, J.E. (1988) 'Child victims of domestic cruelty'. *Bulletin of the Royal College of Psychiatrists*, 12(4), 141–2.

Palmer, A. (2009) Why the vetting and barring scheme is pure madness, *The Telegraph*, 12 September.

Parapelli, S. (2008) Does wearing school uniform change the behaviour of different aged children?, http://childrens-research-centre.open.ac.uk [accessed 16/04/10].

Parton. N. (2004) 'From Maria Colwell to Victoria Climbié: reflections on public inquiries into child abuse a generation apart'. *Child Abuse Review*, 13(2), 80–94.

Parton, N. (2006) *Safeguarding Children*. Basingstoke, Palgrave Macmillan.

Patil, M. (2006) Getting around as the child of a wheelchair user, http://childrens-research-centre.open.ac.uk [accessed 16/04/10].

Pawson, H., Davidson, E., Sesenko, F. et al. (2009) *Evaluation of Intensive Family Support Projects in Scotland*. Edinburgh, Scottish Government.

Percy-Smith, B. and Thomas, N. (eds) (2009) *A Handbook of Children and Young People's Participation: Perspectives from Theory and Practice*. Abingdon, Routledge.

Pickett, K. (2009) 'Health and wellbeing', in *Deprivation and Risk: The Case For Early Intervention*. London, Action for Children.

Prout, A. (2001) 'Representing children: reflections on the Children 5-16 programme'. *Children & Society*, 15(3), 193–201.

Prout, A. (2002) 'Researching children as social actors: an introduction to the Children 5-16 Programme'. *Children and Society*, 16(2), 67–76.

Quinton, D. (2004) *Supporting Families: Child Protection in the Community*. London, NSPCC.

Rabiee, P., Sloper, P. and Beresford, B. (2005) 'Doing research with children and young people who do not use speech for communication'. *Children & Society*, 19(5), 385–96.

Reacroft, J. (2008) *Like Any Other Child? Children and Families in the Asylum Process*. Ilford, Barnardo's.

Reddy, N. and Ratna, R. (2002) *A Journey in Children's Participation*. Bangalore, The Concerned for Working Children.

Reeves, R. (2008) Exploring what people think about water use, http://childrens-research-centre.open.ac.uk [accessed 16/04/10].

Rhodes, H., Mark, L. and Perry, T. (2007) Children's attitudes to literacy home-work, http://childrens-research-centre.open.ac.uk [accessed 16/04/10].

Robertson, J., Hatton, C., Emerson, E. et al. (2010) *The Impacts of Short Break Provision on Disabled Children and their Families*. Centre for Disability Research, Lancaster University/DCSF.

Robinson, C. and Taylor, C. (2007) 'Theorizing student voice: values and perspectives'. *Improving Schools*, 10(1), 5–17.

Roodman, A.A. and Clum, G.A. (2001) 'Revictimization rates and method variance: a meta-analysis'. *Clinical Psychology Review*, 21(2), 183–204.

Rose, J. (2008) *Independent Review of the Primary Curriculum*. London, DCSF.

Rush, C.R. and Baker, R.W. (2001) 'Behavioral pharmacological similarities between methylphenidate and cocaine in cocaine abusers'. *Experimental and Clinical Psychopharmacology*, 9(1), 59–73.

Rutter, J. (2003) *Supporting Refugee Children in 21st Century Britain: A Compendium of Essential Information*. Stoke-on-Trent, Trentham Books.

Santer, J. and Cookson, L. (2009) 'Early years, childcare and Every Child Matters', in R. Barker (ed.) *Making Sense of Every Child Matters: Multi-professional Practice Guidance*. Bristol, Polity Press.

Sayer, T. (2008) *Critical Practice in Working with Children*. Basingstoke, Palgrave Macmillan.

SCAA (School Curriculum and Assessment Authority) (1996) *Desirable Outcomes for Children's Learning on Entering Compulsory Education*. London, DfEE.

Scottish Executive (2005) *Getting It Right for Every Child: Proposals for Action*. Edinburgh, Scottish Executive.

Scottish Executive (2006) *Family Matters: Charter for Grandchildren*, www.scotland.gov.uk/Resource/Doc/112493/0027333 [accessed 24/11/08].

Searing, H. (2007) *'Why Social Workers Oppose The Child Database': Written Evidence to the House of Lords Select Committee on the Merits of Statutory Instruments. Enquiry into ContactPoint*. London, HMSO.

Secretary of State for Social Services (1974) *Report of the Committee of Inquiry into the Care and Supervision Provided in Relation to Maria Colwell*. London, HMSO.

Sharma, N. (2007) *It Doesn't Happen Here: The Reality of Child Poverty in the UK*. Ilford, Barnardo's.

Sharma, N. and Morrison, J. (2008) *Don't Push Me Around: Disabled Children's Experiences of Wheelchair Services in the UK*. Ilford, Whizz-Kidz/Barnardo's.

Shier, H. (2001) 'Pathways to participation: openings, opportunities and obligations'. *Children & Society*, 15(2), 107–17.

Shout out for Sure Start (2010) Sure Start West Riverside Children's Centres – Leanne, http://shoutoutforasurestart.org.uk/archives/425 [accessed 14/01/11].

Siddique, G. (2006) 'Breaking the taboo of child abuse', in *Child Protection in Faith-based Environments: A Guideline Report*. London, Muslim Parliament of Great Britain.

Sinclair, R. (2004) 'Participation in practice: making it meaningful, effective and sustainable'. *Children & Society*, 18(2), 106–18.

Singleton, R. (2009) *Drawing The Line: A Report on the Government's Vetting and Barring Scheme*, http://www.education.gov.uk/publications//eOrderingDownload/DCSF-01122-2009.pdf [accessed 16/01/11].

Siraj-Blatchford, I., Clarke, K. and Needham, M. (2007) *The Team Around the Child: Multi-agency Working in the Early Years*. Stoke-on-Trent, Trentham Books.

Smith, A. (2002) 'Interpreting and supporting participation rights: contributions from sociocultural theory'. *International Journal of Children's Rights*, 10(1), 73–88.

Smith, R. (2010) *A Universal Child?* Basingstoke, Palgrave Macmillan.

Smyth, J. (2006) 'When students have power: student engagement, student voice, and the possibilities for school reform around "dropping out" of school'. *International Journal of Leadership in Education*, 9(4), 285–98.

Social Work Task Force (2009) *Building a Safe, Confident Future: The Final Report of the Social Work Task Force*, http://publications.education.gov.uk/default.aspx?PageFunction=productdetails&PageMode=publications&ProductId=DCSF-01114-2009 [accessed 10/01/11].

Solberg, A. (1996) 'The challenge in child research from "being" to "doing"', in J. Brannen, and M. O'Brien (eds) *Children in Families: Research and Policy*. London, Falmer Press.

Staffordshire County Council (1991) *The Pindown Experience and the Protection of Children*. Staffordshire County Council.

Stainton-Rogers, W. (1994) 'Promoting better childhoods: constructions of child concern', in M.J. Kehily (ed.) *An Introduction to Childhood Studies*, Maidenhead, Open University Press.

Stanley, N., Miller, P., Richardson Foster, H. and Thomson, G. (2010) *Children and families Experiencing Domestic Violence: Police and Children's Social Services' Responses*. London, NSPCC.

Stobart, E. (2006) *Child Abuse Linked to Accusations of 'Possession' and 'Witchcraft'*. London, DfES.

Sullivan, A. and King, L. (1998) 'Conceptualising student empowerment: a sweep through the literature'. *Unicorn*, 24(3), 27–38.

Summit, R.C. (1984) 'Beyond belief: the reluctant discovery of incest'. *American Journal of Orthopsychiatry*, 56.

Sure Start (2006) *Children's Centres: Practice Guidance*, London, DfES.

Sutherland, I. (2007) Children's worries, http://childrens-research-centre.open.ac.uk [accessed 16/04/10].

Sylva, K., Melhuish, E.C., Sammons, P. et al. (2004) *The Effective Provision of Pre-School Education (EPPE) Project: Final Report*. London, DfES/Institute of Education.

Tameside Children and Young People's Strategic Partnership (2007) *Children and Young People's Version of the Children's Plan 2007–2010*, www.tameside.gov.uk/cypp/documents/childrensplan.pdf [accessed 16/04/10].

Tanuli, N. (2008) Are girls and boys treated differently in school?, http://childrens-research-centre.open.ac.uk [accessed 16/04/10].

Tarapdar, S. (2007) I don't think people know enough about me and they don't care: understanding and exploring the needs of young carers from their perspective, http://childrens-research-centre.open.ac.uk [accessed 16/04/10].

Taylor, J. and Daniel, B. (eds) (2005) *Child Neglect: Practice Issues for Health and Social Care*. London, Jessica Kingsley.

Telegraph, The (2008) 'Jim Rose's school's report is flawed: comment', 8 December, http://www.telegraph.co.uk/education/3684693/Jim-Roses-schools-report-is-flawed-Comment.html [accessed 13/01/11].

Thomas, N. (2007) 'Towards a theory of children's participation'. *International Journal of Children's Rights*, 15(2), 199–218.

Thorpe, D. (1994) *Evaluating Child Protection*. Buckingham, Open University Press.

Tobin, J. (2006) 'Beyond the supermarket shelf: using a rights-based approach to address children's health needs'. *International Journal of Children's Rights*, 14(3), 275–306.

Tomlinson, M. and Walker, R. (2009) *Coping with Complexity: Child and Adult Poverty*. London, Child Action Poverty Group.

Townsend, P. (1979) *Poverty in the United Kingdom: A Survey of Household Resources and Standards of Living*. London, Penguin.

Townsley, R., Abbott, D. and Watson, D. (2004) *Making a Difference? Exploring the Impact of Multi-agency Working on Disabled Children with Complex Health Care Needs, their Families and the Professionals who Support them*. Bristol, Policy Press.

Treseder, P. (1997) *Empowering Children and Young People*. London: Save the Children.

UN (United Nations) (1948) *Universal Declaration of Human Rights*. Geneva, UN General Assembly.

UN (1989) *Convention on the Rights of the Child*. Geneva, UN General Assembly.

UNESCO (1994) *Salamanca Statement and Framework for Action on Special Needs Education*. Spain, Ministry of Education and Science.

UNICEF (2007) *Child Poverty in Perspective: An Overview of Child Well-being in Rich Countries*. Florence, Innocenti Research Centre/UNICEF.

Voice (2004) *Start with the Child, Stay with the Child: A Blueprint for a Child-centred Approach to Children and Young People in Public Care*. London, Voice for the Child in Care/National Children's Bureau.

Voice (2005) *Try a Different Way: Sheets*, www.voiceyp.org [accessed 10/01/11].

Waksler, F. (1991) 'Children in an adult world', in F. Waksler (ed.) *Studying the Social Worlds of Children: Sociological Readings*. London, Falmer Press.

Walker, G. (2008) *Working Together for Children: A Critical Introduction to Multi-agency Working*. London, Continuum.

Walker, J., Crawford, J. and Taylor, F. (2008) 'Listening to children: gaining a perspective of the experiences of poverty and social exclusion from children and young people of single-parent families'. *Health and Social Care in the Community*, 16(4), 429–36.

Ward, L. (2004) 'Flags of concern on child database', *The Guardian*, 28 October.

Ward, L. (2005) Churches to attend ritual abuse summit, *The Guardian*, 12 July.

Watson, L. (2004) Recycling and our future: a small scale investigation of the views of 7-11 year olds, http://childrens-research-centre.open.ac.uk [accessed 16/04/10].

Webster, E. (2007) *Development and Evaluation of the 'Getting Sorted' Care Workshops for Young People with Diabetes*. Faculty of Health, Leeds Metropolitan University.

Webster, E. and Newell, C. (2008) *Development and Evaluation of the 'Getting Sorted' Care Workshops for Young People with Asthma*. Faculty of Health, Leeds Metropolitan University.

Welsh Assembly Government (2004) *Children and Young People: Rights to Action*. Cardiff, Welsh Assembly Government.

White, C., Warrener, M., Reeve, A. and La Valle, I. (2008) *Family Intervention Projects: An Evaluation of their Design, Set-up and Early Outcomes*. London, National Centre for Social Research.

White, S., Hall, C. and Peckover, S. (2009) 'The descriptive tyranny of the Common Assessment Framework: technologies of categorization and professional practice in child welfare'. *British Journal of Social Work*, 39(7), 1197–217.

Whitfield, D. (2010) *Global Auction of Public Assets: Public Sector Alternatives to the Infrastructure Market and Public Private Partnerships.* Nottingham: Spokesman.

Whizz-Kidz (2007) Jacob, http://www.whizz-kidz.org.uk/meet-the-kidz/2007/03/jacob/#more-1163 [accessed 13/01/11].

Williams, R. (2009) 'Sure Start Centre shows that mother knows best', *Society Guardian,* 21 October.

Woodhead, M. and Faulkner, D. (2008) 'Subjects, objects or participants? Dilemmas of psychological research with children', in P. Christensen and A. James (eds) *Research with Children: Perspectives and Practice* (2nd edn). London, RoutledgeFalmer.

Woolcock, M. (2001) 'The place of social capital in understanding social and economic outcomes'. *Canadian Journal of Policy Research,* 2(1), 1–17.

Worle Community School (2007) Diet and exercise – is it different on holiday?, http://childrens-research-centre.open.ac.uk [accessed 19/01/11].

Wyness, M. (2006) 'Children, young people and civic participation: regulation and local diversity'. *Educational Review,* 58(2), 209–18.

Wyness, M., Harrison, L. and Buchanan, I. (2004) 'Childhood, politics and ambiguity: towards an agenda for children's political inclusion'. *Sociology,* 38(1), 81–99.

Xiao, B. (2006) Year 6 children's emotions towards the KS2 SATs: What are the symptoms of depressive emotions?, http://childrens-research-centre.open.ac.uk [accessed 22/07/09].

York, A. and Lamb, C. (2005) Building and sustaining specialist CAMHS: workforce, capacity and functions of tiers 2, 3 and 4 specialist child and adolescent mental health services across England, Ireland, Northern Ireland, Scotland and Wales, www.rcpsych.ac.uk/pdf/str_camhs_sep05.pdf [accessed 19/02/07].

Zelizer, V. (2005) 'The priceless child revisited', in J. Qvortrup (ed.) *Studies in Modern Childhood.* Basingstoke, Palgrave Macmillan.

Zito, J.M., Safer, D.J., DosReis, S. et al. (2000) 'Trends in the prescribing of psychotropic medications to preschoolers'. *Journal of the American Medical Association,* 283(8), 1025–30.

Index